ENDGAME IN THE PACIFIC
IWO JIMA AND OKINAWA 1945

American History Archives™

THE HISTORY CHANNEL CLUB

Endgame in the Pacific
Iwo Jima and Okinawa 1945

3 4 5 6 7 8 / 17 16 15 14 13 12
ISBN 978 1 58159 313 6

The History Channel Club
c/o North American Membership Group
12301 Whitewater Drive
Minnetonka, MN 55343
www.thehistorychannelclub.com

Published by North American Membership Group under license from Osprey
Publishing Ltd.

Previously published as Campaign 81: *Iwo Jima 1945: The Marines raise the
flag on Mount Suribachi* and Campaign 96: *Okinawa 1945: The last battle* by
Osprey Publishing, Midland House, West Way, Botley, Oxford OX2 0PH,
United Kingdom

© 2006 Osprey Publishing Ltd.

Editors: Chris Wheatley and Lee Johnson
Page layout by The Black Spot
Index by Glyn Sutcliffe
Cartography by The Map Studio
Colour bird's eye view illustrations by Paul Kime and John Plumer
Battlescene artwork by Jim Laurier and Howard Gerrard
Originated by PPS Grasmere Ltd, Leeds, UK
Printed in China through Worldprint Ltd.

Author DERRICK WRIGHT is the author of Campaign 77: *Tarawa 1943*,
Tarawa: A Hell of a Way to Die (Windrow & Greene, 1997) and *The
Battle for Iwo Jima* (Sutton, 1999). His interest in the Second World
War started in childhood, as he grew up in the Teeside area which
was subjected to so many bombing raids. After national service with
the Army, he became an engineer specializing in Ultrasonics. Retired,
he lives with his wife on the edge of the North Yorkshire Moors. He
has four daughters.

Author GORDON L ROTTMAN entered the US Army in 1967,
volunteered for Special Forces and completed training as a weapons
specialist. He was assigned to the 7th Special Forces Group until
reassigned to the 5th Special Forces Group in Vietnam in 1969–70.
He was a special operations forces scenario writer at the Joint
Readiness Training Center for 12 years and is now a fulltime writer,
living in Texas.

Illustrator JIM LAURIER is a native of New Hampshire. He graduated
with honors from the Paiers School of Art, Connecticut, in 1978 and
has worked as a freelance illustrator ever since, completing
assignments in a wide variety of fields. Jim has a keen interest in
military subjects, both aviation and armor, and is a Fellow member
of the American Society of Aviation Artists, the New York Society of
Illustrators and the American Fighter Aces Association.

Illustrator HOWARD GERRARD studied at the Wallasey School of Art and
has been a freelance designer and illustrator for over 20 years. He has
won both the Society of British Aerospace Companies Award and the
Wilkinson Sword Trophy and has illustrated a number of books for
Osprey including Campaign 69: *Nagashino 1575* and Campaign 72:
Jutland 1916. Howard lives and works in Kent.

Author's Note to Iwo Jima

The author wishes to thank Mr. Taro Kuribayashi, son of the commander of the
Iwo Jima garrison LtGen Tadamichi Kuribayashi, for permission to quote from his
father's writings and for supplying photographs from the family collection.
Thanks also to Mr. Joe Rosenthal for a definitive account of the famous flag
raising on Mount Suribachi and to General Paul Tibbets for information and
photograph. Other photographs are from the National Archives Washington, DC,
USMC, US Navy, US Air Force or as credited in the text.

Editor's Note to Iwo Jima

Many thanks are due to Jim Moran for his invaluable help in supplying references
for the battlescenes and bird's-eye-views which appear in this book.

Acknowledgements to Okinawa

The author is indebted to: Ben Frank, Chief Historian, US Marine Corps
Historical Center; David Bingham, Ft. Polk Military Museum; Freeman Shell,
Ft. Polk Library; Hitoshi Iikawa, Japan Local Government Center, New York;
Nancy O'Leary who led me around Okinawa.

Artist's note to Okinawa

ABBREVIATIONS

AAA	Antiaircraft Artillery
BAR	Browning Automatic Rifle
CAS	Close Air Support
CinCPOA	Commander in Chief, Pacific Ocean Area
CinCPAC	Commander in Chief Pacific Fleet
FA	Field Artillery
FMFPac	Fleet Marine Force, Pacific
IGHQ	Imperial General Headquarters
IIB	Independent Infantry Battalion
IIIAC	III Amphibious Corps
IJA	Imperial Japanese Army
IJN	Imperial Japanese Navy
IMB	Independent Mixed Brigade
IMR	Independent Mixed Regiment
Inf. Div.	Infantry Division (US Army)
LST	Landing Ship, Tank
LVT	Landing Vehicle, Tracked (Amtrac, Amtank)
Mar. Div.	Marine Division
MP	Military Police
TAF	Tactical Air Force, Tenth Army
TF	Task Force
TG	Task Group
UDT	Underwater Demolition Team
USAAF	United States Army Air Forces

US infantry battalions organic to regiments are designated, e.g., 1/4 (1st
Battalion, 4th Marines); 2/32 (2nd Battalion, 32nd Infantry).

KEY TO MILITARY SYMBOLS

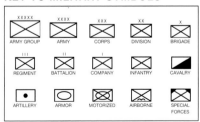

FRONT COVER

**The most famous photograph of World War II. Associated
Press cameraman Joe Rosenthal's superb shot of Marines
raising the flag on the summit of Mount Suribachi on
February 23, 1945. (US Navy)**

ENDGAME IN THE PACIFIC
Iwo Jima and Okinawa 1945

CONTENTS

INTRODUCTION   *4*

Part 1

Iwo Jima   **5**
OPPOSING COMMANDERS   9
OPPOSING FORCES   13
OPPOSING PLANS   15
THE BATTLE   20
AFTERMATH   73
IWO JIMA TODAY   75
CHRONOLOGY   76
SELECT BIBLIOGRAPHY   77
APPENDICES   78

Part 2

Okinawa   **92**
CHRONOLOGY   103
OPPOSING PLANS   104
OPPOSING COMMANDERS   116
OPPOSING FORCES   124
INITIAL OPERATIONS   137
THE OFFENSIVE CONTINUES   147
ACTION AT SEA   162
SEIZING THE SOUTH   166
AFTERMATH   170
THE BATTLEFIELD TODAY   175
ORDER OF BATTLE   176
FURTHER READING   180

INDEX   *181*

INTRODUCTION

By early 1945 the script had been written: Japan was going to lose the war in the Pacific. But the last acts of the drama had yet to play themselves out. The Empire of the Rising Sun was not going to see the end of its day without fighting an epic battle. In 1945 it fought two of them, in fact: one on Iwo Jima, the other on Okinawa.

One of the decisive battles of World War II in the Pacific, Iwo Jima has been aptly described as one of the most costly and savage battles in the history of the United States Marine Corps. But it was a battle that had to be fought. Iwo Jima was situated halfway along the critical B-29 Superfortress bomber route to the Japanese mainland. The Japanese used the island to launch harassing missions against the bomber planes, whose mission was to mount a massive campaign against Japan's industrial heartland. If Iwo Jima could be wrested into American control, those essential bombing missions could continue unfettered.

Okinawa, often called "the last battle," sealed the Imperial army's fate for good. Here, American Marine and Army units clashed with Japanese defenders in an all-out, 82-day battle that proved what was already known on both sides: The victor in this war would have to utterly destroy his opponent. Okinawa provided a glimpse of what would have happened of the United States had been forced to invade the Japanese home islands. The price paid on Okinawa was staggering. The price that would have been paid on the Japanese mainland would have been unbelievable.

So here are the stories of *Iwo Jima and Okinawa 1945*. These epic battles signaled an *Endgame in the Pacific*, which ultimately closed with the dropping of atomic bombs on Hiroshima and Nagasaki later in 1945.

Four Grumman Avenger torpedo-bombers unload their bombs in the area between Airfields Nos. 1 & 2. The cliffs of the Quarry overlooking the East Boat Basin can be seen in the foreground. (National Archives)

PART 1
IWO JIMA

As the final days of 1944 ebbed away the Japanese were facing defeat on all fronts. The heady days of conquest that had followed the attack on Pearl Harbor on December 7, 1941, and the occupation of the Philippines, Singapore, Hong Kong, and the oil rich Dutch East Indies, were little more than a memory as they prepared to defend the homeland at the inner limits of their defensive perimeter.

After suffering staggering defeats at Midway, the Philippine Sea and Leyte Gulf, the Imperial Navy was impotent in the face of the massive US Task Forces that scoured the Pacific and accompanied every amphibious landing.

In the west, British and Commonwealth forces of the 14th Army had pushed the enemy back from the borders of India, and in bitter fighting in some of the worst jungle terrain in the world were driving the Japanese Army along the Irrawaddy River into central Burma.

RIGHT **A flight of B29s head for North Field on Guam after returning from another fire raising attack on the Japanese mainland. (National Archives)**

AREA UNDER JAPANESE CONTROL, END OF SEPTEMBER 1944 (APPROX)

RUSSIA

Sakhalin

Kuril Islands

OUTER MONGOLIA

MANCHURIA

50°

40°

Area under Japanese Control
end of September 1944 (approx)
U.S. movements

Peking

Tientsin

Sea of Japan

KOREA

Hiroshima **Tokyo** JAPAN

TIBET

Yellow Sea

CHINA

East China Sea

Feb 1945: 3rd, 4th & 5th Marine divisions invade Iwo Jima.

30°

Ryukyu Is
Okinawa

Bonin Is

Volcano Is Iwo Jima

TROPIC OF CANCER

Marcus

Formosa

BURMA

Hong Kong

20°

June 1944: Marines invade Marianas.

BAY OF BENGAL

Hainan

20th Air Force raids on Japanese mainland

Mariana Is
Saipan
Tinian
Guam

SIAM

FRENCH INDO-CHINA

Oct. 1944: MacArthur attacks Philippines

Philippine Islands

PACIFIC OCEAN

South China Sea

Palau Is

10°

Caroline Is

Truk

Sept. 1944: 1st Marine division secure Peleliu.

MALAYA

DUTCH EAST INDIES

Sumatra

Borneo

Celebes

EQUATOR

New Guinea

Solomon Is

Java

INDIAN OCEAN

10°

90°   100°   110°   120°   130° AUSTRALIA 140°   150°

In the Central Pacific, Gen MacArthur's army had advanced through the Solomons and across New Guinea and by October, 1944, had invaded Leyte in the Philippines, redeeming his pledge that "I shall return." Through the islands and atolls to the north, Adm Nimitz's Marines swept onward in their "island hopping" campaign that had begun at Tarawa in 1943 and was to climax at Okinawa in 1945. Seizing only those islands that were essential for the support of further operations and bypassing and neutralizing the others, the Marines had by August, 1944, occupied the main islands of the Marianas – Guam, Saipan and Tinian.

The unique strategic location of Iwo Jima, midway along the B29 Superfortress route from the Marianas to Tokyo, made it imperative

that the island should come under American control. Prior to the occupation of Saipan, Tinian and Guam, the B29s had been limited to carrying out raids on southern Japan from bases in central China. With the problem of transporting all of their fuel by air over thousands of miles of inhospitable country and the limitations of small bomb loads, the attacks had little impact. But now, with the construction of five huge airfields 1,500 miles from the Japanese mainland, the way was open for the 20th Air Force to mount a massive campaign against the industrial heartland of Japan.

Initially the 20th Air Force had attempted to duplicate the technique which had been so successfully used by the 8th Air Force in their bombing campaign against Germany – daylight precision bombing. The experiment had failed largely because of unexpectedly high winds as the Superfortresses approached their targets at altitudes of 27,000–33,000ft in the jetstream. The Air Force commander, BrigGen Haywood Hansell, became increasingly frustrated and blamed his crews for the disappointing results; and by January, 1945, the chiefs in Washington had decided that Hansell had to go.

His replacement was Curtis LeMay, a brilliant technician who had previously been in command of the 3rd Division of the 8th Air Force in England. LeMay was to introduce a new term to the aircrews of the 20th Air Force – "area bombing." Widely used by the RAF throughout the war, he proposed to firebomb the main cities of Japan at low level and by night in a dramatic reversal of Hansell's earlier tactics. LeMay was aware that his career was on the line. He had not informed Gen Henry "Hap" Arnold, Commanding General of the Air Force, of this first low altitude raid: "If we go in low, at night, not in formation, I think we'll surprise the Japs, at least for a short period. If it's a failure and I don't produce any results then he can fire me," he said.

The only obstacle on the flight path was Iwo Jima. It housed two airfields with a third under construction, and a radar station that could

ABOVE **The B29 Superfortress bomber was the most advanced aircraft of its day. With pressurized crew compartments, remote control gun turrets, a huge range and bomb load, it was able to reach the Japanese mainland with ease. Here, rows of brand new aircraft stand outside of the plant specially constructed for the B29 program at Wichita, Kansas. (Boeing Company Archives)**

Once their airfields became operational in the Mariana Islands, the B29 bombers began a relentless campaign against the Japanese mainland. Here, a group of B29s passes over one of Japan's most famous landmarks, Mount Fujiyama, on their way to Tokyo. (National Archives)

give two hours warning of an impending raid. The Air Force desperately needed to eliminate the threat of fighter attacks from the Iwo airfields and to neutralize the radar station there. With the island under American control there would be the added bonuses of a refuge for crippled bombers, facilities for air-sea rescue flying boats, and more importantly, a base from which P51 Mustang long range fighters could escort the Superfortresses on the second leg of their long haul to Japan.

At Iwo Jima the amphibious techniques which had been developed over the previous three years were to receive the supreme test as three Marine divisions pitted themselves against more than 21,000 deeply entrenched Japanese troops led by a brilliant and determined commander, LtGen Tadamichi Kuribayashi. "Do not plan for my return," he was to inform his wife from Iwo Jima. Sadly his words would also be the epitaph for nearly 6,000 US Marines.

Lieutenant-General "Howlin' Mad" Smith, Commander Fleet Marine Forces Pacific, called the battle: "The most savage and most costly battle in the history of the Marine Corps." Smith had fronted every amphibious landing in the Central Pacific from Tarawa in 1943 to the Marianas in late 1944 and was eminently qualified to make such a judgment. As the battle reached its climax, Adm Chester Nimitz was to add his now famous phrase: "Among the Americans who fought on Iwo Jima, uncommon valor was a common virtue."

OPPOSING COMMANDERS

Fleet Admiral Chester Nimitz was appointed Commander in Chief Pacific (CICPAC) after the Pearl Harbor debacle. A great organizer and leader, he was by the end of 1945 the commander of the largest military force ever, overseeing 21 admirals and generals, 6 Marine divisions, 5,000 aircraft, and the world's largest navy. (US Navy)

AMERICAN

On October 3,1944, the joint Chiefs of Staff issued a directive to Adm CHESTER NIMITZ, Commander in Chief Pacific (CINCPAC) to occupy the island of Iwo Jima. As with previous amphibious landings in the Marine Corps "island hopping" campaign, he entrusted the planning and implementation of the assault, codenamed "Operation Detachment," to his experienced trio of tacticians, Spruance, Turner, and Smith who had masterminded almost every operation since the initial landing at Tarawa in 1943.

Nimitz was a quiet somewhat introverted Texan who never lost a sea battle. President Roosevelt had been so impressed by him that he bypassed nearly thirty more senior admirals to appoint him CINCPAC after the removal of Adm Husband E. Kimmel following the debacle at Pearl Harbor. One of his greatest abilities was to resolve conflicts with other senior officers. However, his long running disputes with Gen Douglas MacArthur, Supreme Commander of all US Army units in the Pacific Theatre, were legendary. A man of striking contrasts, MacArthur was arrogant, conceited, egotistical, and flamboyant and yet a superb strategist with an amazing sense of where and when to strike the enemy to greatest advantage.

Nimitz and MacArthur disagreed throughout the war on the best way to defeat the Japanese, with MacArthur favoring a thrust through the Philippines and on to Formosa (Taiwan) and China. Nimitz stood by his "island hopping" theory – occupying those islands and atolls that were of strategic importance and bypassing those that had little military value or were unsuitable for amphibious landings.

Admiral RAYMOND A. SPRUANCE had been Nimitz's right hand man since his outstanding performance at the Battle of Midway in June, 1942. His quiet unassuming manner concealed a razor sharp intellect and an ability to utilize the experience and knowledge of his staff to a remarkable degree. He would continue in the role of Operations Commander until the final battle of the Pacific War at Okinawa.

Admiral RICHMOND KELLY TURNER, the Joint Expeditionary Force Commander, was by contrast notorious for his short temper and foul mouth, but his amazing organization skills placed him in a unique position to mount the operation. Dovetailing the dozens of air strikes and shore bombardments, disembarking thousands of troops and landing them on the right beach in the right sequence was an awesome responsibility fraught with the seeds of potential disaster, but Turner had proved his ability time and time again.

Lieutenant-General HOLLAND M. SMITH, Commanding General Fleet Marine Force Pacific, "Howlin' Mad" Smith to his Marines, was on

ABOVE, LEFT **Admiral Raymond Spruance was selected by Adm "Bull" Halsey as his own replacement before the Battle of Midway when Halsey was forced into hospital with dermatitis. His outstanding qualities soon attracted the attention of Nimitz who retained him as his Operations Commander for the remainder of the war. (National Archives)**

ABOVE, CENTRE **The acknowledged master of amphibious warfare, Kelly Turner's organizing skills were legendary. With the exception of Peleliu, he masterminded every landing in the Pacific from Guadalcanal to the final battle at Okinawa. (US Navy)**

RIGHT **Lieutenant-General Holland M. Smith, "Howlin' Mad" to his Marines, was a volatile leader who did not suffer fools gladly. His dismissal of Army Gen Ralph Smith during the Saipan operation was to cause friction between the Army and the Marines for years. Seen here in two-toned helmet alongside Secretary of the Navy James Forrestal (with binoculars) and a group of Iwo Jima Marines. (National Archives)**

the other hand nearing the end of his active career. His aggressive tactics and uncompromising attitude had made him many enemies. In America a powerful clique of publishing barons was running a vitriolic campaign against him in favor of Gen Douglas MacArthur, and his recent dismissal of the Army's Gen Ralph Smith during the Saipan battle for "lack of aggressiveness" had not endeared him to the top brass in the Pentagon. At Iwo Jima he was content to keep a low profile in favor of MajGen Harry Schmidt, V Amphibious Corps Commander: "I think that they only asked me along in case anything happened to Harry Schmidt," he was to say after the battle.

The Iwo Jima landing would involve an unprecedented assembly of three Marine divisions: the 3rd, 4th and 5th. Heading the 3rd Division was MajGeneral GRAVES B. ERSKINE, at 47 a veteran of the battles of Belleau Wood, Chateau Thierry, and St Mihiel during World War I. Later

he was the Chief of Staff to Holland Smith during the campaigns in the Aleutians, Gilbert Islands and the Marianas.

The 4th Division was also commanded by a World War I veteran, MajGen CLIFTON B. CATES, who had won the Navy Cross and two Silver Stars. At Guadalcanal in 1942 he had commanded the 4th Division's 1st Regiment and at Tinian became the Divisional Commander. In 1948 he became the Commandant of the Marine Corps.

Major-General KELLER E. ROCKEY was another Navy Cross holder for gallantry at Chateau Thierry. He won a second Navy Cross for heroism in Nicaragua in the inter-war years and took command of the 5th Division in February, 1944. Iwo Jima was to be the Division's first battle but it boasted a strong nucleus of veterans of the recently disbanded Raider Battalions and Marine Paratroopers.

Responsibility for preparing and executing Marine operations for "Detachment" fell to V Amphibious Corps Landing Force Commander MajGen HARRY SCHMIDT. A veteran of pre-war actions in China, the Philippines, Mexico, Cuba and Nicaragua and later the 4th Division commander during the Roi-Namur and Saipan invasions, he was 58 years old at Iwo Jima and would have the honour of fronting the largest Marine Corps force ever committed to a single battle.

JAPANESE

In May, LtGen TADAMICHI KURIBAYASHI had been summoned to the office of the Japanese Prime Minister, General Tojo, and told that he would be the commander of the garrison on Iwo Jima. Whether by accident or design the appointment proved to be a stroke of genius.

Kuribayashi, a samurai and long serving officer with 30 years distinguished service, had spent time in the United States as a deputy attaché and had proclaimed to his family: "the United States is the last country in the world that Japan should fight." He looked upon his appointment as both a challenge and a death sentence. "Do not plan for my return," he wrote to his wife shortly after his arrival on the island.

Kuribayashi succeeded in doing what no other Japanese commander in the Pacific could do – inflict more casualties on the US Marines than

Along with Admiral Yamamoto, LtGen Tadamichi Kuribayashi must rank as Japan's greatest military commander. His brilliant defense of Iwo Jima, in which he abandoned the traditional tactics of attempting to halt the enemy at the beach, succeeded in achieving his purpose of inflicting massive casualties on the invader. Even Holland Smith was to dub him: "Our most redoubtable adversary." (Taro Kuribayashi)

his own troops suffered. Fifty-four years old at the time of the battle and quite tall for a Japanese at 5ft 9ins, Radio Tokyo described him as having the "traditional pot belly of a Samurai warrior and the heart of a Tiger."

Lieutenant-General Holland Smith in his memoirs was lavish in his praise for the commander's ability: "His ground organization was far superior to any I had seen in France in WWI and observers say it excelled the German ground organization in WWII. The only way we could move was behind rolling artillery barrages that pulverized the area and then we went in and reduced each position with flamethrowers, grenades and demolition charges. Some of his mortar and rocket launchers were cleverly hidden. We learned about them the hard way, through sickeningly heavy casualties. Every cave, every pillbox, every bunker was an individual battle where Marines and Japanese fought hand to hand to the death."

OPPOSING FORCES

AMERICAN

Against the Japanese defense force the Americans were to employ three Marine divisions, the 3rd, 4th and 5th, totalling over 70,000 men most of whom were seasoned veterans of earlier campaigns. Operation Detachment had already been postponed twice because of a shortage of support ships and landing craft due to the massive requirements of MacArthur's Philippines invasion, and it had to be completed in time to release men and materials for the upcoming Okinawa invasion scheduled for April 1,1945

As the plans came to fruition it was time to assemble the invasion force. The 3rd Division were still on Guam having taken the island in August, 1944, while the 4th & 5th Divisions were to be deployed from the Hawaiian Islands. The Navy was scheduled to provide a massive "softening up" bombardment prior to the invasion and many of the fleet's old battleships, the USS *Arkansas, Texas, Nevada, Idaho* and *Tennessee*, too slow for the new Task Forces that were now prowling the Pacific, were ideal for the purpose.

On February 15, the invasion fleet left Saipan, first the LSTs carrying the first waves of troops from the 4th and 5th Divisions and the following day the troop transports with the remainder of the Marines and the plethora of tanks, supplies, artillery, and supporting units. The armada was soon spotted by Japanese naval patrol aircraft and the Iwo Jima garrison went on to immediate alert. General Kuribayashi had earlier issued his troops with a document called "The Courageous Battle Vows"

Another view of the beaches with the East Boat Basin in the distance. The sign says: "Mount Suribachi 169m." (Taro Kuribayashi)

General Kuribayashi wasted no time in re-organizing the inadequate defense system that he discovered upon his arrival on the island. Here he is seen with members of his staff directing operations. (Taro Kuribayashi)

which stated that each man should make it his duty to kill ten of the enemy before dying. With his defenses prepared and his men ready to fight to the death, Kuribayashi waited patiently for the approaching invader.

JAPANESE

The Japanese High Command realized the importance of Iwo Jima and as early as March, 1944, began to reinforce the island. The 145th Infantry Regiment of Col Masuo Ikeda, originally intended to bolster the garrison on Saipan, was diverted to the island and in the period leading up to the Marine attack in 1945, the 109th Division, including the 2nd Mixed Brigade (MajGen Senda), 26th Tank Regiment (LtCol [Baron] Takeichi Nishi), 17th Mixed Infantry Regiment (Maj Tamachi Fujiwara), Brigade Artillery (Col Chosaku Kaido) and additional Anti-Aircraft, Mortar, Cannon and Machine Gun Battalions were drafted to the island. The Naval Units, mainly anti-aircraft, communications, supply, and engineering groups, were under the command of R/Adm Toshinosuke Ichimaru who also had charge of the 27th Air Flotilla. At the time of the Marine landing, February 19, 1945, the total Japanese garrison numbered 21,060, considerably more than the American calculation of 13,000.

OPPOSING PLANS

AMERICAN

The complexity of the underground tunnel system can be judged from this picture of one of the existing passages. (Taro Kuribayashi)

The plan of attack that was devised by MajGen Harry Schmidt's V Amphibious Corps planners looked deceptively simple. The Marines would land on the two-mile long stretch of beach between Mount Suribachi and the East Boat Basin on the south-east coast of the island. These beaches were divided into seven sections of 550yds (914m) each. Under the shadow of Suribachi lay Green Beach (1st and 2nd Bns, 28th Regt), flanked on the right by Red Beach 1 (2nd Bn, 27th Regt), Red Beach 2 (1st Bn, 27th Regt), Yellow Beach 1 (1st Bn, 23rd Regt), Yellow Beach 2 (2nd Bn, 23rd Regt), Blue Beach 1(1st and 3rd Bns, 25th Regt). Blue Beach 2 lay directly under known enemy gun emplacements in the Quarry overlooking the East Boat Basin, and it was decided that both the 1st and 3rd Bns of the 25th Regiment should land abreast on Blue Beach 1. General Cates, the 4th Division commander, said: "If I knew the name of the man on the extreme right of the right hand squad (on Blue Beach), I'd recommend him for a medal before we go in."

The 28th Regiment would attack straight across the narrowest part of the island to the opposite coast, swing left, isolate and then secure Mount Suribachi. On their right, the 27th Regiment would also cross the island and move to the north, while the 23rd Regiment would seize Airfield No. 1 and then thrust northward towards Airfield No. 2. The 25th Regiment, on the extreme right, would deploy to their right to neutralize the high ground around the Quarry overlooking the East Boat Basin.

Kuribayashi and his staff had time to pose for a formal group photograph before the Americans arrived. None was to survive the battle. (Taro Kuribayashi).

JAPANESE

General Kuribayashi's first priority was to reorganize the archaic defense system that was in place when he arrived. All civilians were sent back to the mainland as their presence could serve no useful purpose and they would be a drain on the limited supplies of food and water. With the arrival of more troops and Korean laborers he instigated a massive program of underground defenses. A complex and extensive system of tunnels, caves, gun emplacements, pillboxes, and command posts was constructed in the nine months prior to the invasion. The soft pumice-like volcanic rock was easily cut with hand tools and mixed well with cement to provide excellent reinforcement. Some tunnels were 75ft (23m) under ground, most were interconnecting, and many were provided with electric or oil lighting.

Supply points, ammunition stores, and even operating theaters were included in the system and at the height of the battle many Marines reported hearing voices and movements coming from the ground beneath them. When Mount Suribachi was isolated many of the defenders escaped to the north of the island, bypassing the Marine lines through this labyrinth of tunnels.

The tunnels were constructed at an unprecedented speed. The specification called for a minimum of 30ft (9.1m) of earth overhead to resist any shell or bomb. Most were five feet (1.5m) wide and five feet high with concrete walls and ceilings and extended in all directions (one engineer in his diary said that it was possible to walk underground for four miles). Many tunnels were built on two or even three levels and in the larger chambers, airshafts of up to 50ft (15.2m) were needed to dispel the foul air. Partially underground were the concrete blockhouses and gun

View from the south. The invasion beaches with their black sand stretch away to the right. (Taro Kuribayashi)

With Mount Suribachi in the foreground, the invasion beaches can be seen on the right of the picture, stretching northwards to the East Boat Basin. Isolating the volcano was the number one priority for the Marines and involved crossing the half-mile neck of the island as rapidly as possible. (US Navy)

sites, so well constructed that weeks of naval shelling and aerial bombing failed to damage most of them; and the hundreds of pillboxes, which were of all shapes and sizes, were usually interconnected and mutually supporting.

The General had studied earlier Japanese defense methods of attempting to halt the enemy at the beachhead and had realized that they invariably failed, and he regarded the traditional "banzai" charge as wasteful and futile. In September at Peleliu the Japanese commander, LtGen lnoue, had abandoned these outdated tactics and concentrated on attrition, wearing down the enemy from previously planned and prepared positions in the Umurbrogol Mountains. Kuribayashi approved of these tactics. He knew that the Americans would eventually take the island but he was determined to exact a fearful toll in Marine casualties before they did.

The geography of the island virtually dictated the location of the landing sites for the invasion force. From aerial photographs and periscope shots taken by the submarine USS *Spearfish*, it was obvious that there were only two stretches of beach upon which the Marines could land. General Kuribayashi had come to the same conclusion months earlier and made his plans accordingly.

Iwo Jima is some four and a half miles long with its axis running from south-west to north-east, tapering from two and a half miles wide in the north to a mere half mile in the south, giving a total land area of around seven and a half square miles. At the southern end stands Mount Suribachi, a 550ft (168m) high dormant volcano that affords commanding views over most of the island, and the beaches that stretch northward from Suribachi are the only possible sites for a landing.

On a plateau in the center of this lower part of the island the Japanese built Airfield No. 1, and further north a second plateau roughly a mile in diameter housed Airfield No. 2 and the unfinished Airfield No. 3. The

JAPANESE DEFENSE SECTORS AND US LANDING BEACHES

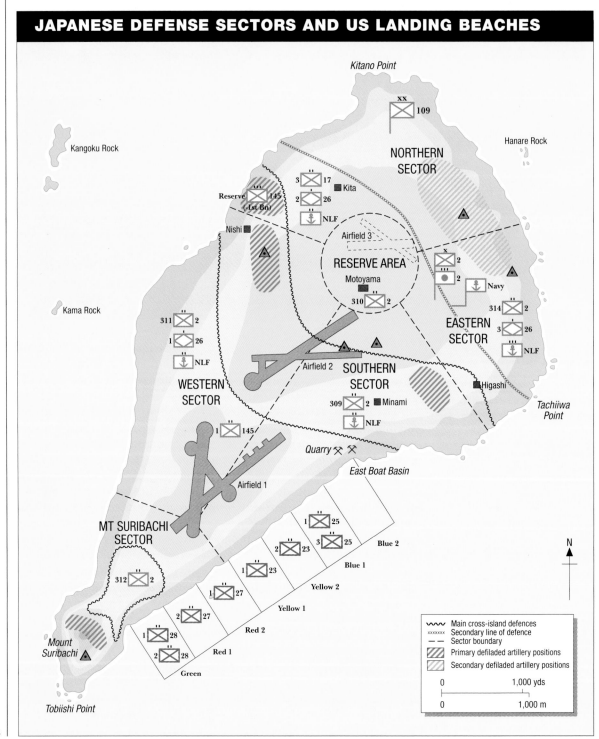

ground that slopes away from this northern plateau is a mass of valleys, ridges, gorges, and rocky outcrops that provide an ideal site for defensive fighting.

Major Yoshitaka Horie, Staff Officer to LtGen Kuribayashi, had many discussions with his superior about the role of anti-aircraft guns. Horie was of the opinion that they would be far better employed as artillery or in an anti-tank role as it was obvious that the Americans would have overwhelming air superiority before and during the battle. His reasoning seems to have impressed the General who overruled the objections of some of his staff officers and implemented some of Horie's ideas.

Horie was interviewed by a Marine officer after the war and his comments were recorded for the Marine Corps Historical Archives. He told Gen Kuribayashi: "We should change our plans so that we can use most of the anti-aircraft guns as artillery and retain very small parts of them as anti-aircraft guns. Anti-aircraft guns are good to protect the disclosed targets, especially ships, but are invaluable for the covering of land defenses," but the staff officers had different opinions. "The staff officers were inclined as follows; they said at Iwo Jima it is good to use anti-aircraft guns as both artillery and anti-aircraft guns. The natural features of Iwo are weaker than of Chichi Jima. If we have no anti-aircraft guns, our defensive positions will be completely destroyed by the enemy's air raids."

Horie continued: "And so most of the 300 anti-aircraft guns were used in both senses as above mentioned, but later, when American forces landed on Iwo Jima, those anti-aircraft guns were put to silence in one or two days and we have the evidence that most anti-aircraft guns were not valuable but 7.5cm anti-aircraft guns, prepared as anti-tank guns, were very valuable."

Horie, in his curious English, went on to describe the initial Japanese reaction to the landings: "On the February 19, American forces landed on the first airfield under cover of their keen bombardments of aircraft and warships. Although their landing direction, strength and fighting methods were same as our judgment, we could not take any counter-measures towards them, and 135 pillboxes we had at the first airfield were trodden down and occupied in only two days after their landing.

"We shot them bitterly with the artillery we had at Motoyama and Mount Suribachi, but they were immediately destroyed by the enemy's counter-firing. At that time we had opportunity to make offensive attacks against the enemy but we knew well that if we do so we will suffer many damages from American bombardments of aircraft and vessels, therefore our officers and men waited the enemy coming closer to their own positions."

THE BATTLE

D-DAY: "A NIGHTMARE IN HELL"

As a prelude to the landings MajGen Harry Schmidt, V Amphibious Corps Commander, had requested ten continuous days of shelling by battleships and cruisers of R/Adm William Blandy's Amphibious Support Force (Task Force 52). Admiral Hill rejected the request on the grounds that there would be insufficient time to re-arm his ships before D-Day. Schmidt persisted and asked for nine days. This was also turned down and he was offered a mere three days of softening up before his Marines went ashore. Spruance's comment – "I know that your people will get away with it" – was to sound hollow as the battle progressed. "Howlin' Mad" Smith was to be scathing in his criticism of the Navy's support during many of the amphibious landings throughout the Pacific campaign: "I could not forget the sight of dead Marines in the lagoon or lying on the beaches of Tarawa, men who died assaulting defenses which should have been taken out by naval gunfire," he was to write after the war.

The first day of the bombardment was a disappointment. Poor weather hampered the gunners and the results were inconclusive. Day two was to be a disaster. The cruiser USS *Pensacola* ventured too close to

Three of the old battleships of the US Navy get into position prior to "softening up" the island in preparation for the landings. Their 16in shells were ideal for reducing the concrete bunkers that dotted the Iwo Jima coastline. (National Archives)

the shore and was engaged by enemy shore batteries. Six hits in rapid
succession killed 17 of the crew and caused substantial damage.

Later in the day 12 gunboats (LCIs) approached to within 1,000yds
(914m) of the shore as part of the support screen for over 100
"frogmen," underwater demolition teams. With distances worked out to
the nearest yard from months of practice, all 12 vessels were hit by
Japanese batteries and scurried away at best speed. The destroyer
USS *Leutze*, which raced to their assistance, was also hit with the loss of
7 crewmen.

The final day of the bombardment was again blighted by poor weather
with rainsqualls and cloud foiling the gunners. Blandy optimistically
signalled Turner: "I believe that landings can be accomplished tomorrow."
Schmidt complained: "We only got about 13 hours worth of fire support
during the 34 hours of available daylight."

By contrast, D-Day, Monday, February 19, 1945, dawned clear and
sunny with unlimited visibility. During the night Adm Marc Mitscher's
Task Force 58, a vast armada of 16 carriers, 8 battleships, and 15 cruisers,
fresh from highly successful attacks against the Japanese mainland,
arrived off Iwo Jima accompanied by Adm Raymond Spruance in his
flagship USS *Indianapolis*. Again Holland Smith was bitter, considering
these raids against Japan to be an unnecessary diversion from the more
important business of occupying Iwo Jima.

As the battleships and cruisers pounded the island and swarms of
carrier-based aircraft mounted air strikes, the disembarkation of
thousands of Marines from troopships and LVTs was gathering

A seven-knot breeze and a calm sea provided the Marines with ideal conditions for the invasion. Admiral Raymond Spruance had arrived during the night with Admiral Mitscher's mighty Task Force 58, and the island was surrounded by over 485 ships of various types to support General Schmidt's Marines. At dawn the battleships and cruisers commenced their final bombardment of Mount Suribachi and the seven invasion beaches as the Amtracs headed for the shore.

momentum. To spearhead the attack 68 LVT(A)s – armored amphibious tractors mounting a 75mm (2.95in) howitzer and three machine guns – were to venture 50yds (46m) onto the beachhead to cover the first wave of Marines, but the first of a number of planning "foul-ups" was to frustrate their deployment. Along the whole of the landing beach the Marines, LVTs, tanks, and other vehicles were to encounter 15ft high terraces of soft black volcanic ash. The troops sank up to their ankles, the vehicles to their hubcaps, and the LVTs and Sherman tanks ground to a halt within yards of the shore. The planners had described the beach conditions in glowing terms: "troops should have no difficulty in getting off the beach at any point," "the isthmus provides excellent landing beaches," and "an easy approach inland," read the pre-invasion reports.

In keeping with Gen Kuribayashi's strategy, Japanese resistance had been relatively subdued; he wanted the Americans to land substantial numbers of men onto the beaches before unleashing his well-rehearsed and co-ordinated bombardment. Many American Naval officers were under the illusion that their rolling barrage over the landing zone was responsible for the limited response.

A steady stream of small arms and machine gun fire whined across the beaches and the occasional crump of a mortar shell sent sand flying, but the most formidable enemy was the sand itself – Marines were trained to move rapidly forward; here they could only plod. The weight and amount of equipment was a terrific hindrance and various items were rapidly discarded. First to go was the gas mask, always regarded as an unnecessary trapping, and many of the Marines decided to dump their pack and retrieve it later; the most important pieces of equipment at that moment were weapons and ammunition.

As the first waves of Marines struggled to move forward, successive waves arrived at intervals of around 5 minutes and the situation rapidly deteriorated. General Kuribayashi had intended to allow the invaders to move towards Airfield No. 1 before commencing his artillery and mortar

ABOVE **War dogs, usually Dobermans or German Shepherds, were used extensively in the Pacific War, carrying messages and locating hidden enemy troops. They provided a very valuable service; sadly they were all destroyed at the end of the battle as it was regarded that they could not be retrained for civilian life. Here a Doberman keeps guard while his handler snatches some sleep. (National Archives)**

barrages. The congestion on the beaches was an added bonus and a little after 1000hrs the full fury of the Japanese defenses was unleashed. From well-concealed positions ranging from the base of Mount Suribachi to the East Boat Basin a torrent of artillery, mortar, and machine gun fire rained down on the crowded beaches. Frantic messages flashed back to the control ship *Eldorado*: "troops 200yds (183m) inland pinned down," "catching all hell from the Quarry," "machine gun and artillery fire heaviest ever seen."

By 1040hrs Harry Hill had 6,000 men ashore and the bulldozers that had arrived in the early waves were hacking away at the terraces. Some tanks were breaking through to solid ground and troops were finally escaping the horror of the beaches where Kuribayashi's artillery and mortars were wreaking havoc. Robert Sherrod, a noted war correspondent for *Time-Life*, aptly described the scene as "a nightmare in hell."

At the extreme left of the beachhead, Green Beach, the terrain was less difficult where the volcanic ash gave way to rocks and stone at the base of Mount Suribachi. Here Col Harry Liversedge's 28th Regiment began their dash across the half-mile isthmus below the volcano in an attempt to isolate this strategically vital position.

On Suribachi, Col Kanehiko Atsuchi with over 2,000 men in his independent command manned a mass of artillery and mortars that were dug in around the lower slopes, and above them there were dozens of caves and tunnels all the way to the summit.

The 1st Battalion, ignoring this threat to their left flank, pressed on towards the far shore but soon encountered Capt Osada's 312th Independent Infantry Battalion and fierce fighting erupted around a series of bunkers and pillboxes. Some were destroyed and others bypassed in the mad dash to cross the island. Dead were abandoned where they lay and the wounded left in the care of the Navy Corpsmen, the heroic medical teams that accompanied all Marine operations. At 1035hrs six men of B Company, 1st Battalion reached the

Abandoned landing craft on the invasion beaches. (National Archives)

General Kuribayashi had intended to let the Marines clear the beaches and head for Airfield No 1 before unleashing his well-rehearsed artillery barrage. However, as the troops became bogged down behind the terraces of volcanic ash, and with further waves of Amtracs arriving every five minutes, he seized the opportunity to rake the beaches from end to end with devastating artillery and mortar fire that caused very heavy casualties.

In a deceptively calm looking sea, rows of landing craft head for the invasion beaches, scheduled to arrive at five-minute intervals. The congestion on the beach afforded General Kuribayashi's gunners a prime target. (US Navy)

west coast, soon to be joined by the remnants of C Company and Suribachi was isolated, albeit precariously. On Red Beaches 1 and 2, the 27th Regiment under Col Thomas Wornham were having great difficulty in moving forward. The Japanese artillery bracketed the crowded beach and casualties mounted by the minute. To their right on Yellow 1 and 2, the 23rd Regiment under Col Walter Wensinger had come face to face with a mass of blockhouses and pillboxes manned by Maj Matsushita's 10th Independent Anti-Tank Battalion and Capt Awatsu's 309th Infantry Battalion. Battling against shredding machine gun fire, Sgt Darren Cole, armed only with grenades and a pistol, single-handedly silenced five pillboxes before being killed by a hand grenade and became the first of the Marine Corps 27 Medal of Honor recipients during the battle.

At the extreme right, Blue Beach 1, Col John Lanigan's 25th Regiment moved straight ahead to avoid the obvious danger presented by the high ground at the Quarry on their right flank, making a two-pronged attack with the 1st Battalion pressing inland as the 3rd Battalion swung right to assault cliffs at the base of the Quarry.

2nd Lt Benjamin Roselle, part of a six-man naval gunfire team, was to suffer a horrendous D-Day. Reaching the second row of terraces, they were pinned down by heavy artillery fire. As they attempted to move forward, the radio operator went down and Roselle strapped his equipment to his back and moved on. Within a minute a mortar shell exploded among the group. Others were able to move but the Lieutenant could not, his left foot and ankle hung from his leg, held on by a ribbon of flesh. Pinned down and with no hope of advancing, he rode out the storm of mortar shells that were blasting the area. Within

Instead of the straightforward exit from the beaches that the Marines had been led to expect, they came upon terraces of black volcanic ash, some of them up to 15 feet high and there were long delays in getting troops, tanks, and artillery inland. (National Archives)

minutes a second round landed near him and fragments tore into his other leg. For nearly an hour he wondered where the next shell would land. He was soon to find out as a shell burst almost on top of him, wounding him for the third time in the shoulder. Almost at once another explosion bounced him several feet into the air and hot shards ripped into both thighs. Remarkably, he wondered what time it was and as he lifted his arm to look at his watch a mortar shell exploded only feet away and blasted the watch from his wrist and tore a large jagged hole in his forearm: "I was beginning to know what it must be like to be crucified," he was to say later. Eventually recovered by a medical team, he was taken to an offshore LST hospital ship where his fractured arm was set and his foot amputated.

A few tanks of the 4th Tank Battalion had succeeded in getting ashore on Blue 1 at around 1020hrs. A tank-dozer scooped a passage through the first terrace and the remainder passed through in single file, only halting when they reached a large minefield.

At 1400hrs the 3rd Battalion under their commander "Jumpin' Joe" Chambers began scaling the cliffs around the Quarry. The enemy resistance was fanatical and the Marines were soon down to 150 men from the original 900 who had landed at 0900hrs.

At the base of Mount Suribachi the 28th Regiment were consolidating their positions. LT Keith Wells' 3rd Platoon were ordered to cross the isthmus to reinforce the 1st Platoon whose position was in danger of being overrun. Under heavy fire from their left the four squads sprinted forward, coming across many dead and wounded Marines who had to be left behind until the base of the volcano had been secured. By afternoon a few Sherman tanks that had penetrated the beachhead were moving up to provide valuable assistance by destroying many Japanese pillboxes with their 75mm (2.95in) guns, and by evening Suribachi was securely isolated from the rest of the island.

The grim task of occupying this formidable bastion would have to wait until later.

In the center, the 27th and 25th Regiments were gradually extricating themselves from the Red and Yellow beaches and moving towards Airfield No. 1. The Seabees (Naval Construction Battalions), largely recruited from the civilian construction industry and manned by volunteers usually in their 40s or early 50s, were performing miracles on the beaches. Landing with the early waves of assault troops they attacked the terraces with their bulldozers carving passages through which the tanks, artillery, and transport could pass and cleared the masses of bogged down landing craft and vehicles that cluttered the shoreline. There was a joke: "Protect your Seabees. One of them could be your dad." Turner had had to halt the landings around 1300hrs as there was nowhere to get more Marines ashore, but the heroic efforts of the Seabees, who suffered heavy casualties on D-Day, allowed the flow of men and materials to resume after two hours. Even so, in virtually every shell hole there lay at least one dead Marine and at the foot of the terraces scores of wounded lay among the exploding shells and mortars, waiting for evacuation by the landing craft which were running the gauntlet of the terrific barrage.

By 1130hrs some Marines had reached the southern end of Airfield No. 1 which was sited on a plateau whose perimeter rose steeply on the eastern side. The Japanese mounted a fierce defense, hundreds being killed and the remainder pouring across the runway or disappearing into the pipes of the drainage system. At one point over a hundred Japanese charged down the runway to be met by a hail of machine gun and rifle fire.

As evening approached, the Marines held a line running from the base of Mount Suribachi across the southern perimeter of Airfield No. 1 and ending at the foot of the Quarry, (See Map). The 0-1 line, the D-Day

On the beach a Marine in pensive mood sits with his M1 rifle. (National Archives)

objective, had not been reached but it was always an unrealistic goal. Perhaps if Adm Nimitz had prised some of his deskbound planners away from their comfortable offices in Hawaii and given them a spell with the assault troops they may have come up with more realistic projections.

The Marines habitually sought to consolidate their positions during the night while the Japanese, on the other hand, were adept at nighttime infiltration and favored darkness for their famous "banzai" charges. Throughout the night destroyers fired flares to illuminate the front lines. As they descended on parachutes they cast an eerie glow over the scene. The Japanese kept up their mortar and artillery fire, while at sea a shuttle service of landing craft brought in supplies and evacuated the wounded.

Aboard the command ship *Eldorado*, "Howlin' Mad" Smith studied the day's reports. Progress had not been as good as he had hoped and the casualty figures made grim reading: "I don't know who he is, but the Japanese General running this show is one smart bastard," he announced to a group of war correspondents.

D+1 – D+5: "INFLICT MUCH DAMAGE TO THE ENEMY"

D+1

A four-foot high surf on the beaches and a bitterly cold wind did little to raise the spirits of either the Marines or their commanders on Tuesday, D+1. Having isolated Mount Suribachi, the 28th Regiment were faced with the unenviable task of capturing it, while to the north the remainder of the invasion force were poised to mount a concerted attack to secure Airfields 1 and 2.

With daylight came the carrier planes, pounding the volcano with bombs and napalm while destroyers shelled the gun positions directly to

Section Chief Marine Private First Class R. F. Callahan calls in 155mm (6.1in) artillery fire against a Japanese position. (USMC)

the front of the 28th Regiment. Attacking on a broad front with artillery support, the Marines could only gain 75yds (69m) of ground by 1200hrs in the face of fierce resistance from Col Atsuchi's defenders. Tanks had joined the battle at around 1100hrs following long delays in refuelling and added valuable support, but the Japanese had a huge advantage in their prepared positions on the higher ground. Looking ahead, Lt Wells said: "I saw little or nothing to shield us from the enemy's fire power; my men would be open targets all the way."

Colonel Atsuchi radioed Gen Kuribayashi that the American bombardments from both artillery and offshore naval units were very fierce and suggested that he and his men should attempt a "banzai" charge. The General had expected the garrison on Mount Suribachi to maintain control for at least ten days and did not even bother to reply, but suspected that Atsuchi was beginning to waver.

Little progress was made in the afternoon and the Marines dug in and awaited reinforcements and additional tanks for an all-out assault the following day. The Japanese were determined that there should be no respite for the enemy and commenced a barrage all along the front line. "The shells continued walking up our lines, exploding only a few feet away. All I could think about was the great loss of men. What made it even more horrifying, it stopped soon after passing through us and started back again," said Wells. During the night, Japanese troops began to gather near the eastern slopes of the volcano but the destroyer USS *Henry A. Wiley* blasted them under the glare of searchlights, and the anticipated nighttime counterattack was nipped in the bud.

To the north, the other three regiments began their offensive at around 0830hrs, with the right flank anchored at the Quarry and the left swinging north in an attempt to straighten the line. The Marines encountered strong opposition from the mass of bunkers, pillboxes, and landmines that had been so carefully prepared. Mid-afternoon saw the arrival of the brand new battleship USS *Washington* which blasted the cliffs around the Quarry with its massive 16in guns causing a landslide that blocked dozens of enemy caves.

By 1200hrs the majority of Airfield No. 1 was in American hands, a bitter blow to Gen Kuribayashi who had not anticipated such a rapid advance, and the Marines now had an almost straight front line across the island although the D-Day 0-1 objective still eluded them. General Schmidt decided to commit the 21st Regiment of the 3rd Division, an indication that the top brass did not consider that progress had been swift enough. (The Joint Chiefs of Staff had hoped to keep the whole of the 3rd Division intact for the upcoming invasion of Okinawa.) However, the high seas and congested beaches frustrated the landings and after six hours in their landing craft the Regiment were ordered back to their transports.

As the second day drew to a close the Marines had control of almost a quarter of the island but the cost had been very heavy. Kuribayashi's orders, "Each man should think of his defense position as his graveyard, fight until the last and inflict much damage to the enemy" was bearing fruit. Heavy rain began to fall in the afternoon and continued throughout the night, filling foxholes with water and collapsing their sides. The old hands among the Marines shivered and wished themselves back among the hot sands of the atolls that they had so recently liberated.

D+2

Wednesday's plan looked straightforward – the 28th Regiment would begin their final assault on Mount Suribachi and the remainder would

The beaches were already beginning to become congested with swamped jeeps, trucks, and tanks as this group of Marines await their chance to move out. (National Archives)

A machine gun crew sit among a pile of spent ammunition somewhere just south of Mount Suribachi. (National Archives)

move north on a broad front: in the west, the 26th and 27th Regiments, in the center the 23rd and in the east the 24th, but simple plans seldom develop smoothly. The bad weather of the previous day had deteriorated even further as a howling gale tore through the island and rain clouds scurried overhead. Six-foot waves crashed down onto the beaches forcing Adm Turner to close them down again.

For an 18 year old Marine in his first battle, Iwo Jima was a trying experience for "Chuck" Tatum, a member of a machine gun squad with the 27th Regiment: "Dawn on D+2 greeted us with a cold rain and we were still next to Airfield No. 1. I worked this out to be a grand total of 1,000yds (914m) advance from the beach in two days – we wouldn't be arrested for speeding! The terrain we were in was flat from the edge of the runway to the western shoreline, probably the only flat ground in Iwo. The dark overcast sky filled with rain, soaked us, and transformed the volcanic soil into a gooey sticky mess. Vehicles and men struggled to move and finally bogged down. On the landing beaches to our right chaos continued as increasing winds and seas smashed derelict, broached landing craft. Beaches remained closed to all but emergency traffic and wounded lay patiently in hastily prepared shelters while Corpsmen did what they could to save lives. At 0800hrs the frontal attack northward was renewed. The 5th Division objective was the left flank of the island, the entire area between the runways and the beaches. As we had the day before, we mopped up bypassed positions and consolidated the gains made."

Supported by a blistering artillery barrage, fire from Navy cruisers and destroyers, and napalm and machine gun fire from over 40 carrier planes, the 28th Regiment launched their assault on Mount Suribachi at

0845hrs. The gunfire denuded the ground before them, revealing chains of blockhouses and connecting trenches with little or no cover between the two front lines. There was the additional hazard of rows of barbed wire that the Marines had placed in front of their own lines during the night to prevent enemy infiltration. It had been assumed that the morning's advance would be spearheaded by tanks which would flatten all before them but again they were delayed by fuelling problems.

The 3rd Platoon in the center met heavy opposition but the late arrival of tanks and halftrack 75mm (2.95in) guns helped their progress. By evening the regiment had formed a semi-circle around the north side of the volcano and moved forward 650yds (594m) on the left, 500yds (457m) in the center and 1,000yds (914m) on the right, – good progress under the circumstances.

"We had nothing to protect us but the clothes on our back," said Wells who was in the thick of the fighting, reducing enemy bunkers with hand grenades and receiving severe wounds to his legs. "I could feel myself running out of energy, my wounds were beginning to take their toll. I had not eaten, drunk water, or defecated in two and a half days."

To the north, 68 Navy planes blasted the Japanese lines with bombs and rockets, and at 0740hrs a massive barrage of artillery and naval gunfire added their weight as the 4th and 5th Marine Divisions moved against a complex of well-hidden enemy positions and casualties soon began to mount. Near the west coast, Sherman tanks led an advance of over 1,000 yards by the 26th and 27th Regiments and the D-Day 0-1 line was finally reached. On the east side of the island, the 4th Division could only take 50yds (46m) of ground in the rugged terrain around the Quarry despite being reinforced by an extra company. Fighting among the cliffs and caves in the Quarry area was a hazardous business and involved heavy casualties. Capt "Jumpin' Joe" McCarthy, commanding officer of G Company 2nd Battalion of the 24th Regiment states: "We

landed with 257 men and received 90 replacements. Of that total of 347 only 35 men were able to walk off the island when the fighting was over." McCarthy's men were under terrific fire all morning and were suffering heavy losses and in the afternoon he assigned an assault squad to clean out the pillboxes that had kept his advance to a standstill.

One of the group was Pfc Pete Santoro who recalls: "I took it on myself to go to my left as the others moved right, and below me was the entrance to a tunnel. I saw two Japs with rifles crawling out on their hands and knees. I shot them both in the back I'm sorry to say as I don't know how to say turn around in Japanese. Captain McCarthy came around the other side and shot them again and I said I got them already. As we went to take more high ground I found the entrance to another tunnel. I fired a rifle grenade but it fell short so I fired my last one. As I started to move in I was shot in the back. It felt like I was hit with a sledgehammer. I couldn't move my legs. I crawled out to two of our men who asked if I had been hit by a shotgun. The Jap had hit my M1 ammunition clip and my shells had shattered and penetrated all over my back." Santoro was eventually taken to the hospital ship *Solace* and after treatment returned to the beach.

It was here that he disposed of a Japanese sniper who had been taking potshots at airmen from Airfield No. 1, and from there he returned to his unit much to the surprise of McCarthy who put him in charge of the ammunition dump. On March 9, a mortar round exploded close by and Santoro was severely concussed. Returning again to the *Solace*, he swore that he would not be returning to that island.

General Schmidt again disembarked the 21st Regiment of the 3rd Division and they came ashore on Yellow Beach. The Japanese continued their disruptive fire throughout the night and between 150 and 200 troops gathered at the end of the runway of Airfield No. 2 and rushed the lines of the 23rd Regiment at 2330hrs. A combination of artillery and naval gunfire annihilated them before they could reach the Marines.

The ships of the Navy Task Force supporting the landings were to become the targets of one of the early kamikaze attacks of the war. As the light began to fade, 50 Japanese aircraft approached from the north-west. They were from the 2nd Milate Special Attack Unit based at Katori Airbase and had refuelled at Hachijo Jima 125 miles south of Tokyo. They were picked up by the radar of the USS *Saratoga*, a veteran carrier of the Pacific War, and six fighters were sent to intercept. They shot down two Zeros (Mitsubishi AGM fighters), but the remaining Zeros plowed on through the low lying cloud, two of them trailing smoke, and slammed into the side of the carrier turning the hangers into an inferno. Another solitary attacker smashed into the flight deck leaving a gaping hole 100yds (91m) from the bow. Damage control teams worked wonders and within one hour the fires were under control and the Saratoga was able to recover a few of her planes. The others were taken aboard the escort carriers USS *Wake Island* and USS *Natoma Bay*.

Another aircraft, a "Betty" twin engined bomber (Mitsubishi G4M), tore into the escort carrier USS *Bismarck Sea*. The decks were full of aircraft and the ensuing explosion caused uncontrollable fires. Abandon ship was sounded and 800 men went over the side. Within a few minutes a huge explosion ripped off the entire stern of the carrier and she rolled over and sank. Three other ships were also damaged: the escort carrier

USS *Lurga Point* was showered with flaming debris as four aircraft were blasted out of the sky; the minesweeper *Keokuk* was damaged when a "Jill" dive bomber (Nakajima B6N) hit her deck; and LST 477 loaded with Sherman tanks received a glancing blow.

The *Saratoga*, with destroyer escort, returned to Pearl Harbor, but by the time the damage was repaired the war was over. The kamikazes had done their work: 358 men killed, one carrier sunk, and another severely damaged. It was a grim preview of the mayhem they would later cause during the invasion of Okinawa in April.

D+3

There was no let-up in the weather on Wednesday as Marines of the 28th Regiment, drenched to the skin and bent by the wind, prepared to renew the attack on Suribachi. Fresh supplies of ammunition had been brought to the front during the night, but the Shermans were mired in mud and the Navy declined to supply air support in the appalling weather. It was to be up to the foot soldier with rifle, flamethrower, grenade, and demolition charge to win the day.

Colonel Atsuchi still had 800–900 men left and they had no intention of allowing the Americans an easy victory. Major Youamata announced: "We are surrounded by enemy craft of all sizes, shapes and descriptions, enemy shells have smashed at our installations and defenses, their planes bomb and strafe yet we remain strong and defiant. The Americans are beginning to climb the first terraces towards our defenses. Now they shall taste our steel and lead."

Throughout the day the Marines attacked the Japanese positions on the lower slopes of Mount Suribachi. There was little room for maneuver and it was impossible to use support fire from artillery and tanks to maximum advantage because of the close proximity of the lines. By

afternoon, patrols from Companies G and E had worked their way around the base of the volcano and it was surrounded. The bitter fighting on the northern slopes had reduced the Japanese garrison to a few hundred men and many were infiltrating the Marine lines through the maze of tunnels and joining Kuribayashi's forces in the north. Others moved upwards towards the summit. The final assault would have to wait until the following day.

The sweep to the north continued with Harry Schmidt placing the newly landed 3rd Division reinforcements, the 21st Regiment, in the center of the line between the 4th and 5th Divisions around Airfield No. 2. Here Col Ikeda with his 145th Regiment had the strongest section of the Japanese defenses. Lack of sleep and hot food, heavy casualties, and terrible weather were affecting the fighting efficiency of the men who had landed on D-Day and many of the hard pressed units were replaced. The new 3rd Division men had a baptism of fire as they stormed the heavily defended ground south of the airfield and the day's gains amounted to a mere 250yds (229m) – F Company of the 2nd Battalion were so badly mauled that they only lasted one day.

On the eastern flank near the Quarry, "Jumpin' Joe" Chambers had rocket firing trucks brought forward to pound the enemy hideouts, resulting in dozens of Japanese fleeing to the lower ground where they were decimated by machine gun fire. Chambers was himself badly wounded in the afternoon and evacuated to a hospital ship.

The Japanese mounted a series of strong counterattacks throughout the day which were repulsed by heavy artillery fire, and as the weather

The Sherman tanks had great difficulty coming ashore until the bulldozers could clear a way for them through the soft sand. Here. "Cairo," fitted with wooden planks as protection against magnetic mines, has shed a track. (National Archives)

deteriorated further with icy rain and low mists preventing the Navy from providing gunfire and air support, the fighting died down. Casualties still crowded the beaches as the rough seas prevented LSTs from evacuating the wounded, and behind the lines near Airfield No. 1, the 4th Division cemetery was inaugurated. Up till now the dead had been left in rows under their ponchos, "stacked like cordwood" as one Marine described it.

"Howlin' Mad" Smith aboard the USS *Auburn* was counting the cost. Three days of battle and the Regimental Returns listed 2,517 casualties for the 4th Division and 2,057 for the 5th: 4,574 dead and wounded and the 0-1 line had just been reached. Little did he know that as his Marines approached the hills, ravines, canyons, gullies, and cliffs of the north the worst was yet to come.

D+4

February 23 was the day that the 28th Regiment captured Mount Suribachi. General Kuribayashi had not expected this strategically important feature to fall so early in the battle and when the survivors who had infiltrated the American lines arrived in the north they were severely reprimanded.

With much improved weather, LtCol Chandler Johnson gave the order to occupy and secure the summit and Marines from the 3rd Platoon started out at 0800hrs. A forty-man patrol led by Lt Hal

ABOVE **Near the beach, rows of dead lie under their ponchos: burial parties check identification and personal possessions. (National Archives)**

RIGHT **Marine artillery was vital in the support of the front line troops. Most of the Marine advances were accompanied by massive bombardments from both offshore naval units and forward artillery. (National Archives)**

Schrier labored up the northern slopes, laden with weapons and ammunition. The going became increasingly difficult but the opposition was surprisingly light. At 1000hrs they reached the rim of the crater and engaged a number of the enemy who attacked them with hand grenades. At 1020hrs the Stars and Stripes were raised on a length of pipe and *Leatherneck* photographer Lou Lowery recorded the moment. Throughout the southern half of the island the shout was "the flag is up" and troops cheered and vessels sounded their sirens. Around 1200hrs, a larger flag was raised to replace the smaller one and the event was photographed by Associated Press cameraman Joe Rosenthal, and this became the most famous picture of World War II. (For a full account of the flag raisings on Mount Suribachi see Appendix 3.)

With about one third of Iwo Jima in American hands and a great improvement in the weather, Gen Harry Schmidt and Gen Cates came ashore to set up their HQs (Gen Rockey had come ashore the previous day), and the three met to discuss the situation. It was decided that the 3rd Division would maintain the center with the 5th Division in the west and the 4th in the east. The Navy would continue to add support with gunfire and carrier aircraft, and the tanks of all three divisions would come under a single command, LtCol William Collins of the 5th Division.

D+4 was largely a day of consolidation and replenishment although fighting continued south of Airfield No. 2 and north of the Quarry. Schmidt was planning a major offensive for the following day in an attempt to break the stalemate.

D+5

True to his word, Harry Schmidt provided a tremendous barrage all along the front line. From the west the battleship USS *Idaho* blasted the

Flamethrowers were invaluable on Iwo Jima where the enemy had to be prised out of every cave, pillbox, and bunker by groups of Marines. A flamethrower was always accompanied by a number of riflemen to protect him against snipers. (US Navy)

Colonel Kenehiko Atsuchi had established a formidable defense sector on Mount Suribachi. At the base a network of cave defenses, mortar, artillery and machine-gun positions thwarted the advance of the 28th Marines for four days, while further up the volcano, numerous emplacements were to hamper the Marines right up to February 23rd, when the flag was raised on the summit.

By D+1, the 28th Marines had established a secure line across the island and were supported by heavy 103mm (4.1in) artillery fire from the 13th Marines to their rear. General Kuribayashi knew that severing Mount Suribachi from the northern plateau had done little to damage his overall defense system, and had decided that the volcano should be a semi-independent sector capable of continuing the battle without his assistance.

The only route to the top of Mount Suribachi lay up the north face in the 2nd Battalion's zone. At 0900hrs on D+4, Col Johnson sent out two patrols from Companies D and F to reconnoiter suitable routes and little resistance was forthcoming. A 40-man detachment followed them and the rim of the volcano was reached at about 1015hrs, where a short fierce skirmish developed with the few remaining defenders, who were soon overwhelmed.

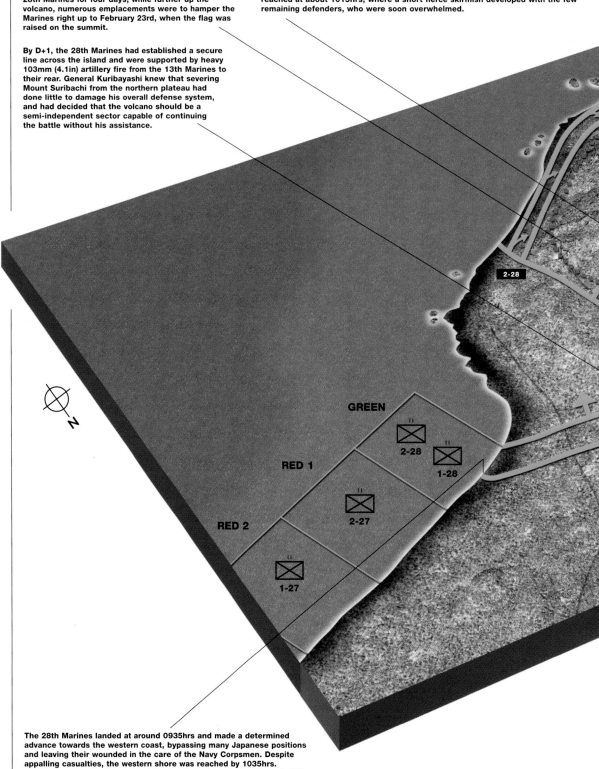

The 28th Marines landed at around 0935hrs and made a determined advance towards the western coast, bypassing many Japanese positions and leaving their wounded in the care of the Navy Corpsmen. Despite appalling casualties, the western shore was reached by 1035hrs.
At 1039hrs, Gen Rockey ordered the 3rd Battalion, who had been held in reserve, to land in support of the 1st and 2nd.

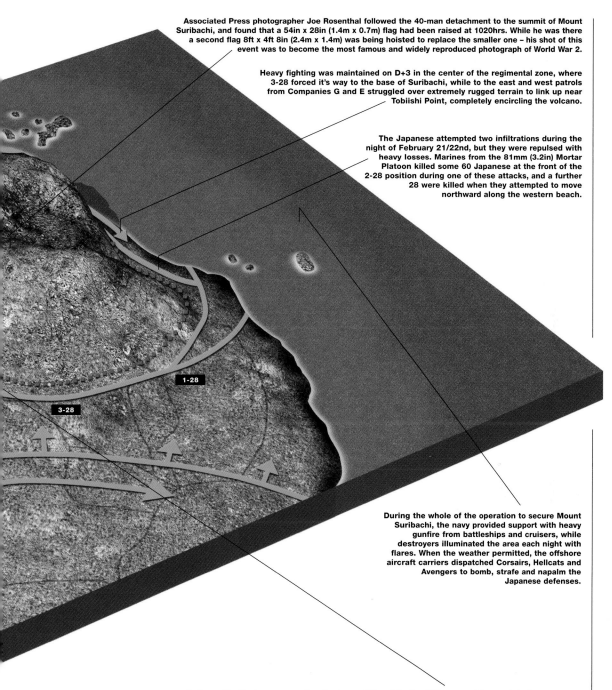

Associated Press photographer Joe Rosenthal followed the 40-man detachment to the summit of Mount Suribachi, and found that a 54in x 28in (1.4m x 0.7m) flag had been raised at 1020hrs. While he was there a second flag 8ft x 4ft 8in (2.4m x 1.4m) was being hoisted to replace the smaller one – his shot of this event was to become the most famous and widely reproduced photograph of World War 2.

Heavy fighting was maintained on D+3 in the center of the regimental zone, where 3-28 forced it's way to the base of Suribachi, while to the east and west patrols from Companies G and E struggled over extremely rugged terrain to link up near Tobiishi Point, completely encircling the volcano.

The Japanese attempted two infiltrations during the night of February 21/22nd, but they were repulsed with heavy losses. Marines from the 81mm (3.2in) Mortar Platoon killed some 60 Japanese at the front of the 2-28 position during one of these attacks, and a further 28 were killed when they attempted to move northward along the western beach.

1-28

3-28

During the whole of the operation to secure Mount Suribachi, the navy provided support with heavy gunfire from battleships and cruisers, while destroyers illuminated the area each night with flares. When the weather permitted, the offshore aircraft carriers dispatched Corsairs, Hellcats and Avengers to bomb, strafe and napalm the Japanese defenses.

D+2 saw the Marines surrounding the base of Mount Suribachi from coast to coast. In the west were 1st Battalion, in the center the 3rd Battalion, and in the east the 2nd Battalion. Tanks did not participate in the early phases of this assault because they were unable to refuel and rearm in time as their maintenance section had not yet come ashore.

ASSAULT ON MOUNT SURIBACHI D-DAY - D+4

The 28th Marines landed on Green Beach and advanced across the 700yds (640m) wide isthmus at the base of Mount Suribachi. Despite fierce opposition and very heavy casualties, they had isolated the volcano and its defenders by 1035hrs. General Kuribayashi had anticipated that Suribachi would be cut off early in the battle, but was very disappointed that Col Atsuchi's garrison held out for only four days.

An armored Amtrac, "Old Glory"
somewhere on the island.
(National Archives)

area north of the airfield with her 14in guns as the cruiser USS *Pensacola*, repaired after her D-Day battering, joined in from the east coast. Masses of aircraft added bombs and rockets, and the Marine artillery and mortars expended huge amounts of ammunition.

The attack was spearheaded by the 21st Regiment deployed in the area between the two airfields. Massed tanks were scheduled to precede the infantry but Col Ikeda had anticipated this move, and the taxiways of both airfields were heavily mined and covered by anti-tank guns. The first two tanks were disabled by mines and the remainder ground to a halt. Deprived of their armor, the Marines had no alternative but to clear the mass of bunkers and pillboxes the hard way, with small arms, grenades and flamethrowers. In what looked more like an episode from World War I, the Marines charged the high ground and the Japanese retaliated by leaving their positions and engaging the Americans in hand-to-hand fighting. In a frenzied mêlée of clubbing, stabbing, kicking and punching, arms and legs were broken, swords slashed, bodies fell and blood spurted until over fifty of the enemy lay dead and the Marines occupied the higher ground.

With only four hours of daylight remaining, the Marines, exhausted and desperately short of ammunition, were determined to hold on to their gains. As the light faded the redoubtable Seabees came forward with tractors and trailers loaded with ammunition, food, and water and the troops settled in for the night. Warrant Office George Green remembers the incident well: "The Seabees had loaded trailers with supplies and ammunition and brought them to the limit of Airfield No. 1, only 200yds (183m) from the battlefront. As darkness fell the entrenched Marines stared in wonder as a tractor trundled towards them towing a trailer with ammunition, water, and containers of hot food preceded by two men on foot carrying flashlights to show the way. How they did it I don't know. After dark we heard the tractor coming, and sure enough there's a guy driving the thing in pitch-black night. To this day I don't know how he knew where he was going. To me that guy had guts."

On the right flank, the 24th Regiment of the 4th Division were battling for "Charlie Dog Ridge," an escarpment south of the main runway of Airfield No. 2. Backed up by howitzers and mortars they blasted and burned their way to the top sustaining heavy casualties. At 1700hrs Col Walter Jordan ordered the men to dig in for the night. By Iwo Jima standards the overall gains for the day had been impressive, but so too had the casualty figures. Between D+1 and D+5, 1,034 men had died, 3,741 were wounded, 5 were missing and 558 were suffering from battle fatigue. Less than half of the island had been secured and the battle had a further 30 days to run.

D+6 – D+11: INTO THE MEATGRINDER

D+6

Having secured a front across the island that approximated to the 0-1 line, Harry Schmidt was intent on pressing northward across the plateau and the unfinished Airfield No. 3 to the north coast to split the enemy in two. Other factors also influenced the commander's choice. The west coast of the island had accessible beaches which were desperately needed to unload the vast amount of equipment and

The opening up of the beaches on the west side of the island was vital. Little could be landed on the east coast until the masses of vehicles and equipment was cleared. (National Archives)

supplies still stacked in the armada of transports. With Okinawa only two months away these ships were urgently needed elsewhere, but at the moment the Japanese still commanded the heights north-west of Airfield No. 2 from which they could shell the western coast with impunity.

Even though the southern end of the island was still within range of many of the Japanese guns, the area around Airfield No. 1 was being turned into a gigantic construction site. Over 2,000 Seabees were extending the runways to make them capable of handling the giant B29 Superfortress bombers, P51 Mustang fighters, and P61 Black Widow night fighters. Off the shores of Mount Suribachi, a base was being established for the Catalina and Coronado flying boats engaged in rescue operations between the Marianas and Japan. Elsewhere a "city" of Nissan huts, tents, workshops, and supply dumps was replacing what only days earlier had been a bloody battlefield.

The thrust to the north began on D+6, Sunday, February 25 – no day of rest for the Marines. As the 3rd Battalion moved against high ground at the end of the main runway of Airfield No. 2, 26 Shermans rumbled out to spearhead the attack and ran into a fusillade of artillery, anti-tank gun, and mortar fire. Three of the leading tanks burst into flames and were abandoned. The strongest point in the Japanese defenses was "Hill Peter," a 360ft high prominence just off the runway. This was stormed repeatedly but by 1430hrs the Marines had only gained 200yds (183m). The 2nd and 1st Battalions had slightly better luck and were north of the airfield, although "Hill Peter" remained in enemy hands. Nine Shermans had been knocked out and Marine casualties stood at nearly 400 dead and wounded.

The 5th Division on the left were already 400yds (366m) ahead of the 3rd Division lines and were ordered to stay where they were, but on the right the 4th Division faced a complex of four formidable defense positions that became known collectively as the "Meatgrinder." The first was Hill 382 (named from its elevation above sea level), with its slopes peppered with countless pillboxes and caves. Four hundred yards to the south lay a shallow depression called the "Amphitheater," and immediately to the east

Rocket firing trucks were used extensively on Iwo Jima where the terrain permitted. It was usual for the trucks to line up, fire off their rockets as fast as possible, and get the hell out before the Japanese mortars located them. (National Archives)

The most famous photograph of World War II. Associated Press cameraman Joe Rosenthal's superb shot of Marines raising the flag on the summit of Mount Suribachi on February 23, 1945. (US Navy)

was "Turkey Knob," a hill surmounted by a massive blockhouse. The fourth obstacle was the ruins of the village of Minami, long reduced to rubble by naval gunfire and now studded with machine gun emplacements. This collective killing ground was defended by MajGen Senda and his 2nd Mixed Brigade which included the men of Baron Nishi's 26th Tank Regiment, now largely devoid of tanks but still full of fight.

The 23rd and 24th Regiments, some 3,800 men of the 4th Division, little knowing that this was the island's most impregnable fortress, prepared to take on the "Meatgrinder" and at 0800hrs the now customary naval barrage and armada of carrier planes preceded the assault on Hill 382. One platoon battled their way to the summit only to be surrounded when the Japanese mounted a massive counterattack. Vicious hand to hand fighting ensued as the survivors withdrew under cover of smoke. Ten of the wounded were recovered after dark by gallant volunteers, and day one in the "Meatgrinder" was a complete stalemate. About 100yds (91m) had been gained at the cost of nearly 500 casualties.

D+7

Monday, February 26, dawned bright but chilly. The Marines could not believe that they had only been on the island for a week; it seemed like months. "Hill Peter" remained defiant and at 0800hrs the 9th Regiment advanced with tank support. One flamethrower tank got behind the enemy lines and incinerated a number of the enemy who were escaping through a tunnel, but the day's gains were insignificant.

To the west the 5th Division set their sights on Hill 362A, 600yds (549m) south of the village of Nishi and surrounded by pillboxes and

Bogged down tank, Amtracs blown over by shellfire – a view on the beaches taken some days after the landing. (National Archives)

caves. Tanks from the 5th Tank Battalion ground through the rocks and boulders to give support but the complex proved impregnable. A little to the right, the tanks smashed through the enemy defenses to a depth of 100yds (91m), and the 27th Regiment advanced up the west coast assisted by gunfire from the Amphibious Battalions from offshore. Day two of the battle for Hill 382 in the "Meatgrinder" saw the 24th Regiment replaced by the 25th Regiment. The initial attack looked promising with a gain of over 100yds (91m) until heavy machine gun fire from "Turkey Knob" brought the advance to a halt.

The 23rd Regiment to the left worked its way through a minefield beside the perimeter track of the airfield and advanced towards a ruined radio station at the foot of the hill. A massive fusillade of mortar and machine gun fire from nearby "Turkey Knob" and Hill 382 brought the Marines to a grinding halt as 17 men lay dead and 26 were wounded. Under cover of smoke grenades, stretcher-bearers evacuated the survivors. It was during this engagement that Pvt Douglas Jacobson silenced sixteen enemy positions using a bazooka single-handedly. The 19-year-old had killed 75 of the enemy in less than 30 minutes and earned himself the Medal of Honor.

D+8

"Hill Peter" still stood out like a sore thumb at the front of the 3rd Division line and at 0800hrs two battalions of the 9th regiment, LtCol Randall's 1st and LtCol Cushman's 2nd, moved forward to secure the complex. Inching forward against murderous machine gun and

mortar fire the 1st reached the top of the hill but were pinned down by fire from bypassed positions at their rear. In the early afternoon another concerted effort was launched and elements of both battalions relieved the beleaguered Marines.

To the east the 4th Division appeared to be bogged down before the seemingly impregnable "Meatgrinder." General Cates committed five battalions to the area, two against Hill 382 and three against "Turkey Knob," and all day the battle seesawed up and down the slopes of the hill. Rocket launching trucks blasted the hill with over 500 rockets before having to scurry away under a torrent of enemy mortar fire, and at one point a small group of Marines actually reached the summit until shortage of ammunition and vicious counterattacks forced them to fall back. At the foot of the hill the Marines finally completed an encircling maneuver after bitter hand-to-hand fighting, and the last hours of daylight were spent in consolidating their precarious gains.

As the battle moved further north the tanks found it more and more difficult to operate among the gullies and boulder-strewn terrain. Tankdozers, Shermans fitted with bulldozer blades, were constantly in action clearing paths through the rubble and scrubland but the battle was developing into a horrific man-to-man slog in which casualties escalated by the day and prisoners were a novelty. The only grim consolation for the Marines was that their casualties could be replaced.

During the night, Japanese aircraft made a desperate attempt to get supplies to their garrison. In the only attempt that was made during the battle to support their troops, the aircraft succeeded in dropping a few parachutes containing medical supplies and ammunition. Three of the planes were shot down by carrier based night fighters. General Kuribayashi was moved to say: "I pay many respects to these brave aviators. It is difficult to express how the fighting youth of Iwo Jima who stood before their death felt when they saw these brave flyers."

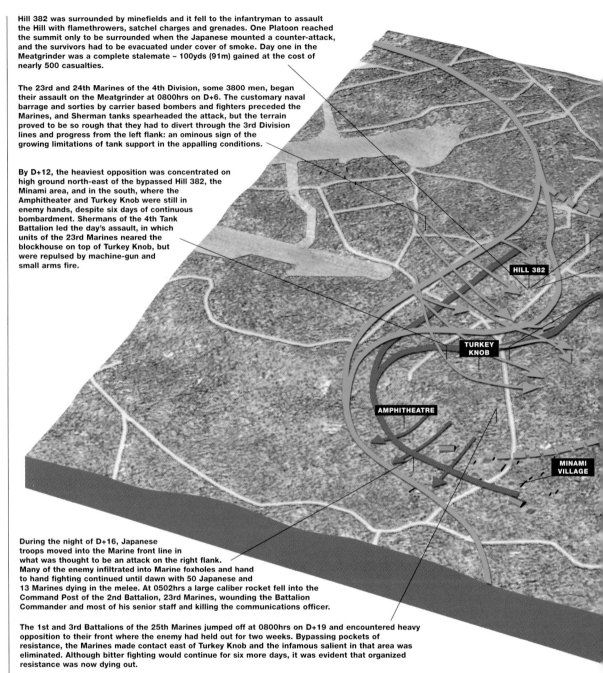

Hill 382 was surrounded by minefields and it fell to the infantryman to assault the Hill with flamethrowers, satchel charges and grenades. One Platoon reached the summit only to be surrounded when the Japanese mounted a counter-attack, and the survivors had to be evacuated under cover of smoke. Day one in the Meatgrinder was a complete stalemate – 100yds (91m) gained at the cost of nearly 500 casualties.

The 23rd and 24th Marines of the 4th Division, some 3800 men, began their assault on the Meatgrinder at 0800hrs on D+6. The customary naval barrage and sorties by carrier based bombers and fighters preceded the Marines, and Sherman tanks spearheaded the attack, but the terrain proved to be so rough that they had to divert through the 3rd Division lines and progress from the left flank: an ominous sign of the growing limitations of tank support in the appalling conditions.

By D+12, the heaviest opposition was concentrated on high ground north-east of the bypassed Hill 382, the Minami area, and in the south, where the Amphitheater and Turkey Knob were still in enemy hands, despite six days of continuous bombardment. Shermans of the 4th Tank Battalion led the day's assault, in which units of the 23rd Marines neared the blockhouse on top of Turkey Knob, but were repulsed by machine-gun and small arms fire.

HILL 382

TURKEY KNOB

AMPHITHEATRE

MINAMI VILLAGE

During the night of D+16, Japanese troops moved into the Marine front line in what was thought to be an attack on the right flank. Many of the enemy infiltrated into Marine foxholes and hand to hand fighting continued until dawn with 50 Japanese and 13 Marines dying in the melee. At 0502hrs a large caliber rocket fell into the Command Post of the 2nd Battalion, 23rd Marines, wounding the Battalion Commander and most of his senior staff and killing the communications officer.

The 1st and 3rd Battalions of the 25th Marines jumped off at 0800hrs on D+19 and encountered heavy opposition to their front where the enemy had held out for two weeks. Bypassing pockets of resistance, the Marines made contact east of Turkey Knob and the infamous salient in that area was eliminated. Although bitter fighting would continue for six more days, it was evident that organized resistance was now dying out.

During the period when the 4th Division was pitted against the Meatgrinder, they were engaged in head-on assaults and fought a bloody path from Charlie Dog Ridge past Hill 382, the Amphitheater, Turkey Knob, through the ruins of Minami Village and almost to the east coast. The right flank, the hinge, advanced only 1000yds (914m), while the rest of the Division, the door, turned upon it and attacked north-east, east and south-east to close and sweep trapped enemy forces towards the sea.

ASSAULT ON THE MEATGRINDER D+6 – D+19

As Harry Schmidt's three Divisions fought slowly northward through Iwo Jima, the 4th Division came up against a complex of four formidable defense positions to the east of Airfield No2, that soon became known to the Marines as "The Meatgrinder". Defended by MajGen Senda's 2nd Mixed Brigade and elements of Baron Nish's 26th Tank Regiment, Hill 382, Turkey Knob, The Amphitheater and the ruins of Minami Village were to hold out until March 15 and be the scene of some of the bloodiest actions of the whole battle.

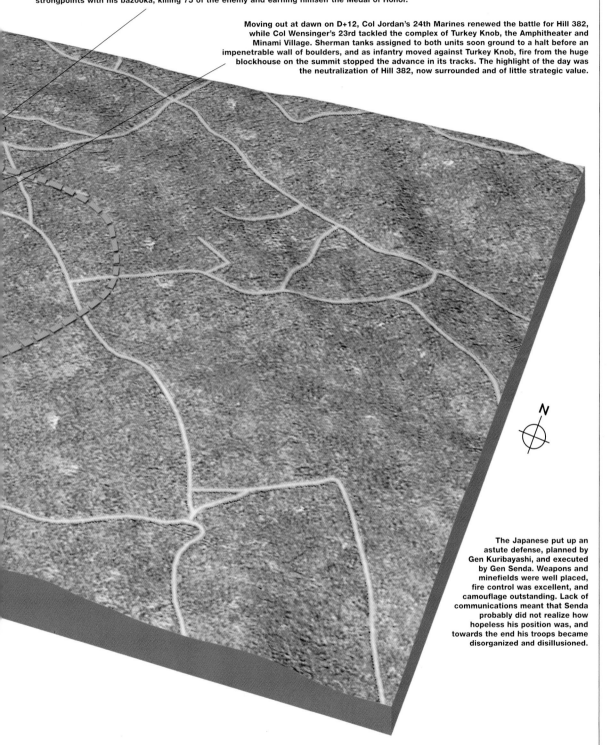

On D+7, Gen Cates alerted the 25th Marines to replace the battered 24th and three Battalions attacked behind an artillery barrage. Things went well for the first 100yds (91m) before a wall of extremely heavy machine-gun fire from the Amphitheater and Turkey Knob brought the advance to a grinding halt. The 23rd Marines on the left flank worked their way through a minefield and occupied a shattered radio station below Hill 382. On this day, Pfc Douglas Jacobson silenced sixteen strongpoints with his bazooka, killing 75 of the enemy and earning himself the Medal of Honor.

Moving out at dawn on D+12, Col Jordan's 24th Marines renewed the battle for Hill 382, while Col Wensinger's 23rd tackled the complex of Turkey Knob, the Amphitheater and Minami Village. Sherman tanks assigned to both units soon ground to a halt before an impenetrable wall of boulders, and as infantry moved against Turkey Knob, fire from the huge blockhouse on the summit stopped the advance in its tracks. The highlight of the day was the neutralization of Hill 382, now surrounded and of little strategic value.

N

The Japanese put up an astute defense, planned by Gen Kuribayashi, and executed by Gen Senda. Weapons and minefields were well placed, fire control was excellent, and camouflage outstanding. Lack of communications meant that Senda probably did not realize how hopeless his position was, and towards the end his troops became disorganized and disillusioned.

D+9

The last day of February was to be a good one for the 3rd Division in the center of the island. Although this was the day that Harry Schmidt had predicted as the end of the battle, his orders for the day were for the 3rd to press forward towards the north coast. Relieving the battered 9th, the 21st Regiment moved out at 0900hrs and, under a huge naval and artillery barrage that appeared to have stunned the enemy, made good progress. At one point they were confronted by some of the few remaining "Ha-Go" tanks of Baron Nishi's 26th Regiment, but these flimsy vehicles were wiped out by bazookas and marauding aircraft leaving the Baron with only three serviceable tanks on the island. The Japanese soon recovered and by afternoon resistance had stiffened to such an extent that a second massive artillery barrage was called in and by 1300hrs the troops were again on the move. This time the momentum was maintained as the Marines stormed their way into the ruins of the village of Motoyama, once the largest settlement on Iwo Jima. The machine gunners and snipers who had taken over the ruins were soon ousted and Col Duplantis' 3rd Battalion swept on to occupy the high ground overlooking the unfinished Airfield No. 3.

As the 3rd Battalion advanced, the 1st and 2nd Battalions were busy dealing with the mass of overrun enemy positions and in an afternoon of grim fighting the flamethrowers and demolition teams secured the flanks. The flamethrower was the most practical weapon for clearing the enemy from caves, pillboxes, and bunkers. Horrific in its effect, it saved the lives of countless Marines who would otherwise have had to prise the enemy out in hand-to-hand fighting with an opponent who did not consider surrender an option. Pfc Hank Chamberlain describes an attack that was typical: "I was cover for a flamethrower near a row of caves. A grenade came flying out towards us and we dived behind an outcrop of rocks to our left and the grenade exploded harmlessly. The flamethrower was now alongside the cave entrance and sidestepped in front of it and let off a long blast. A single Jap came tearing out. He was a mass of flames from head to foot and his shrieks were indescribable. Both Buckey and I had emptied our guns into the cave and we reloaded as fast as we could. The Jap was now writhing on the ground with his arms flaying the air. We put him out of his agony with enough bullets to kill a dozen men."

Over on the 5th Division front, the Marines were still confronted with Hill 362A – the top dotted with anti-tank guns and mortars, the slopes bristling with machine guns, and the base lined with bunkers and pillboxes. Two battalions of the 27th Regiment, supported by tanks, assaulted the hill with demolition charges and flamethrowers, but little progress was made and at 1200hrs six rocket firing trucks added salvos of 4.5in rockets. Some men reached the top but were driven back by determined enemy troops. The only gains of the day were made by the 1st Battalion who pushed back strong opposition to gain 300yds (274m) near the base.

The impasse at the "Meatgrinder" continued as the 4th Division continued to batter Hill 382 and "Turkey Knob." Attempts to encircle these positions were frustrated, and as smoke shells covered the withdrawal of forward troops, the operation was closed down for the day at 1645hrs.

The most memorable event of the day came at 1400hrs when a Japanese shell landed in a large ammunition dump near Airfield No. 1, and the whole of southern Iwo Jima erupted in a spectacular display of pyrotechnics. Shells exploded with a deafening bang, bullets popped and crackled, and huge clouds of smoke rolled out to sea. Miraculously there were no casualties, but the 5th Division lost almost a quarter of it stocks.

D+10

After a night overlooking Airfield No. 3, the 21st Regiment of the 3rd Division moved forward against surprisingly light resistance and by 1200hrs were across the main runway. Tanks rolled forward to stiffen the attack and all went well until the forward troops reached Hills 362B and

362C, two more heavily defended bastions barring the way to the coast, and the advance ran out of steam.

On the west coast, the 28th Regiment, the conquerors of Mount Suribachi, were now bolstering the 5th Division front as all three battalions were pitted against the complex of strongpoints north of Hill 362A. The day started with shelling by a battleship and three cruisers, and as the dust settled the 1st and 2nd Battalions stormed the slopes and reached the summit. The Japanese had abandoned the site through a labyrinth of caves and taken up new positions on Nishi Ridge, a ragged cliffline 200yds (183m) further north.

For the 4th Division, Hill 382 was the key to the impasse. Until it was taken the whole of the eastern side of Iwo Jima would be firmly in enemy hands, and in the pre-dawn darkness the 24th Regiment moved up to replace the 23rd. In a day of unremitting savagery the battle flowed back and forth. An early advance by the 1st and 2nd Battalions was stalled by a hail of mortar fire. The Japanese then took to their caves as a barrage from naval guns, artillery and carrier planes swept the area. As the 1st Battalion resumed the attack the enemy emerged from the depths and resumed their machine gun, mortar, and small arms fire from the high ground. By afternoon it was obvious that there was yet another stalemate.

The Generals were becoming increasingly concerned about the combat efficiency of their units. It was not unusual to see command pass from captain to lieutenant to sergeant and in some cases to Pfc (Private First Class). A confidential report of the 3rd Battalion 25th Regiment makes note of the situation at the front around this time: "Special note must here be made of the mental condition and morale of our troops. We have been in the assault for a period of ten days during which we

A couple of Marines utilize a captured Japanese Nambo machine gun as the fighting in the north intensifies. (National Archives)

Two flamethrowers, Pvt Richard Klatt on the left and Pfc Wildred Voegeli, demonstrate the terrifying effect of their weapons. (National Archives)

have shown a gain of approx. 800yds (732m). Initially, we had relieved troops whose position on the ground was far short of the position they showed themselves to occupy on the map. Throughout the assault we have suffered heavy casualties. One company commander and two platoon leaders have been killed in action. While it was true we did not move from D+11 to D+17, nevertheless throughout that period of time enemy mortar fire of various calibers fell in our zone of action inflicting many casualties. On D+8, without warning a strafing and napalm strike was made behind and within our lines although our front line panels were clearly displayed. On D+11, a TBF (Avenger Torpedo Bomber) accidentally dropped a lone bomb behind our lines. On D+12, without warning in any way, a rocket barrage, apparently from a rocket jeep, fell directly on our flank platoon. All of this contributed to make our troops "jittery." It is common knowledge that we were relieving a unit which had been unable to accomplish its mission."

General Erskine was scathing in his criticism of the quality of the replacements: "They get killed the day they go into battle," he said. The problem was the use of "battle replacements" as opposed to "organic replacements."

"Battle replacements were recruits who had gone through Parris Island in the summer of 1944, where they had fired for qualification once. In early September they were formed into an Infantry Training Unit at Camp Lejeune where they went through 'musketry range' once, threw one live grenade, fired one rifle grenade and went through one live fire exercise. Designated the 30th Replacement Draft in October, they went to Camp Pendleton and straight on to Maui in Hawaii where they worked on mess duties or working parties with no additional training. The day after Christmas Day they began boarding for Iwo Jima. Those who survived went back to Maui and began receiving the training that might have helped them before the operation," writes author and Iwo Jima veteran John Lane. The situation was typified by one replacement who was placed with a machine gun unit. When asked if he had any questions he replied, "Yes, how do you fire this thing?"

As the 5th Division advanced up the west coast, many enemy gun positions were captured. Here a Marine stands guard over a Japanese coastal artillery piece. (National Archives)

D+11

The pressure continued on Hill 382 and "Turkey Knob." The 1st Battalion of the 25th Regiment made pre-dawn infiltrations but were driven back by mortar shells raining down from the heights above. Sherman tanks and "Zippos" (flamethrower tanks) pounded the blockhouse on the top of "Turkey Knob" and the "Zippos" expended over 1,000 gallons of fuel on the caves, but the Japanese simply retired to the depths of their tunnels and sat out the inferno. Meanwhile the 26th Regiment, in some of the fiercest fighting of the day, secured a

Utilizing an enemy installation, Navy doctors perform front line surgery somewhere in the 4th Division sector. Note the doctor with scissors in his top pocket and kneepads. Conditions were primitive until the casualties could be evacuated. (National Archives)

foothold on the summit of Hill 382. Casualties were horrendous, one unit losing five officers in rapid succession – two fatally wounded, two seriously wounded and the other loosing his leg below the knee.

In the center, hopes of a dash to the north coast were fading. Although the sea was only 1,500yds (1372m) away the 3rd Division had yet to deal with Hills 362B and C. Four thousand men headed out in a two-pronged assault, one group headed for Hill 362B while the other deployed around Airfield No. 3. The approach to the hill was a flat area overlooked by artillery and offering virtually no cover. Tanks were brought forward and under their cover an advance of 500yds (457m) was made to the base of the hill.

On the right the 2nd Battalion moved towards the east of the airfield but made little progress as they came face to face with Baron Nishi's lines. Without his tanks the Baron was resigned to dying on the front line with the remains of his command. The glory days when he had won an Olympic medal on his horse Uranus and socialized with Los Angeles society and Hollywood stars were only a memory.

Colonel Chandler Johnson's 28th Regiment on the west coast were determined to secure Nishi Ridge. Advancing along the left side of Hill 363A they came under heavy fire but pushed on to the ravine between the hill and the ridge where they had a clear area from which the Shermans could blast the cliff face. Johnson, well known for being up front with his men, fell victim to what was probably a misplaced American round which blew him to pieces.

D+12 – D+19: DEADLOCK

D+12

Casualty figures were reaching epidemic proportions. By D+12 the Marine figure stood at 16,000 of whom more than 3,000 were dead. The Japanese numbers were staggering. Of the 21,000 troops in Gen Kuribayashi's command on D-Day, a mere 7,000 remained. The battle was dragging on far longer than the forecast of the Chiefs of Staff, deteriorating into an inexorable slog from gully to gully, ridge to ridge, and cave to cave.

The 5th Division kept up the pressure on the west coast as the 26th Regiment attacked Hill 362B (previously located in the 3rd Division sector but now re-allocated to the 5th), and the 28th Regiment confronted Nishi Ridge. In a grim day's fighting during which they suffered severe casualties, the 26th finally stormed to the top of Hill 362B although the enemy still occupied much of the surrounding area. But the best news of the day came with the capture of Nishi Ridge by the 28th Regiment, an achievement that pleased Gen Rockey who had envisaged a prolonged struggle for this strategically important location.

The 3rd Division again pitted themselves against the "Meatgrinder." Colonel Jordan's 24th Regiment renewed their assault on Hill 382 as Col Wensinger's 23rd tackled "Turkey Knob," the Amphitheater and Minami Village. Shermans of the 4th Tank Battalion had been assigned to both units, but the increasingly rocky terrain was taking its toll as a large proportion of the tanks ground to a halt before impenetrable mounds of rocks and boulders. Engineers braved heavy enemy fire in an

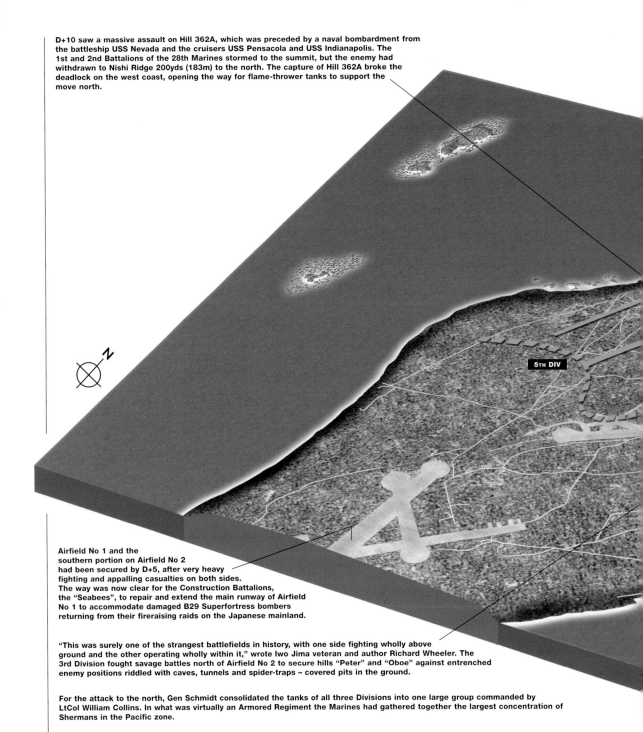

D+10 saw a massive assault on Hill 362A, which was preceded by a naval bombardment from the battleship USS Nevada and the cruisers USS Pensacola and USS Indianapolis. The 1st and 2nd Battalions of the 28th Marines stormed to the summit, but the enemy had withdrawn to Nishi Ridge 200yds (183m) to the north. The capture of Hill 362A broke the deadlock on the west coast, opening the way for flame-thrower tanks to support the move north.

5TH DIV

Airfield No 1 and the southern portion on Airfield No 2 had been secured by D+5, after very heavy fighting and appalling casualties on both sides. The way was now clear for the Construction Battalions, the "Seabees", to repair and extend the main runway of Airfield No 1 to accommodate damaged B29 Superfortress bombers returning from their fireraising raids on the Japanese mainland.

"This was surely one of the strangest battlefields in history, with one side fighting wholly above ground and the other operating wholly within it," wrote Iwo Jima veteran and author Richard Wheeler. The 3rd Division fought savage battles north of Airfield No 2 to secure hills "Peter" and "Oboe" against entrenched enemy positions riddled with caves, tunnels and spider-traps – covered pits in the ground.

For the attack to the north, Gen Schmidt consolidated the tanks of all three Divisions into one large group commanded by LtCol William Collins. In what was virtually an Armored Regiment the Marines had gathered together the largest concentration of Shermans in the Pacific zone.

THE ATTACK NORTH D+5 - D+16

Mount Suribachi, with it's commanding views over most of Iwo Jima, was now secure and MajGen Harry Schmidt, the V Amphibious Corps Commander, planned to attack the Japanese on a broad front with his three Divisions abreast – the 5th in the west, the 3rd in the center, and the 4th in the east. It immediately became apparent that the Marines had reached Gen Kuribayashi's main defense belt, and the fighting degenerated into small unit actions of incredible savagery.

On D+15 the Navy and Marines produced the heaviest bombardment of the battle. Marine artillery expended 22500 rounds in 67 minutes working across the Japanese lines from west to east. The Navy battleships, cruisers and destroyers lobbed 14in (356mm) and 8in (203mm) shells into known enemy strongpoints and Corsair and Dauntless fighters and bombers attacked with bombs and napalm cannisters for over one hour. The pounding appeared to have little effect and only marginal progress was achieved.

In the northern sector of the 3rd Division zone all the high-ground north-east of Airfield No 3 had been seized by D+12 after harrowing close-quarter fighting, and Gen Erskine ordered the 9th Regiment to advance against Hill 357 in an attempt to reach the north coast and split the enemy forces through the middle of the island.

By D+16 Marine casualties stood at 2777 dead and 8051 wounded and Gen Schmidt was a worried man. At 0500hrs the 3rd Battalion of the 9th Regiment, 3rd Division silently advanced towards Hill 362C – the last obstacle between the Marines and the sea. The enemy counter-attacked at 0530hrs, but the objective was secured by 1400hrs after heavy fighting, and with the coast only 800yds (732m) beyond the front line there was an excellent prospect of splitting the enemy down the middle.

DIV

APPROX. FRONT LINE. D+16

APPROX. FRONT LINE. D+5

4TH DIV

Near the east coast the 23rd and 24th Regiments of the 4th Division deployed to the east and then swung south, trapping around 1500 troops of Gen Senda and Navy Capt Inouye between them and the 25th Regiment. Strictly against Gen Kuribayashi's orders, Inouye opted for a night-time "banzai" attack, and around midnight they advanced towards the Marine front line. By the light of star shells, the Japanese died in their hundreds under a barrage of artillery, machine-gun and small arms fire.

With Airfield No 1 now fully operational, the first B29 Superfortress bomber to land on Iwo Jima was able to put down. With bomb bays jammed in the open position and a malfunctioning fuel tank valve, "Dinah Might" was the first of many bombers to make emergency landings on the island. General Paul Tibbets, pilot of the "Enola Gay", estimated that over 22000 aircrew owed their lives to the valor of the Marines in securing the island.

The advance on D+6 brought the 4th Division face to face with a complex of formidable positions defended by MajGen Senda's 2nd Mixed Brigade and elements of Baron Nishi's 26th Tank Regiment (now devoid of tanks). Hill 382 to the east of the main east-west runway was peppered with caves and pillboxes, the "Amphitheater": a bowl-shaped depression bristling with artillery and mortar positions, and "Turkey Knob": a hill surmounted by a huge blockhouse – here was a complex 600yds (549m) diameter killing ground that the Marines were to aptly name "The Meatgrinder".

The Superfortress "Dinah Might" was the first B29 to land on the island. The arrival attracted a great deal of attention, as crowds of Marines and Seabees gathered to see the huge bomber. (National Archives)

attempt to clear a path but with little success. As the 24th Regiment advanced they were confronted by a nest of concrete pillboxes but, with the help of the few tanks that had broken through, surrounded Hill 382. This was to be the only significant gain of the day as the 23rd came to a grinding halt from enfilading fire from the remaining positions.

Although the day had been disappointing in material gains it had been one of incredible valor, five Medals of Honor being awarded for acts of heroism that almost defy belief. Two Marines died saving the lives of their companions by throwing themselves onto hand grenades. Two Corpsmen enhanced the reputation of the Navy medics by outstanding acts of self-sacrifice. One ministered to the wounded until he had to be dragged to the rear to have his own life-threatening wounds attended to, and the other died as he refused aid so that he could continue tending wounded Marines. The fifth, Sgt William Harrell, won his medal defending his front line position against nighttime infiltrators, suffering horrific wounds including the loss of both hands.

D+13

In deteriorating weather, icy drizzle, and leaden clouds, carrier plane sorties and naval bombardments were called off because of poor visibility. An overall weariness seemed to permeate the entire front as the Marines battled with a seemingly invisible enemy which spent most of its daylight hours in their caves and tunnels, emerging at night to infiltrate the American line, more intent on foraging for food and water than killing the enemy.

In the knowledge that the battle was swinging irrevocably in favor of the Americans, Gen Kuribayashi radioed Tokyo: "Our strongpoints might be able to fight delaying actions for several more days. I comfort myself a little seeing my officers and men die without regret after struggling in this inch-by-inch battle against an overwhelming enemy …". The General's predictions were, if anything, on the pessimistic side as his garrison would prolong the battle for another three weeks.

As tanks and rocket launchers pounded the Amphitheater in the east, the 3rd Division in the center were unable to make any significant progress. In the west the 5th Division continued to engage the more exposed positions with flamethrowers and grenades, but little progress could be reported over the entire front. A communiqué at 1700hrs from the Command Posts of Generals Rockey, Erskine, and Cates: "There will be no general attack tomorrow … Divisions will utilise the day for rest, refitting, and re-organization in preparation for resumption of action on March 6." It was clear that the Marines desperately needed a break after two weeks of the bloodiest fighting the Corps had ever experienced.

The highlight of the day was the arrival of "Dinah Might," the first B29 Superfortress bomber to land on Iwo Jima. With bomb bays jammed in the open position and problems with the fuel transfer valve, the aircraft had struggled back from a mission south-west of Tokyo. As she ground to a halt at the northern end of the main runway on Airfield No. 1, the Japanese directed a steady hail of artillery fire in the general direction, causing the huge plane to swing around and retire rapidly to the Mount Suribachi end of the airfield. The bloody sacrifices of the Marine Corps in securing the island were beginning to pay dividends in the lives of what were to be thousands of Air Force crewmen.

D+14

The day was one of "consolidation, replenishment, and rest." Unfortunately, no one had informed the Japanese who continued to lob artillery rounds and mortar shells into the Marine lines all day. Tank crews serviced their machines; ammunition, food, and fresh water were brought to the front; hot coffee and doughnuts arrived from the newly

As the battle moved further north, the terrain became increasingly difficult. Here a group examine an abandoned Japanese car among a mass of boulders and rocks. (National Archives)

installed bakery in the rear, and replacements filtered through to relieve many of the exhausted troops who had slogged for fourteen days in hell.

With undue optimism the Navy began to run down its support. Admiral Spruance in his flagship USS *Indianapolis* departed for Guam, along with the 3rd Regiment of the 3rd Division, seasoned troops that Harry Schmidt would have preferred to the green replacements from Hawaii. However, there were some newcomers. Army units who were to garrison Iwo Jima after the departure of the Marines began to disembark, and the first of the Mustang and Black Widow fighters took their places on the handstands of the airfield

D+15

If the Generals had hoped that the day of rest and replenishment would mean big advances on Tuesday they were to be bitterly disappointed.

The Navy and Marine artillery mounted one of the heaviest bombardments of the battle and within 67 minutes the artillery fired 22,500 rounds. A battleship, a cruiser, and three destroyers added a further 450 rounds of 14in and 8in shells, while Dauntless and Corsair carrier planes strafed and dropped bombs and napalm canisters.

Between 0800hrs and 0900hrs the 4th and 5th Divisions moved forward but resistance was as fierce as ever. The 21st and 27th Regiments on the west coast were halted by shredding machine gun and mortar fire before they had gone more than a few yards, and support from "Zippo" flamethrower tanks had little effect. Marine Dale Worley wrote: "They have almost blown Hill 362 off the map. There are bodies everywhere and the ground is spotted with blood. The smell is sickening."

In the center the 3rd Division made little progress. One element of the 21st Regiment, under Lt Mulvey, battered their way to the top of yet another ridge and saw before them the prize that had so long eluded them – the sea. He estimated that it was less than a quarter of a mile away and called for reinforcements. A dozen men came forward but before they could reach the Lieutenant six were killed and two wounded, and the group had to retire under a storm of enemy fire. In the east the best advance of the day was a mere 350yds (320m) by the 3rd Battalion of the 24th Regiment aided by four "Zippo" flamethrower tanks.

D+16

General Erskine had, for a long while, been toying with the idea of a night attack. As a veteran of World War I he had witnessed many such actions and was aware that the Japanese knew that the Marines usually confined their fighting to daytime. His plan was to infiltrate the enemy lines for about 250yds (229m) and capture Hill 362C, the last major obstacle between the 3rd Division and the sea.

At 0500hrs the 3rd Battalion of the 9th Regiment under the command of LtCol Harold Boehm moved silently forward and for thirty minutes their luck held until an alert enemy machine gunner opened up on their left. Pressing forward, Boehm and his men stormed to the top of the hill and radioed back to Erskine who said: "We caught the bastards asleep just as we thought we would." But the euphoria was short lived, as Boehm checked his maps and realised that he was atop Hill 331 and not 362C. In the darkness and driving rain, one Iwo Jima hill looked much like another. Calling in artillery support, Boehm and his battalion

pushed forward despite heavy opposition from the front and both flanks, and by 1400hrs finally reached the correct objective.

As he was moving towards Hill 362C, the 1st and 2nd Battalions were advancing on his right flank, but soon encountered heavy resistance from their front and from bypassed positions. LtCol Cushman and his 2nd Battalion had stumbled across the remains of Baron Nishi's Tank Regiment and soon found themselves surrounded. It was not until the next day that the remains of Cushman's battalion could be extricated with the aid of tanks. Bitter fighting was to continue in this area for another six days in what was to become known as "Cushman's Pocket."

On the 5th Division front, the 26th Regiment, approaching a ridge just north of the ruins of Nishi Village, found the enemy opposition to be almost nonexistent. Cautiously proceeding to the summit they expected a fusillade of fire from the far side as had often happened in the past. Instead, the whole ridge disappeared in a massive explosion that could be heard for miles around. The Japanese had mined their Command Post and it was left to the Marines to recover the bodies of 43 of their comrades.

In a clever maneuver in the 4th Division sector, the 23rd and 24th Regiments moved to the east and then swung sharply south, edging the Japanese towards the 25th Regiment which had assumed a defensive line. Realizing that they were trapped, Gen Senda and Navy Capt Inouye, with 1,500 men, elected for a "banzai" attack, strictly against the instructions of Gen Kuribayashi. At around 2400hrs a large column of men armed with grenades, small arms, swords, and bamboo spears moved south in a bizarre attempt to infiltrate the American lines, scale Mount Suribachi and raise the Japanese flag. Caught in the nightly display of flares provided by offshore destroyers, the column was decimated by artillery and machine gun fire. The morning light was to reveal scores of bodies littering the area.

The story of Inouye's "banzai" attack was revealed years later by two of his orderlies who survived and were captured. Many of his troops

Corpsmen and stretcher-bearers evacuate some of the wounded to landing craft on the beach, from where they went either to offshore LVTs or to hospital ships. (National Archives)

believed that Inouye was a superior leader who inspired his men to perform outstanding feats of bravery – others thought he was a maniac. The sight of the Stars and Stripes flying on top of Mount Suribachi had filled him with increasing rage. He is quoted as saying: "We shall destroy their banner, we shall replace it with ours in the name of the great Emperor and the great people of Japan."

Inouye was in charge of the Naval Guard Force who manned the shore guns that sank and damaged many of the US warships and landing craft, and was described as a bombastic and temperamental character, a fine swordsman, heavy drinker, and womanizer. His bizarre plan almost beggars belief. The Captain was certain that the airfields would be lightly defended by service troops. He and his men would move southward, destroying B29 bombers as they passed; climb Mount Suribachi and tear down the Stars and Stripes; and replace it with the Rising Sun as an inspiration to all Japanese troops on the island.

General Sendra radioed Kuribayashi to seek approval for the attack but the General was furious and declared it impractical and stupid. Sendra and Inouye consulted and decided to go ahead anyway. As night fell, the Marines of the 23rd and 24th Regiments became aware of increasing activity in the enemy lines. First voices, and after about two hours, a barrage of artillery fire thundered across the front line as large numbers of Japanese troops began to infiltrate the American lines. Some, probably the officers, wielded sabres, a few had machine guns, most had rifles and grenades, and some of the sailors carried crude wooden spears or had demolition charges strapped to their chests. In the chaos that followed, the Marines fired flares and star shells to illuminate the sky as they shredded the onrushing enemy with machine gun fire, rifles, and 60mm (2.36in) mortars. Some of the Japanese wore Marine helmets, others shouted "Corpsman" in English and throughout the night bitter hand-to-hand struggles and grenade-throwing contests erupted all along the line. The morning revealed the extent of the carnage. A body count showed almost 800 Japanese dead, probably the largest number of casualties that they suffered in a single day and a justification of Gen Kuribayashi's reluctance to sanction the attack. Marine casualties were 90 dead and 257 wounded.

D+17

March 9 saw two more Marines earn the Medal of Honor. Nineteen year old Pfc James LaBelle flung himself on a spluttering grenade and died saving the lives of his two companions, while in a push up the west coast towards Kitano Point, Lt Jack Lummus silenced two enemy emplacements and then ran ahead of his men urging them forward. As he did he stepped on a mine and both his legs were blown off. When the dust and debris settled, his men were amazed to see him still standing on his bloody stumps waving them on. Lummus died that afternoon in the 3rd Division hospital from shock and loss of blood.

The day saw steady if unspectacular progress. Cushman's Pocket still barred the progress of the 3rd Division, and the 4th were still confronted with "Turkey Knob" and the Amphitheater.

D+18

The final breakthrough to the sea was achieved by a 28-man patrol led by Lt Paul Connally. As the men swilled their faces in the icy water, mortar rounds began falling among them and there was a mad scramble back to the safety of the cliffs. Connally had filled his water bottle with sea water and passed it back to his CO, Col Withers, who in turn sent it to Gen Erskine with the message "for inspection, not consumption."

With the battle now confined to the north of the island, the Divisional cemeteries were established. The 5th Division cemetery is flanked on the left by that of the 3rd Division and on the right, the 4th Division; Mount Suribachi looms in the distance. (USMC)

That same night, as the Marines bedded down after another frustrating day which saw only minor gains on the 4th and 5th Division fronts, the drone of hundreds of aircraft was heard as they skirted the east of Iwo Jima. Three hundred and twenty-five B29s from Saipan, Tinian, and Guam were heading for Tokyo for the first of Gen Curtis

US GAINS BY END OF D+19

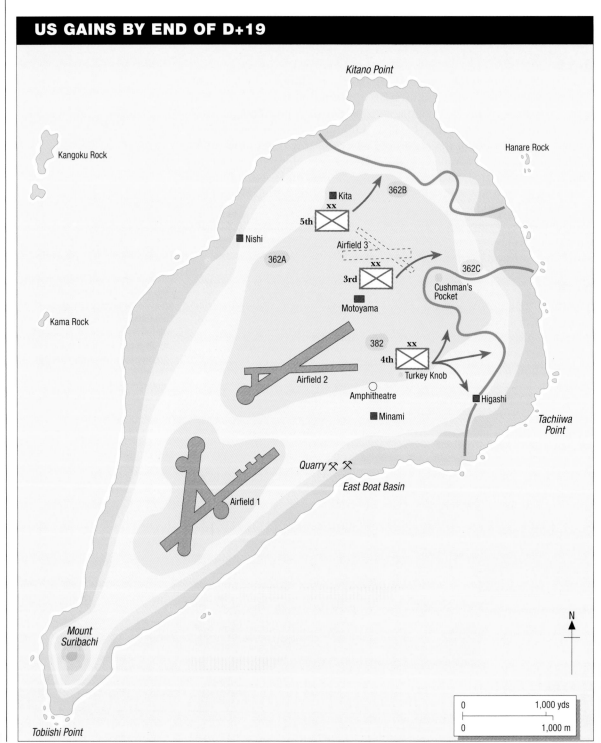

LeMay's "fire raising" raids. In a dramatic change in policy, daylight precision bombing had been abandoned in favor of "area bombing" which had been practiced by the RAF against Germany since 1941. In a spectacular raid that destroyed almost a quarter of Tokyo and killed 83,793 people, LeMay had spelled out his intentions for the future of the 20th Air Force's assault against the Japanese mainland.

D+19

It was obvious to both sides that, by March 10, the battle was reaching its climax. Cushman's Pocket was proving a tough nut to crack and the "Meatgrinder" and "Turkey Knob" were still to be taken. However, the Japanese were nearing the end of their endurance as diminishing numbers, chronic shortages of ammunition, food, and water were taking their toll. In the north-west corner of the island Gen Kuribayashi prepared his final enclave, one which was significantly to be called "Death Valley" by the Marines. Located about 500yds (457m) south of Kitano Point, it was a nightmare of rocks, caves and gullies where the 1,500 remaining troops prepared for the end. The General informed Tokyo: "The enemy's bombardments are very severe, so fierce that I cannot express or write it here. The troops are still fighting bravely and holding their positions thoroughly."

D+20 – D+36: "GOODBYE FROM IWO"

The Japanese were now confined to three distinct areas: one was Cushman's Pocket, the second an area on the east coast between the village of Higashi and the sea, and the other was Death Valley on the north-west coast where Gen Kuribayashi and the remains of his command were entrenched. Conventional battle was abandoned as the infantry slugged it out with a desperate enemy. Tanks could only operate in the few areas where bulldozers could clear a path for them. Artillery fire was reduced dramatically as the front lines merged, and many gunners found themselves donning combat gear. The heavy elements of the Navy

This photograph dramatically shows the type of terrain in which the final phase of the battle was fought. Every rock and boulder could hide a sniper; tank warfare was impossible; the fighting descended into a hand-to-hand slog between opposing infantrymen. (USMC)

Prisoners were rare on Iwo Jima. A group of curious Marines stop to stare at one of the few Japanese taken alive. (National Archives)

departed for Guam, and the Mustangs took over from the carrier aircraft in providing ground support with bombs, rockets and napalm.

In a cynical move to placate public alarm at the mounting casualty figures released by the War Department, Iwo Jima was declared "secure" on March 14. In a ceremony held in the shadow of Mount Suribachi, Harry Schmidt's personnel officer read the statement as an artillery barrage thundered in the north of the island, almost drowning out his words. The irony of the situation was obvious to all.

In the north-west, the 5th Division regrouped and re-armed in preparation for the final assault on Gen Kuribayashi's headquarters in Death Valley (or "The Gorge" as the Marine maps labeled it). Meanwhile the 3rd Division fought a bloody battle in Cushman's Pocket, slowly grinding down the fanatical remnants of Baron Nishi's command. The Baron, partially blinded in the fighting, held out until the end using dug-in tanks as artillery and fighting from a maze of caves until the Pocket finally fell silent. The Baron's fate is uncertain as his body was never identified and none of his staff survived.

General Senda, who had declined to take part in the mad "banzai" attack of D+16, was still holding out in an area east of Higashi. Prisoners estimated his strength at around 300 men, and in an attempt to reduce the carnage, Gen Erskine arranged for loudspeakers to broadcast to the

Japanese to explain the futility of further resistance. However, the equipment failed to work and his efforts were in vain. The slaughter continued four more days until the whole garrison were eliminated. The body of General Senda was never found.

With only Death Valley to secure, Harry Schmidt could be forgiven for thinking that the battle was all but over. He sadly misjudged Kuribayashi, and another ten days of savage fighting and 1,724 casualties lay ahead. Death Valley was around 700yds (640m) long and between 300 (274m) and 500yds (457m) wide with dozens of canyons and gullies leading off on both sides. In a cave somewhere in this labyrinth the General planned his final stand.

Colonel Liversedge's 28th Regiment moved up the coast and took up their positions on the cliffs overlooking the Valley, while the remainder of the division attacked from the center and from the east. In a week of attrition the Marines painfully squeezed the Japanese further and further back until, by March 24, the enemy had been reduced to an area of around 50yds (46m) square. Flamethrower tanks had expended over 10,000 gallons of fuel per day burning out caves and crevices. So badly mauled was the 2nd Battalion that they ceased to exist as a fighting force, and the 1st Battalion was on its third commander in nine days. The first was decapitated, the second maimed by a mine, and the third lost his left arm to a burst of machine gun fire.

Again Gen Erskine tried to persuade the enemy to give up the hopeless struggle, sending Japanese POWs and Nisei (Japanese Americans) to contact the defenders. General Kuribayashi, in radio contact with Major Horie on Chichi Jima, said: "We only laughed at this childish trick and did not set ourselves against them." On March 17, Horie had contacted the General informing him of his promotion to full General, and on the evening of March 23 received a final message: "All officers and men of Chichi Jima, – goodbye from Iwo."

In the pre-dawn darkness of March 26, the final act of the tragedy was performed. Between 200 and 300 Japanese troops from Death Valley and other scattered positions on the west coast silently crept through the ravines of the 5th Division sector headed for a tented area between Airfield No. 2 and the sea occupied by a mixture of Seabees, Air Force personnel, Shore Parties and AA Gunners. Most of them were sleeping, secure in the knowledge that the battle was virtually over. In a three-pronged attack they slashed tents, stabbed sleeping men, threw grenades, and fired pistols and rifles at the hapless sleepers. The noise soon alerted troops from the surrounding area, and Marines from a nearby Pioneer Battalion, Negro troops from a Shore Party, and soldiers from the 147th Infantry joined battle in a frenzy of shooting, punching, kicking and stabbing. Dawn revealed the full extent of the carnage in the ruined encampment: 44 Airman and 9 Marines lay dead with a further 119 wounded; of the attackers 262 were killed and 18 captured. Lt Harry Martin of the 5th Pioneers had hurriedly organized a defense line during the attack and single-handedly killed four enemy machine gunners before dying himself. He was to be Iwo Jima's final Medal of Honor hero, bringing the total to an incredible 27.

The circumstances of Gen Kuribayashi's death have always been shrouded in mystery. Over the years various sources have suggested that he died in the fighting around Death Valley or that he killed himself in

The thousands of Japanese dead that were found throughout the north of Iwo Jima were collected in tractors and unceremoniously dumped in any convenient shell hole or pit. (USMC)

The handsome and dashing LtCol (Baron) Nishi, commander of the 26th Tank Regiment, was something of a legend in Japan. He had won a gold medal in the equestrian event at the 1932 Olympic Games in Los Angeles, and was a member of a very wealthy and influential family with links to the Emperor. Around D+20, in Cushman's Pocket, the Baron and the remains of his command were resisting strongly from a complex of caves as the 5th Division began the final onslaught. Partially blinded, the Baron and his men held out for longer than most until the Pocket fell silent. Some say that he was killed leading a raid, others that he committed hara-kiri. The exact nature of his death will never be known.

A memorial stands near the site of General Kuribayashi's cave in Death Valley. (Taro Kuribayashi)

his HQ. In a letter to the author, his son Taro offers the following version, which is probably the more authoritative: "It seems that it was after sunset on March 25 to the dawn of the 26th that surviving Imperial Japanese forces were obliged to stand still under the US onslaught and showering shells. Under such circumstances, he had his sword in his left hand and ordered the chief staff officer, Col Takaishi, who was beside him, 'Send snipers to shoot' (Sgt Oyama heard the order.). Oyama, who was seriously wounded in the last combat, fell unconscious, was hospitalized by the US and after having served as a POW came back and testified the dreadful account of the night to me. My father had believed it shameful to have his body discovered by the enemy even after death, so he had previously asked his two soldiers to come along with him, one in front and the other behind, with a shovel in hand. In case of his death he had wanted them to bury his body there and then. It seems that my father and the soldiers were killed by shells, and he was buried at the foot of a tree in Chidori Village, along the beach near Osaka Mountain. Afterwards Gen Smith spent a whole day looking for his body to pay respect accordingly and to perform a burial, but in vain."

What is without doubt is that he proved to be Japan's greatest wartime general and in Holland Smith's opinion: "Our most redoubtable adversary."

AFTERMATH

Operation Detachment was planned and executed in accordance with the necessities of the time. Iwo Jima posed a major threat to the 20th Air Force's campaign against the Japanese mainland and its occupation was imperative as subsequent statistics proved. A total of 2,251 B29 Superfortress bombers made forced landings on the island during and after the battle. This represented 24,761 crewmen who would otherwise have had to ditch in the 1,300-mile expanse of ocean between Japan and the Marianas with a minimal chance of survival.

In an interview with the author, General Paul Tibbets, pilot of the Superfortress "Enola Gay" which dropped the Hiroshima bomb says: "On March 4, 1945, when the first B29 in distress landed on Iwo Jima, until the end of the war, more than 2,200 aircraft made emergency landings on Iwo. Many wounded crewmen on board would not have made the return trip to their home bases. Had it not been for the heroic valor of the Marines in securing the island and the Navy Seabees who built the runways, more than 22,000 pilots and air crew would have perished in crash landings at sea."

The B29 Superfortress "Enola Gay" (named after the pilot's mother) with Colonel Paul Tibbets, its pilot. The atomic bombing of Hiroshima and Nagasaki brought the war to an end. Few Marines have any regrets about the events and consider that they owe their lives to the bombings. (Paul Tibbets)

73

The capture of the Philippine Islands and the invasion of Okinawa in April accelerated the pace of the war. The 20th Air Force fire raising raids and the dropping of the atomic bombs on Hiroshima and Nagasaki ended it, and the island of Iwo Jima, secured at a terrible cost in Marine lives, played a major role in these events.

Since the end of the war many revisionists have condemned the dropping of the atomic bombs as acts of terrorism against helpless civilians; few have considered the alternative. Operation Downfall, the invasion of the Japanese mainland by the Marine Corps and the US Army, was already planned and filled the Government, Army, and USMC with foreboding. Knowing the ethos of fanatical commitment to Emperor and country that was prevalent at that time, and drawing from experience gleaned at Saipan, Iwo Jima, and Okinawa, the military knew that every beach, town, village, and field would be defended to the death by both the armed forces and the civilian population.

Japan still had 2,350,000 regular troops, 250,000 garrison troops, 7,000 aircraft, 4,000,000 employees of the armed services and 23,000,000 men, women, boys and girls sworn to fight to the death. Adding the kamikazes and the remnants of the navy provided the ingredients for a bloodbath that would make previous battles pale into insignificance. The Joint Chiefs were expecting 70 percent casualties in the landing force and the war was projected to last until 1946 or even 1947. Troops, ships, and aircraft (Tiger Force) were already on their way from the European theater when the war ended. The author, who has corresponded and talked to hundreds of Marine veterans, has yet to meet one who does not consider that he owes his life to the dropping of those bombs.

IWO JIMA TODAY

Evidence of the battle remains around this cave entrance with the mass of bullet holes. (Taro Kuribayashi)

With the exception of Pearl Harbor on the Hawaiian island of Oahu, the majority of the Pacific World War II battlefields are remote, and difficult and expensive to visit. In the case of Iwo Jima it is almost impossible.

After the war the US Air Force maintained a base on the island for twenty years and a US Coast Guard contingent remained until 1968 to operate the LORAN (Long Range Aid to Navigation) station situated near Kitano Point in the north. This token presence vanished in 1993 when the island was turned over to the Japanese Maritime Safety Agency and Iwo Jima was returned to Japanese jurisdiction and is now a government installation and a national war memorial. With no visitor facilities or civilian airport the only access for westerners is via the annual one-day trips, organized by Marine Corps oriented tour companies, which are almost exclusively allocated to Iwo Jima veterans.

All American dead were removed prior to the handover and re-interred in either the Punchbowl Cemetery in Hawaii or returned to the United States. No such service could be provided for the Japanese dead most of whom were either buried in mass graves or sealed in caves and tunnels during the battle. For many years groups of "bone diggers" from Japan, led by Tsuenzo Wachi, former Imperial Navy Captain and one time commander on Iwo Jima, returned to recover the remains of the garrison.

The island now bears little resemblance to the wartime battlefield. The three airfields have been replaced by one huge north to south runway with adjacent hangers and living quarters. Once-familiar locations like Cushman's Pocket, Nishi Ridge, the Quarry, the "Meatgrinder" and Motoyama Village have vanished under the bulldozer, and Mount Suribachi is studded with monuments. Only the landing beaches with their familiar black ash are tangible reminders, for the veterans who make their pilgrimages, of the carnage that took place here more than half a century ago.

CHRONOLOGY

1941

December 7	Japanese attack Pearl Harbor. US declares war on Japan.
December 8	Japanese assault Philippines, Hong Kong, Malaya and Wake Island.
December 11	Germany and Italy declare war on the United States.

1942

February 15	Singapore falls to Gen Yamashita.
March 12	General MacArthur leaves Philippines vowing "I shall return."
May 6	All US forces in Philippines surrender.
May 7	Battle of the Coral Sea – first Japanese setback of the war.
June 4–7	Battle of Midway – Japanese lose four carriers; turning point of the Pacific War.
August 7	US Marines land on Guadalcanal in Solomon Islands.

1943

February 1	All Japanese troops evacuate Guadalcanal.
June 30	Operation Cartwheel – operations against remainder of Solomon Islands.
November 20-23	Battle of Tarawa – start of Marines "island hopping" operations.

1944

February 2	Marines assault Kwajalein in Marshall Islands.
June 11	US Task Force 58 bombards Mariana Islands.
June 15	Invasion of Marianas begins at Saipan.
June 19	Battle of the Philippine Sea – destruction of Japanese naval air power.
August 8	Island of Guam in Marianas occupied.
September 15	1st Marine Division assault Peleliu in Palau Islands.
October 20	US Army under MacArthur land on Leyte in Philippines.
November 27	B29 Superfortress bombers firebomb Tokyo.

1945

February 19	Three Marine divisions assault Iwo Jima.
March 26 - June 30	Battle of Okinawa.
August 6	Atomic bomb dropped on Hiroshima.
September 2	Japanese surrender aboard USS *Missouri* in Tokyo Bay.

SELECT BIBLIOGRAPHY

Alexander, Col Joseph *Closing In – Marines in the Seizure of Iwo Jima*,
   Marine Corps Historical Center (Washington, DC, 1994)
Alexander, Col Joseph *A Fellowship of Valor*, HarperCollins (New York, 1997)
Bartley, LtCol Whitman S *Iwo Jima, Amphibious Epic*,
   USMC Official History 1954.
   Reprinted by Battery Press (Nashville, Tennessee, 1988)
Lane, John *This Here is G Company*, Bright Lights Publications
   (Great Neck, NY, 1997)
Newcomb, Richard F *Iwo Jima*, Holt, Rinehart & Winston (New York, 1965)
Ross, Bill D *Iwo Jima – Legacy of Valor*, Random House (New York, 1985)
Vat, Dan van der *The Pacific Campaign*, Simon & Schuster (New York, 1991)
Waterhouse Col Charles *Marines and Others*, Sea Bag Productions
   (Edison, NJ, 1994)
Wells, John Keith *Give Me 50 Marines Not Afraid to Die*,
   Quality Publications (1995)
Wheeler, Richard *Iwo*, Lippincott & Crowell (New York, 1980)
Wright, Derrick *The Battle for Iwo Jima 1945*, Sutton Publishing,
   (Slough, Glos., 1999)

APPENDICES

APPENDIX NO. 1

US COMMAND AND STAFF LIST

Expeditionary Troops (TF 56)
Commanding General   LtGen Holland M. Smith

V Amphibious Corps (VACLF)
Commanding General   MajGen Harry Schmidt

3rd Marine Division
Commanding General   MajGen Graves B. Erskine

3rd Regiment   Col James A. Stuart

(This regiment did not land on Iwo Jima and did not actively participate in that operation.
The 3rd Reg. remained in the area as Ex Trp Pac Reserve until March 5, 1945, when it returned to Guam.)

9th Regiment   Col Howard N. Kenyon
  1st Battalion   LtCol Cary A. Randell
  2nd   "   LtCol Robert E. Cushman
  3rd   "   LtCol Harold C. Boehm

21st Regiment   Col Hartnoll J Withers
  1st Battalion   LtCol Marlowe Williams
  2nd   "   LtCol Lowell E. English
  3rd   "   LtCol Wendell H. Duplantis

4th Marine Division
Commanding General   MajGen Clifton B. Cates

23rd Regiment   Col Walter W. Wensinger
  1st Battalion   LtCol Ralph Haas
  2nd   "   Maj Robert H. Davidson
  3rd   "   Maj James S. Scales

24th Regiment   Col Walter I. Jordan
  1st Battalion   Maj Paul S. Treitel
  2nd   "   LtCol Richard Rothwell
  3rd   "   LtCol Alexander A. Vandegrift, Jr.

25th Regiment   Col John R. Lanigan
  1st Battalion   LtCol Hollis U. Mustain
  2nd   "   LtCol Lewis C. Hudson, Jr.
  3rd   "   LtCol Justice M. Chambers

5th Marine Division

Commanding General | MajGen Keller E. Rockey

26th Regiment. | Col Chester B. Graham
   1st Battalion. | LtCol Daniel C. Pollock
   2nd   " | LtCol Joseph P. Sayers
   3rd   " | LtCol Tom M. Trotti

27th Regiment. | Col Thomas A. Wornham
   1st Battalion. | LtCol John A. Butler
   2nd   " | Maj John W. Antonelli
   3rd   " | LtCol Donn J. Robertson

28th Regiment. | Col Harry B. Liversedge
   1st Battalion. | LtCol Jackson B. Butterfield
   2nd   " | LtCol Chandler W. Johnson
   3rd   " | LtCol Charles E. Shepard, Jr.

Of the battalion commanders who landed on D-Day, only seven remained unwounded and in command at the end of the battle.

US Task Force Organization

Overall Command of Iwo Jima Operation | Adm Raymond A. Spruance
Task Force 51 (Joint Expeditionary Force) | V/Adm Richmond K. Turner
Task Force 52 (Amphibious Support Force) | R/Adm William H. P. Blandy
Task Force 53 (Attack Force) | R/Adm Harry W. Hill
Task Force 54 (Gunfire & Covering Force) | R/Adm Bertram J. Rogers
Task Force 56 (Expeditionary Troops) | LtGen Holland M. Smith
Task Group 56-1 (Landing Force) | MajGen Harry Schmidt
Task Force 58 (Fast Carrier Force – 5th Fleet) | V/Adm Marc A. Mitscher
Task Force 93 (Strategic Air Force –
   Pacific Ocean Area) | LtGen Hillard F. Harmon
Task Force 94 (Forward Area – Central Pacific) | V/Adm John H. Hoover

Aerial view of Mount Suribachi from the west in March, 2000. (Taro Kuribayashi)

APPENDIX NO. 2

JAPANESE COMMAND AND STAFF LIST

Commander in Chief	LtGen Tadamichi Kuribayashi
Chief of Staff	Col Tadashi Takaishi

ARMY UNITS

109th Division	LtGen Tadamichi Kuribayashi
145th Infantry Regiment	Col Masuo Ikeda
17th Mixed Infantry Regiment	Maj Tamachi Fujiwara
26th Tank Regiment	LtCol (Baron) Takeichi Nishi
2nd Mixed Brigade	MajGen Sadasue Senda
Brigade Artillery	Col Chosaku Kaido
Army Rocket Unit	Capt Yoshio Yokoyama

NAVY UNITS

Commanding Officer	R/Adm Toshinosuke Ichimaru
Naval Guard Force	Capt Samaji Inouye
125th Naval Anti-Aircraft Defense Unit	Lt Tamura
132nd Naval Anti-Aircraft Defense Unit	En Okumura
141st Naval Anti-Aircraft Defense Unit	Lt Doi
149th Naval Anti-Aircraft Defense Unit	Not known
Operations.	Comm Takeji Mase
Communications	LtComm Shigeru Arioka
Engineering	LtComm Narimasa Okada
Supply	LtComm Okazaki
Suribachi Commander	Capt Kanehiko Atsuchi

Total number of Japanese forces on Iwo Jima – February 19, 1945 (D-Day). – 21060.

Associated Press photographer Joe Rosenthal with his Speed Graphic camera stands atop Mount Suribachi minutes after taking the picture that was to make him famous. (USMC)

Pvt Robert Campbell took this photograph of the first flag being lowered as the second flag was raised. Rosenthal and Genaust were standing a few yards to his left. (USMC)

APPENDIX NO. 3

FLAGS OVER SURIBACHI

The Second World War produced many outstanding photographs – Cecil Beaton's picture of the dome of St Paul's Cathedral surrounded by a ring of fire during the London Blitz, the mushroom cloud over Hiroshima, Gen Douglas MacArthur wading ashore in the Philippines, and the horrific pits full of emaciated bodies at Belsen concentration camp to name a few – but none of them achieved the fame of Joe Rosenthal's picture of US Marines raising the flag on the summit of Mount Suribachi.

When it was first seen in America it became an instant sensation and lent itself to an issue of three-cent stamps that had the largest sale in history. A painting was used for the 7th War loan drive that raised $220,000,000, it appeared on 3,500,000 posters, and 175,000 car cards, was portrayed in films, re-enacted by gymnasts, and a float won first prize in the Rose Bowl Parade. The greatest accolade was the 100-ton bronze statue by Felix de Weldon that stands near the northern end of Arlington National Cemetery in Washington, DC, as a memorial to the United States Marine Corps.

Because of its outstanding composition and the fact that it was the second flag to be raised that day, there has always been speculation that the picture was posed, a view compounded by many books and magazine articles over the years. In correspondence with the author, Joe Rosenthal gives the true story of the events of that day and clears up the misconceptions for good.

On the February 23, Joe boarded an ICT along with Bill Hippie, a magazine correspondent, and landed near Mount Suribachi where the boatswain told them that a patrol was going up Suribachi with a flag. They went to the 28th Regiment command post and learned that a 40-man detachment had already left following two patrols that had reached the top at 0940hrs. At the command post were Bob Campbell, a combat photographer, and Sgt Bill Genaust, a cine photographer (killed nine days later at Hill 362); and Rosenthal, Genaust and Campbell started the tough climb, stopping occasionally while Marines dealt with enemy troops holed up in caves.

About half way up they met four Marines coming down. One was Lou Lowery, a photographer for *Leatherneck*, the Marine Corps magazine, who told them that a flag had been raised on the summit and that he had photographed the event. Joe was in two minds whether to continue but decided to press on and take a picture anyway. Reaching the top of the volcano, he saw the flag flying and also saw a group of men dragging a long iron pipe and holding another neatly folded flag. "What are you doing?" he asked. "We're going to put up this bigger flag and keep the other as a souvenir," they said. This second flag came from IST 779 which was beached at the base of Suribachi. Ensign Alan Wood who was aboard told the author: "A dirty, dusty, battle-worn Marine (2nd Lt Albert Tuttle) asked for a flag. It was one that had been salvaged from a supply depot at Pearl Harbor. I hadn't the slightest idea that one day it would become the symbol of one of the war's bloodiest battlefields."

Rosenthal toyed with the idea of a shot showing the first flag coming down and the second one going up, but left that to Campbell and concentrated on a picture of the second flag being raised. He moved back but the sloping ground masked his view and he had to build a platform of sandbags and

Joe Rosenthal assembled a group of Marines for a posed shot after taking his famous flag raising picture. It was this that was to start the rumours that his famous picture was "posed." (USMC)

stones (he is only 5ft 5in tall). With Genaust standing on his right, he saw the men start to raise the flag and shouted, "There she goes," and swung his camera and caught the scene. He also took pictures of a group of Marines under the flag waving and cheering before he and Campbell made their way back to the 28th Regiment command post.

Back on the USS *Eldorado*, he wrote captions for the day's pictures and handed them in to go on the daily mail plane to Guam. When his picture reached the United States via radiophoto it was an immediate sensation. Ironically, Joe was not to see it for another nine days when he returned to Guam where he was congratulated by a group of correspondents. "It's a great picture," they said. "Did you pose it?" "Sure," he said – he thought that they were referring to the shot with the waving and cheering Marines, but then someone showed him the picture. "Pose that one?" "Gee," I said. "That's good alright, but I didn't pose that one." It was here that the first misunderstandings about the picture started. Someone heard him say that he had posed a picture and wrote that the shot was a phoney and that Rosenthal had posed it.

Joe Rosenthal's life was completely changed by that photo. He was recalled to America by Associated Press where he became a celebrity, got a raise in salary, was awarded the Pulitzer Prize, and met President Harry Truman. Speaking engagements followed, at one of which he was bizarrely introduced as "Mr. Joe Rosenberg who raised the flag at Okinawa."

The accusations of a posed photograph have been a sore point since the end of the war as the old misconceptions continued to re-appear in books and magazines over the years. The "posed" myth is easily discounted by looking at Bill Genaust's five-second cine film taken at the same time which shows one frame identical to Rosenthal's photograph. Joe Rosenthal's final words on the subject are: "I can best sum up what I feel by saying that of all the elements that went into the making of this picture, the part I played was the least important. To get that flag up there, America's fighting men had to die on that island and on other islands, and off the shore, and in the air. What difference does it make who took the picture? I took it, but the Marines took Iwo Jima."

The six flag raisers in the picture are all now deceased. They were from left to right: Pfc Ira Hayes, Pfc Franklin Sousley, Sgt Michael Strank, Pharmacist's Mate 2nd Class John H. Bradley, Pfc Rene A. Gagnon and Cpl Harlon H. Block (Sousley, Strank and Block were all killed on Iwo Jima). Both flags now hang in the Marine Corps Historical Center in Washington, DC.

RIGHT **Aerial picture of the Marine Corps Memorial on the day of the dedication ceremony, November 10, 1954. The ceremony was conducted by President Dwight D. Eisenhower accompanied by Vice President Richard Nixon and the then Commandant of the Marine Corps, General Lemuel C. Shepherd, Jr. (USMC)**

APPENDIX NO. 4

THE MARINE CORPS MEMORIAL

This 100-ton bronze statue designed by Felix de Weldon is the memorial to the United States Marine Corps at Arlington National Cemetery in Washington, DC. (USMC)

Directly inspired by Joe Rosenthal's famous Iwo Jima photograph, a Memorial to the United States Marine Corps was erected at Arlington National Cemetery in Washington, DC, in 1954. The sculptor, Felix de Weldon, chose the Iwo Jima image as the Marine Corps symbol most familiar to the American public although the Memorial of course represents the nation's tribute to the dead of the Corps since its formation in 1775. Three years in the making, the figures are 32ft high and stand on a Swedish granite base surrounded by polished black granite blocks listing the names and dates of all major Marine Corps engagements since the Corps was founded. Also engraved on the base is Adm Chester Nimitz's famous tribute to the Marines of Iwo Jima: "Uncommon Valor was a Common Virtue."

The Memorial was official dedicated on November 10, 1954, by President Dwight D. Eisenhower, accompanied by Vice President Richard Nixon and the then Commandant of the Marine Corps, Gen Lemuel C. Shepherd, Jr. Also present at the ceremony were the three surviving flag raisers from Rosenthal's picture, John H. Bradley, Ira Hayes and Rene A. Gagnon. Surprisingly, Rosenthal's name was not mentioned on the monument and it was many years before it was acknowledged that the statue was based on his photograph and a plaque was added to the base.

Pharmacist's Mate 2nd Class John H. Bradley (US Navy) seldom spoke of his part in the flag raising, even to his family, and lived a quiet post-war life in his home town of Antigo, Wisconsin. The longest surviving member of the six who raised the second flag on Mount Suribachi, he died aged 70 in January 1994.

Corporal Ira H. Hayes, a Pima Indian from the Gila River Reservation in Arizona, enlisted in the Corps in 1942 as a member of the Parachute Regiment. When this unit was disbanded in 1944 he was transferred to the 5th Division with which he served at Iwo Jima. Ordered back to the US after the flag raising to promote a War Bond selling tour, he found the publicity overwhelming and welcomed the return to his unit. In later life he had major problems with alcoholism and died aged 32 in 1955 and is buried in Arlington National Cemetery.

Rene Gagnon, a 5th Division Marine, was also co-opted to the Treasury Department to promote the 7th War Loan Drive and, after he returned to his unit, served with the occupation forces in China until his discharge in 1946. He died in 1979 and was buried in Manchester, New Hampshire. In 1981 at the request of his widow he was re-interred in Arlington Cemetery.

All three survivors had posed for de Weldon who modeled their faces in clay. Photographs of the deceased flag raisers were used to depict their likenesses. The castings of the figures took almost three years to complete and were made at the Bedi-Rassy Art Foundry in Brooklyn, New York.

The Monument was funded by US Marines, Reservists, friends of the Marine Corps and members of the Naval Service at a cost of $850,000 – no public funds were used. Now one of Washington's major tourist attractions and certainly the most striking War Memorial in the capital, the monument has stood for over four decades in tribute to the Corps.

A major controversy arose recently when the US Air Force attempted to secure an area near the Memorial for their own monument. It was rightly judged that another large structure so close to this one would be obtrusive and detract from the Marine Corps Memorial. After much inter-service and political in-fighting, the Air Force were obliged to find a location elsewhere on the Arlington site.

LEFT The three surviving flag raisers were invited to the ceremony. They are, from left to right, John H. Bradley, Ira Hayes and Rene A. Gagnon. All are now deceased. (USMC)

OPPOSITE This dramatic shot from the rear of a landing craft shows the chaos into which the Marines were deposited – volcanic ash up to their ankles, enemy pillboxes and bunkers straight ahead, and more troops arriving every five minutes. (National Archives)

APPENDIX NO.5

THE MEDAL OF HONOR – UNCOMMON VALOR

The United States' highest decoration, the Medal of Honor, was awarded to 27 combatants at Iwo Jima, a figure that represents a third of the total number of awards to members of the United States Marine Corps during the whole of World War II. Admiral Chester Nimitz's words: "Among the Americans who served on Iwo Jima, uncommon valor was a common virtue," could not have been more appropriate.

Cpl CHARLES J.BERRY – *1st Battalion 26th Regiment 5th Division* (Posthumous)
On the night of March 3, Berry and two other riflemen were in a foxhole close to Nishi Ridge. A group of Japanese made an infiltration and lobbed a hand grenade into the foxhole whereupon Berry immediately threw himself on to it and was killed instantly, saving the lives of his comrades.

Pfc WILLIAM CADDY – *3rd Battalion 26th Regiment 5th Division* (Posthumous)
North of Airfield No. 3, a Japanese sniper had Caddy and his two companions pinned down for two hours in a shell hole. Around 1600hrs one of the Marines scrambled to the edge of the hole to try to locate the enemy but was spotted. The sniper threw a hand grenade, and Caddy threw himself onto it and took the full blast in his chest and stomach, dying immediately.

LtCol JUSTICE M.CHAMBERS – *3rd Battalion 25th Regiment 4th Division*
At 38, "Jumpin' Joe" Chambers was one of the old men of the battle. Determined to take "Charlie Dog Ridge," he called in a salvo of rockets and rushed to the head of his men in a wild charge towards the summit, but was hit in the chest by a burst of machine gun fire and was dragged back to his observation post. After a long convalescence in America he received his medal from President Truman at the White House.

Sgt DARRELL S.COLE – *1st Battalion 23rd Regiment 4th Division* (Posthumous)
Storming the beaches on D-Day, Cole's platoon came under very heavy fire from pillboxes on Yellow Beaches 1 and 2. Armed with hand grenades and a .45cal pistol he silenced six positions, returning to his lines twice for more ammunition before being killed by an enemy grenade that exploded at his feet.

Capt ROBERT H.DUNLAP – *1st Battalion 26th Regiment 5th Division*
Dunlap's company were pinned down near Airfield No. 1 under a hail of mortar fire. Grabbing a field telephone he advanced to an isolated position only 50yds (46m) from the enemy and for the next 48 hours called in devastating fire on the Japanese positions from various directions, playing a significant role in clearing the western section of the island.

On the fourth day of the battle the 21st Regiment were faced with a stubborn complex of bunkers and anti-tank guns adjoining Airfield No 2 in the center of the island. Maj Houser called upon 21-year-old Cpl Hershel Williams, the last of his flamethrowers, to go forward escorted by riflemen. With complete disregard for his own safety, Williams moved from one position to another, burning out bunkers and strongpoints, until the way ahead had been cleared. He was the first 3rd Division Marine on Iwo Jima to be awarded the Medal of Honor.

Sgt ROSS F. GRAY – *1st Battalion 25th Regiment 4th Division*
When his platoon became bogged down in fighting around Airfield No. 2, Gray grabbed a satchel charge and silenced the nearest emplacement. In short order he repeated the process until all six adjacent positions lay silent and the way was clear for an advance. Later in the day Gray cleared a path through a dangerous minefield single-handedly.

Sgt WILLIAM G. HARRELL – *1st Battalion 28th Regiment 5th Division*
Manning a front line foxhole near Nishi Ridge, Sgt Harrell and Pfc Carter were attacked by nighttime infiltrators. Four of them were swiftly disposed of before a hand grenade was thrown into the position and almost blew off Harrell's left hand and caused other serious injuries. Carter's gun had jammed and he left to get another. Meanwhile two more Japanese charged into the foxhole, one placed a grenade next to Harrell and attempted to leave. Harrell shot him with his pistol and lobbed the grenade out, but it exploded blowing off his right hand. The indomitable sergeant was evacuated next morning and after the war, with the aid of mechanical hands, became a rancher in his native Texas.

Lt RUFUS G. HERRING – *USNR LGI(G) 449*
The first of Iwo Jima's medal winners, Herring was the captain of Gunboat 449 which was laying down a carpet of rockets in support of frogmen two days before D-Day. A direct hit from Japanese artillery killed 12 of the crew and seriously wounded Herring. Bleeding profusely he struggled for thirty minutes to steer his vessel and wounded crew away from the enemy barrage and alongside the destroyed USS *Terror*, remaining propped up by empty shell cases until all of his men had been evacuated.

Pfc DOUGLAS T. JACOBSON – *3rd Battalion 23rd Regiment 4th Division*
Battling to take Hill 382, 19 year old Jacobson seized a bazooka and began to wage his own war on the enemy. For thirty minutes he ran from blockhouse to blockhouse, blasting each one in turn until sixteen positions fell silent and 75 of the enemy lay dead, opening up a gap for his company to reach the top of the hill. Using a bazooka is a two-man operation, but Jacobson achieved his remarkable feat alone.

Sgt JOSEPH R. JULIAN – *1st Battalion 27th Regiment 5th Division* (Posthumous)
In vicious fighting around Kitano Point on the 18th day of the battle, Julian silenced four enemy emplacements and a machine gun nest. Dashing back to his lines he collected demolition charges and a bazooka and once more charged the enemy, this time destroying four more strongpoints before being killed by a burst of machine gun fire.

Pfc JAMES D. LaBELLE – *2nd Battalion 27th Regiment 5th Division* (Posthumous)
It seems that LaBelle was destined to die on Iwo Jima. On D-Day he missed death by inches when three companions were mown down by machine gun fire; three days later he was the only one unhurt when a grenade landed in a shell hole he was sharing with four other Marines; and on day ten his best friend died at his side near Nishi Ridge. While they were standing behind an outcrop of boulders with

ABOVE **Douglas Jacobson, seen here at an Iwo Jima reunion in Wichita Falls, Texas, in March, 2000, proudly displays his Medal of Honor. (Author)**

The twelve LCI gunboats supporting the activities of the Navy frogmen came in for lethal enemy gunfire. Made largely of wood, the frail craft were easy targets for Japanese gunners who had had months to practice. Here a crewman lies dead among the spent ammunition on the vessel. (US Navy)

Mr. Taro Kuribayashi, son of the Japanese commander of Iwo Jima, stands beside the 5th Division memorial. Mr. Kuribayashi is a frequent visitor to the island and actively promotes American–Japanese reconciliation. (Taro Kuribayashi)

two friends, a solitary Japanese soldier lobbed a grenade into their midst. Shouting a warning, Labelle threw himself on the grenade saving the lives of the others.

2nd Lt JOHN H. LEIMS – *1st Battalion 9th Regiment 3rd Division*
Attacking Hill 362C, east of Cushman's Pocket, Leims and his company were cut off. He personally advanced and laid telephone lines across an exposed expanse of fire-swept terrain. Later, learning that several casualties were still behind enemy lines, he made two trips under heavy fire to bring back his wounded.

Pfc JACKLYN H. LUCAS – *1st Battalion 26th Regiment 5th Division*
A born rebel, Lucas had enlisted in the Corps when he was only 14; now at 17 he was wanted by the Military Police in Hawaii for being AWOL. On D+1 near Airfield No. 1 he was one of three men pinned down by enemy fire. When grenades fell among them he grabbed one and smothered it with his body and then grabbed a second and pulled it underneath. Miraculously he survived the blasts and after spending months in hospital recovered with only a partially paralysed arm.

1st Lt JACK LUMMUS – *2nd Battalion 27th Regiment 5th Division* (Posthumous)
Determined to keep up the momentum while attacking a complex of enemy caves and bunkers near Kitano Point, Lummus, a 29 year old ex-professional football star from Texas, spearheaded an attack and was soon blown to the ground by a grenade. Jumping to his feet, he attacked the position to his front killing the occupants. Waving his men forward for another charge, he stepped on a mine and both legs were blown off. As the debris settled, his men were horrified to see him upright on his stumps still urging them forward. He died several hours later in a field hospital

1st Lt HARRY L. MARTIN – *5th Pioneer Battalion* (Posthumous)
Before dawn on the March 26, between 200 and 300 Japanese troops, the remnants of Gen Kuribayashi's command, launched a massed attack against a rest area occupied by aircrews, Seabees and other non-combat troops west of Airfield No. 2. Martin immediately formed a defense line manned mainly by Black troops and held many of the enemy in check. He recovered a number of wounded and attacked a machine gun position killing four of the enemy before being seriously wounded by a grenade. As dawn revealed the carnage, the body of Martin was recovered from among the hundreds strewn around the camp.

Capt JOSEPH J. McCARTHY – *2nd Battalion 24th Regiment 4th Division*
Another "Jumpin' Joe", 33 year old McCarthy, rallying his men on the approach to Airfield No. 2, filled bags with grenades, mustered a three-man flamethrower team, and headed for the enemy yelling: "Let's get the bastards before they get us." Thrusting grenades through the firing vents, he personally silenced four pillboxes allowing his company to advance.

Pvt GEORGE PHILLIPS – *2nd Battalion 28th Regiment 5th Division.* (Posthumous)
On the very day that Iwo Jima was officially declared "secure," Pfc Phillips, an 18 year old replacement who had only landed on the island two days earlier, threw himself onto a grenade and died instantly, saving the lives of the three companions that he barely knew.

Pharmacist's Mate 1st Class FRANCIS PIERCE, Jr. – *2nd Battalion 24th Regiment 4th Division*
Corpsman Pierce and a party of stretcher-bearers were ambushed while evacuating wounded on March 15. He engaged the enemy with rifle fire and carried a wounded Marine to safety, returning for another while under constant fire from Japanese snipers. Badly wounded the following day, he refused aid and continued to minister to casualties until he collapsed. Pierce's actions were typical of Iwo Jima's Corpsmen, and show why they were held in such high regard by the Marines.

Pfc DONALD J. RUHL – *2nd Battalion 28th Regiment 5th Division* (Posthumous)
21 year old Ruhl showed conspicuous gallantry from the day that he landed on Iwo Jima. On D-Day he killed nine of the enemy while charging a blockhouse. The following morning he dragged a wounded Marine to safety across 40yds (37m) of ground swept by heavy fire and later occupied an enemy gun emplacement and secured it overnight to prevent the enemy from re-occupying it. He met his death on D+2 when he and his platoon sergeant were in a camouflaged bunker bringing fire to bear on the enemy. A grenade landed between the pair, and without a thought for his own safety he threw himself upon it to protect his companion.

Pvt FRANKLIN E. SIGLER – *2nd Battalion 26th Regiment 5th Division*
In the final stage of the battle in Death Valley, Sigler took command of his leaderless squad and led an attack against a gun emplacement that was causing chaos among the 2nd Battalion. In the face of

murderous fire he silenced the position with hand grenades, killing the entire enemy crew, but was severely wounded by fire from nearby caves. Continuing the attack, he sealed several caves before withdrawing to his lines. Refusing medical treatment, he carried three wounded Marines to safety and continued to direct rocket and machine gun fire at the enemy until ordered to the rear for medical treatment.

Cpl TONY STEIN – *1st Battalion 28th Regiment 5th Division*
During the advance across the island at the base of Mount Suribachi on D-Day, Stein, armed with an improvised aircraft .50cal machine gun that he called his "stinger," attacked five enemy positions killing at least 20 of the enemy. When his ammunition ran out he made repeated trips to the beach for more, carrying a wounded marine back each time. Although wounded by shrapnel, he continued to fight, supervising the withdrawal of his platoon although having his "stinger" twice shot from his hands. Stein was killed near Hill 362A later in the battle, never knowing of his citation.

Gunnery Sgt WILLIAM G. WALSH – *3rd Battalion 27th Regiment 5th Division* (Posthumous)
During the attack on Hill 362A, Walsh led his platoon to the summit in the face of heavy enemy fire, but his success was short lived when they were forced to withdraw under devastating machine gun fire from three enemy positions. Undeterred, Walsh mounted a counterattack, again reaching the top where the six men in his squad took cover in a trench. The Japanese retaliated by lobbing hand grenades and when one fell in their midst Walsh threw himself upon it and died instantly.

Pvt WILSON D. WATSON – *2nd Battalion 9th Regiment 3rd Division*
Two hills, codenamed Peter and Oboe, near Airfield No. 2 were formidable stumbling blocks for the 3rd Division. Watson was the first man atop Hill Oboe, having silenced a bunker and a machine gun nest on the way. Aided by only one other Marine, he staved off repeated enemy attacks for thirty minutes until reinforcements arrived in support. Pressing forward, he destroyed another bunker and was attacking a second when he was wounded by mortar fire and had to be evacuated for treatment. In two days he had killed over 90 of the enemy and played a major role in the reduction of these key positions.

Pharmacist's Mate 2nd Class GEORGE E. WHALEN – *2nd Battalion 26th Regiment 5th Division*
Another of Iwo's gallant Corpsmen, Whalen was wounded on February 26, but continued tending the injured despite intense enemy fire. Wounded again on March 3, he refused aid and was wounded for a third time but crawled among the casualties to administer aid until he had to be carried to the rear for urgent treatment. When evacuated, Whalen had been treating wounded Marines non-stop for five days and nights.

Cpl HERSHEL W. WILLIAMS – *1st Battalion 21st Regiment 3rd Division*
Confronted with a complex of bunkers and anti-tank guns adjoining Airfield No. 2, Maj Robert Houser called upon 21 year old Williams, the last of his flamethrowers. Escorted by riflemen, he incinerated the occupants of the first pillbox and a group of Japanese troops who attempted to shoot him down. Moving from one position to another he burned out bunkers and pillboxes and in four hours had cleared the way for his regiment to move forward. Williams was the first 3rd Division Marine on Iwo Jima to win the Medal of Honor.

Pharmacist's Mate 3rd Class JACK WILLIAMS – *3rd Battalion 28th Regiment 5th Division* (Posthumous)
Williams, a 21-year-old from Harrison, Arkansas, added to the prestige of Iwo's Corpsmen on March 20. Under heavy fire he went to aid a wounded Marine, screening him from enemy fire with his own body while attending to his wounds. Inevitably he was wounded himself, receiving gunshots to the abdomen and groin, but continued treating his patient before attending to his own injuries. He then moved on to a second casualty and although bleeding profusely, administered aid before attempting to return to the rear but was killed by an enemy sniper.

Pharmacist's Mate 1st Class JOHN H. WILLIS – *3rd Battalion 27th Regiment 5th Division* (Posthumous)
Willis had been tending the wounded all day around Hill 362 on February 28 until he was wounded by shrapnel and was ordered to the rear for treatment. Within hours he was back with the troops attending a seriously wounded Marine in a shell hole. With his rifle stuck in the ground, he was administering plasma when a grenade rolled down beside him. He threw it out, but seven more followed in rapid succession and each was quickly thrown out until the last one exploded in his hand killing him instantly.

Herschel "Woody" Williams still attends Iwo Jima reunions and is one of the diminishing number of Iwo Jima Medal of Honor recipients. (Author)

RIGHT **Here seen in the setting sun, the Memorial is one of Washington's most striking images and a very popular tourist attraction. (USMC)**

PART 2
OKINAWA

The spring of 1945 found Allied fortunes in the Pacific very much in the ascendant. A series of victorious campaigns had reclaimed many of the islands and territories seized by the Imperial Japanese forces at the end of 1941 and the early months of 1942. The dark days of humiliating defeats were long behind the unstoppable Allied juggernaut. There was no doubt who would be the ultimate victor. The only questions remaining were when the final battle would be fought and how many more men would have to die to set right a grievous wrong.

Allied strategy entailed three thrusts across the Pacific. In the North Pacific Area the US Army and Navy, backed by Canadians, cleared the Japanese from Alaska's Aleutian Islands. In the Southwest Pacific Area, General Douglas MacArthur had at his disposal combined US Army, US Marine, Australian, and New Zealand forces with the Third and Seventh Fleets mainly supported by land-based aircraft. They first secured the line of communications between the US and Australia. Then they seized the Solomon Islands, with the main objective being Rabaul on New Britain, and thrust along New Guinea's north coast aiming at the Philippines.

In the Central Pacific Area the Fifth Fleet, supported by carrier-based aircraft, secured the Gilberts in late 1943, with the ultimate objective being the Japanese base at Truk Atoll in the Carolines. The Japanese bastions at Rabaul and Truk were neutralized by air power and bypassed. The Fifth Fleet went on to seize the Marshalls in early 1944. The Fifth and Third Fleets' next target was the Mariana Islands. The seizure of the Marianas proved to be an extremely serious blow to Japan. Part of the Mandated Territories bequeathed to Japan by the League of Nations in 1919, the former German possessions were considered part of the Japanese Empire. The fall of Saipan and neighboring Tinian in July 1944, followed by the liberation of Guam in August, led to such an outcry in Japan that General Shigenori Tojo was forced to resign as prime minister and a new cabinet was formed.

MacArthur invaded Leyte in the Philippines in October 1944 with the Sixth Army and Seventh Fleet. By the end of the year they had secured several solid footholds in the massive archipelago. The Philippines was finally declared liberated on 5 July 1945, two weeks after Okinawa was secured. In the meantime the Third Fleet took Iwo Jima between February and March 1945.

The Japanese knew what was coming next. What they did not know was exactly where the Americans would strike. The Imperial General Headquarters (IGHQ) narrowed the possible targets to Formosa off the Chinese mainland or Okinawa southwest of the Home Islands. The Japanese began to reinforce both areas as the American Fifth Fleet and Tenth Army marshaled at island bases across the Pacific.

A photograph of the Katchin Hanto (Peninsula) area on the east coast taken on 2 June 1945 shows the open areas encountered on much of southern Okinawa. (US Army)

PLANNING *ICEBERG*

The battle for Okinawa is said by some to have begun in May 1944; a year before the landing. During the lull before the Marianas landings, Admiral Earnest J. King, Chief of Naval Operations and Commander-in-Chief, US Fleet, met with Admirals Chester W. Nimitz, Commander-in-Chief, Pacific Fleet/Commander, Pacific Ocean Area (CinCPAC/POA), and William F. Halsey, Commander, Third Fleet, in San Francisco to discuss future Pacific Theater strategy. A major concern was the possibility that Japan might conclude a separate peace with a hard-pressed China. Nimitz suggested establishing US positions on the coast of China and opening supply lines to the interior. Supplying the massive, but ill-equipped, Chinese Army would force Japan to reinforce the mainland and stretch its forces. Consideration was given to invading Formosa, 670 miles (1,079 km) southwest of Japan, before it could be reinforced, and thereby bypass the Philippines.

Formosa, basically a Japanese colony, had its advantages. Bypassing the Philippines would prevent a potentially protracted campaign requiring a massive commitment of US forces. Formosa would provide a base from which to invade the mainland, protect sea routes to China, and launch long-range bombers at Japan. B-29 Superfortresses of the Twentieth Air Force were operating out of southern China at extreme range and experiencing major difficulties receiving supplies and fuel from India.

Formosa could be a problem as well, however. It was well within range of Japanese air bases on mainland China, was garrisoned by substantial forces[1], could be easily reinforced from the mainland only

93

STRATEGIC SITUATION, MARCH 1945

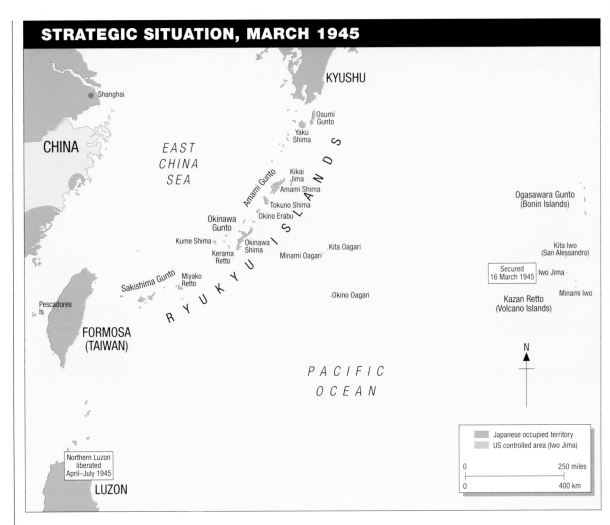

KYUSHU

Shanghai

CHINA

EAST
CHINA
SEA

Osumi
Gunto

Yaku
Shima

Kikai
Jima

Amami Gunto

Amami Shima

Tokuno Shima

Okino Erabu

Okinawa
Gunto

Kume Shima

Okinawa
Shima

Kerama
Retto

Minami Oagari

Kita Oagari

Sakishima Gunto

Miyako
Retto

Pescadores
Is

Okino Oagari

FORMOSA
(TAIWAN)

R Y U K Y U   I S L A N D S

Ogasawara Gunto
(Bonin Islands)

Kita Iwo
(San Alessandro)

Secured
16 March 1945   Iwo Jima

Minami Iwo

Kazan Retto
(Volcano Islands)

PACIFIC
OCEAN

N

Northern Luzon
liberated
April–July 1945

LUZON

Japanese occupied territory
US controlled area (Iwo Jima)

0   250 miles
0   400 km

100 miles (161 km) away, and was a large mountainous land mass 240 miles (386 km) long and 90 miles (145 km) wide, with elevations to 13,000 ft (3,943 m). It promised to be a tough campaign; Formosa was about the size of Kyushu, the southernmost island of Japan.

In July 1944, with the Marianas campaign winding up, President Roosevelt met with Admiral Nimitz and General MacArthur. Nimitz, as Commander, Pacific Ocean Area, controlled the South, Central, and North Pacific Areas from his headquarters at Pearl Harbor. MacArthur commanded forces coming out of Australia in the Southwest Pacific and New Guinea[2]. He opposed the plan to bypass the Philippines contending that, with additional naval support, he had the forces to liberate them. Nimitz agreed to an alternate plan that included recapturing much of the Philippines between October and December 1944. Depending on the situation, either Luzon would be invaded in February 1945 or Formosa–Amoy Area (on mainland China) in March. This would be followed by the Bonins (Chichi Jima) in April and the Ryukyus (with Okinawa) in May. MacArthur insisted on liberating Manila on Luzon, determined to fulfil the promise he made to return on his departure in March 1942.

Soon after the proposed plan was developed, Lieutenant-General Millard F. Harmon, Army Air Forces, Pacific Ocean Area, proposed that Operation *Causeway* – Formosa – be abandoned with compelling arguments that air operations could more effectively be conducted against Japan from the Marianas. He pointed out the threat posed by remaining hostile forces (it was not to be completely occupied because

LEFT **An aerial view of Okinawa Shima looking north. The island's southern tip, Cape Kiyan, is cut off, but most of the south of the island, where the battle was largely fought out, is shown. (US Army)**

This aerial photograph of the Motobu Peninsula on Okinawa's upper west coast where the 6th Mar. Div. fought, demonstrates the ruggedness of Okinawa's terrain. Sesoko Shima can be seen in the background; this is a comparatively small area when viewed in the context of the entire 640 sq mile (1,658 sq km) island and provides an idea as to the island's magnitude. (USMC)

A typical Okinawan rural village with thatch-roofed houses surrounded by mud or stone walls. Windbreaks of hedges and large bushes grow along the walls. Camouflaged Japanese trucks can be seen at the top of the photograph. (US Army)

of its size), possible interception from the Chinese mainland along the entire route to Japan, and less favorable weather. Harmon proposed that Iwo Jima in the Volcano Islands (south of Japan) be seized in January 1945 and Okinawa (southwest of Japan) in June, simultaneous with the invasion of Luzon. General Robert C. Richardson, US Army Forces, Pacific Ocean Area, agreed with Harmon. Other key commanders tagged for *Causeway* favored the proposal. General Simon B. Buckner, Tenth Army, stated sufficient combat and service troops were not available to secure a significant lodgment on Formosa. Admiral Raymond A. Spruance also preferred to avoid Formosa.

In October 1944, Nimitz advised Admiral King of his subordinate commanders' views. The Joint Chiefs of Staff evaluated the proposals and directed MacArthur to land on Luzon on 20 December 1944, and Nimitz to assault Iwo Jima on 20 January 1945 and Okinawa on 1 March. This last operation before the November invasion of Japan was code-named *Iceberg*. The Ryukyu Islands Group was codenamed *Bunkhouse* and Okinawa itself was designated *Scattering*.

A ridge-side gorge in the Awacha Pocket viewed from Wilson Ridge in May. This area, 2,000 yds (1,829 m) north of Shuri, was a maze of gorges and steep hills. Such gorges were honeycombed with dugouts and fighting positions covering the approaches and both sides. A force attacking one side was fired on from the other as well as from above. It took the 5th Marines, 1st Mar. Div. from 3–11 May to seize the pocket held by elements of the Japanese 62nd Division. (USMC)

With the US fully securing the Philippines, Japanese forces in the Dutch East Indies would be cut off from the Home Islands. B-29s could ceaselessly bomb Japan from their bases in the Marianas with the Japanese denied bases in the Ryukyus from which to intercept them. American bases in the Ryukyus would further protect the flank by intercepting enemy aircraft from Formosa and China, and they could attack Japan as well. Seizing Iwo Jima, midway between the Marianas and Japan, would allow fighters to rendezvous with and escort the bombers, and provide stricken B-29s with emergency airfields. The forces and command structure devised for Formosa would be retained for the invasion of Okinawa Gunto. In the meantime, the Third Fleet and III Amphibious Corps assaulted the Palau Islands in September 1944 to secure MacArthur's eastern flank while he conducted initial operations in the Philippines[3]. The Fifth Fleet and V Amphibious Corps assaulted the critical target of Iwo Jima on 19 February 1945, over a month and a half late due to operational necessity, in a vicious battle presaging future events on Okinawa. It would not be secured by V Corps' three Marine divisions until 16 March. Within days the initial operations for *Iceberg* began, delayed by the hold-ups in the Iwo Jima operation.

RYUKYU ISLANDS

The Nansei Shoto (Southwestern Islands) is a curving string of widely spaced islands stretching southwest from Kyushu, the southernmost of the Japanese Home Islands, across the East China Sea to Formosa. Ryukyu Retto comprises most islands in the Nansei Shoto string. The Ryukyus consists of 161 islands in five major groups: Osumi, Torkara, Amami, Okinawa, and Sakishima Guntos. Okinawa is the centerpiece and largest jewel of the Ryukyus[4].

Okinawa Gunto includes several islands and groups satellited around the main island: Kerama Retto (eight islands 15 miles/24 km west of Okinawa), Kume Shima (55 miles/89 km west), Agunia Shima (40 miles/64 km west), Ie Shima (4 miles/6.5 km west), Iheya Retto (four islands 15 miles/24 km north), Yoron Shima (15 miles/24 km northeast), and an unnamed group of eight scattered islands called the Eastern Islands by the Americans (5–10 miles/8–16 km east). Most of these islands would play important roles in the Okinawa campaign.

Okinawa Gunto is approximately 320 miles (515 km) southwest of Kyushu. It lies 350 miles (564 km) northeast of Formosa and 450 miles (725 km) east of the Chinese mainland. It is in time zone 21, the same as Japan, what the US called time zone *Item* or *Zulu-9, Zulu* being Greenwich meantime.

The Chinese intermittently raided the Ryukyus for hundreds of years beginning in the 6th or 7th century. The Dragon Empire never attempted to attain complete sovereignty over the islands, but in 1368 demanded tribute and the Ryukyuan king declared himself a subject of China. Okinawa also had relations with Japan but managed to remain at least partly independent of both its dominating imperial neighbors. Japan gained partial control of the islands in the 1500s. In 1609, after Okinawa refused to provide troops for Japan's war against Korea, Japan invaded and devastated the island kingdom. Okinawa still maintained a semi-independent status, paying tribute to both Japan and China. Commodore Matthew Perry used Okinawa as a supply base during his 1853 effort to establish trade with Japan. He raised an American flag on a hill near Shuri Castle that Americans would die for almost 100 years later. The opening up of Japan quickly established the country as a regional power, and it took control of Okinawa in 1867. The Okinawan king was given a permanent residence in Tokyo and in 1874 the Japanese Home Ministry took total control of the islands. A Japanese governor was installed in 1879 and the islands given prefecture *(ken)* status. China still claimed the islands and Okinawans preferred their fence-sitting status between the two powers, but they were now solidly part of the Empire of the Rising Sun. Okinawa was granted a prefecture assembly and a seat in the Diet in 1920. In 1943, the Prefecture of Okinawa was consolidated with seven others into the Home Islands District of Kyushu.

Okinawa Shima is oriented northeast to southwest with a length of 64 miles (100 km). Its width varies from 18 miles (29 km) at the Motobu Peninsula *(hanto)* extending east from the island's northern portion to 2 miles (3.2 km) at the Ishikawa Isthmus just south of the island's mid-point. Several smaller peninsulas extend from the island's southern portion protecting excellent anchorages. The Ishikawa Isthmus divides Okinawa into two contrasting regions.

The sparsely populated north is covered with rugged, ridge-like 1,000–1,500-ft (300–450 m) high hills branching off a central ridge. The areas around the hills are bisected by deep ravines and gullies terminating at the coast in steep cliffs. The northwest coast's Motobu Peninsula is a dominant feature and was the center of Japanese resistance in the north. The entire area is covered by dense forests of pine, live oak, and thick underbrush. The road system was extremely limited, with only one single-track road following the northwest shore to

The Japanese used every available natural terrain and manmade feature for defensive purposes. These concrete-lined rainwater catchment basins, linked to the rice paddy irrigation system, were used as fighting positions. Here marines examine an Arisaka rifle. (USMC)

the north end. Cross-country vehicle movement was impossible. The soil is red clay and sandy loam and is well drained by the many small streams. This difficult terrain stretches south past the Ishikawa Isthmus to the island's southern one-third.

The heavily populated south is characterized by rolling hills, sometimes terraced, gradually climbing to over 500 ft (152 m) high at the island's southern end. The hills are cut by ravines and shallow, narrow streams that provide poor drainage. Caves (gama), cut by underground streams, honeycomb the hills and ridges. The further south one goes, the more hilly and broken the terrain becomes. The central plains south of the Ishikawa Isthmus are open and gently rolling. Further south, small scattered, irregular knolls dot the area, and these were incorporated into the Japanese defenses. The hills can be steep in some areas and several escarpments and twisting limestone ridges cut across the island providing successive cross-compartment defensive lines as one advances south. There were few long fields of fire, so conditions were ideal for Japanese short-range weapons. While some areas were lightly wooded, four-fifths of the south was cultivated with sweet potato, sugar cane, rice, and soybean fields in the valleys and on hills and plateaus. Although secondary to farming, fishing was also one of the island's principal industries. Villages and towns were scattered across the southern region and connected by a network of single-track roads and trails; some of which were surfaced with crushed coral, but most were dirt cart tracks. A single two-lane limestone road connected the island's only two cities of Naha and Shuri. Because of the clay soil conditions, the largely unimproved roads were totally incapable of supporting military traffic during the rainy season. Off-road traffic was impossible in most areas when the rains came. A narrow-gauge (60-cm) railroad connected Naha,

An aerial view of the north end of Tokashiki Shima looking south. This is the largest island in the Kerama Retto. The islands unsuccessfully served the Japanese as a suicide boat base and the US as a fleet base. The small bay on the upper right coast is one of the 27 March US landing beaches. (US Army)

Kobakura, Kobuba, and Yonabaru with branches linking Kobakura to Kadena and Kokuba with Itoman. The 30 miles (48 km) of track mainly hauled produce, and some of it would be returned to operation by American engineers.

Much of the coastline was fronted by limestone cliffs and scattered coral heads. The most desirable landing beaches were on the west coast, south of the two-mile (3.2-km) wide Ishikawa Isthmus, the Hagushi Beaches[5] edging the central plains. The usual coral-reef shelf paralleled the shore with a higher seaward crest 200–700 yds (183–640 m) offshore that deepened closer to shore. At low tide, trucks could easily drive across it. The area's mean tides are 4 ft 1 in. (1.24 m), but at the time of the landing a spring tide would raise the water level to 5 ft 11 in. (1.79 m). The eight miles (13 km) of landing beaches were gently sloping with few natural obstacles, although there were extensive sea walls 3–10 ft (0.9–3 m) high. The beaches were not continuous, but separated into lengths between 100 and 900 yds (90–820 m) long by low-cliff headlands. At low tide the beaches were 10–45 yds (9–41 m) wide, but at high water were completely awash. Behind the beaches sparsely vegetated and cultivated ground rose gradually to 50 ft (15 m). The beaches were selected because of their proximity to Yontan and Kadena airfields 2,000 yds (1,820 m) inland. Their early seizure would allow land-based fighters to fly close air support and aid in the defense of the fleet.

The population of Okinawa was 435,000 and included thousands of Japanese immigrants serving as government officials, administrators, managers, and merchants. Even with representation in the government, Okinawans had little real say in their affairs. Naha is Okinawa's prefectural capital and commercial center with a pre-invasion population of over 60,000. It was the island's main seaport. Shuri was slightly smaller and was the Ryukyu's traditional capital. Shuri Castle is perched on the massive

ABOVE **A marine intelligence team examine a weapon first encountered on Iwo Jima, the 320-mm spigot mortar. The black-painted projectile with a thin red band, weighed 675 lb and had a range of barely 1,000 yds. Manned by the Japanese 1st Independent Mortar Regiment, its 24 mortars were inaccurate and proved to be none too effective despite their massive warhead. (USMC)**

ABOVE, RIGHT **The embrasure of a concrete and limestone 10.5-cm Model 14 (1925) gun emplacement dug into the side of a hill. While provided with a limited field of fire, it and other widely dispersed guns were able to concentrate their fires on specific areas through which it was predicted the enemy would advance. Similar positions were constructed of logs rather than concrete. They were also built for 15-cm Model 89 (1929) guns and Model 96 (1936) howitzers. Small in size, the embrasures were difficult to detect from the air and hard to knockout from the ground as they required multiple direct hits. The gun could be pulled well back into the tunnel when fire was directed at the embrasure. The scattered logs had probably been stacked in front as camouflage. (USMC)**

ridge cutting across the island and was the ancient throne of the Ryukyuan kings. It would become a vicious battleground.

Most population centers were villages ranging from fewer than 100 inhabitants to over 1,000. The towns of Itoman, Nago, and Yonabaru were simply large villages with few modern buildings. Concrete and stone government and commercial buildings were numerous in Naha and Shuri, but most urban buildings and dwellings were one-storey wood, surrounded by low stone walls. Dwellings in villages had clay walls, thatch roofs, and were surrounded by bamboo windbreaks or low stone or mud walls overgrown with tropical vegetation. Unique to Okinawa were the stone, lyre-shaped family tombs, which were an important part of the indigenous animistic cult, emphasizing the veneration of ancestors. Dug into hillsides, they did not offer all-around defense, but provided protection from artillery and their vulnerable sides could be covered from other fighting positions.

The two main airfields, Yontan and Kadena (also known as Yara Hikojo), were on the central plains while Machinato Airfield was just north of Naha. Across from it on the east coast was abandoned Yonabaru Airfield. An Imperial Navy airfield was located on Oroku Peninsula. Two airfields were located on Ie Shima.

Before the invasion 80,000 Okinawans were shipped to Kyushu aboard returning supply ships to work in factories (some were sunk en route by US submarines). Another 60,000 were forced to relocate to the sparse north, reducing the burden on Japanese forces in the heavily populated south.

Temperatures are moderate with a winter night low of 40°F $(4.4°C)$[6]. At the time of the battle, day temperatures ranged from the 70s to the 80s (degrees fahrenheit). Humidity is high all year around. Rain is frequent, but irregular, with the heaviest occurring from May to September during the summer monsoon – 93 in. (23.6 cm) per year. Rain was to have a major impact on the coming battle. Moderate winds varied from south to east at the time of the battle. Between May and November one or two typhoons may pass Okinawa each month.

Japanese and Okinawans lay claim to the same basic racial origins – the Ainu aborigines – but Okinawans have more Mongoloid and Malayan blood. Okinawans bear a physical resemblance to the Japanese, but there the similarity ends. Their languages have the same roots, but are mutually unintelligible (Japanese was taught in schools, but few Okinawans were proficient). The native language is Luchuan. Bearing extensive Chinese influence, Okinawa's culture and religion were distinctly different from Japan's. Furthermore, the Japanese viewed the Okinawans as inferior and there was wide disparity between the two races socially, economically, and politically, resulting in much resentment. Japanese on the island enjoyed many privileges not conferred on Okinawans. This secondary status did not, however, exempt Okinawans from military conscription to serve the Emperor. The coming battle for Okinawa could be described as a clash between three cultures, the effects of which still reverberate today. Ryukuans caught in the American storm sweeping across Okinawa would refer to the assault as the *tetsu no bofu*– "Typhoon of Steel."

---

1 Formosa was defended by 479,313 troops of the 10th Area Army under General Rikuchi Ando with the 9th, 12th, 50th, 66th, and 71st Divisions, 8th Air Division, 1st Air Fleet (IJN), and 12th, 75th, 76th, 102nd, and 103rd IMBs.
2 The existence of two "sub-theater" commanders in the Pacific Theater caused numerous conflicts and difficulties. It prevented complete unity of command and even made logistics distribution difficult. It was a political arrangement due to the personalities involved. The Twentieth Air Force's strategic B-29 bombers were directed by the Joint Chiefs of Staff rather than one of the service commanders to prevent either from appearing to possess a further strategic reach than the other.
3 In May 1944, the Pacific Fleet was reorganized to allow the Third and Fifth Fleets to be rotated, thus accelerating the war's tempo. One fleet planned, refitted, and trained for the next operation while the other fought. There was no decrease in operational tempo since as soon as one fleet had completed an operation, the other immediately went into action. The Fast Carrier Force, however, operated almost continuously and would be assigned to the operational fleet, although individual ships were rotated as required.
4 Translations of Japanese terms are: Shoto – groups of islands, Retto – archipelago, Gunto – group, Shima and Jima– island. Terms for settlements are: shi – city, sho – town, mura – village. Ryukyu is derived from the Chinese Liuchiu ("loochoo"), meaning something like "precious floating stones on the horizon" (almost every source gives a different meaning), and the Japanese inability to pronounce "L" resulted in Ryukyu.
5 The beaches were named after centrally located Hagushi Village at the mouth of the Bishi Gawa (stream). Hagushi, however, was actually a mistranslation. The village's real name was Togushi. The Japanese called them the Kadena Beaches.
6 Japanese forces were well supplied with warm clothing and blankets, while US troops were ill-prepared for the chilly nights.

CHRONOLOGY

1944

16–17 February, Task Force (TF) 58 aircraft strike and neutralize Truk.

15 June–9 July, V Amphibious Corps assaults and captures Saipan.

21 July–10 August, III Amphibious Corps assaults and captures Guam.

10 October, First carrier raid on Okinawa.

23–26 October, Japanese fleet is eliminated as a threat during the Battle of Leyte Gulf.

25 October, CinCPOA issues joint staff study for Operation *Iceberg*.

24 November, First B-29 bomber raid on Tokyo. Raid launched from Saipan.

1945

6 January, Tenth Army issues Tentative Operation Plan 1-45 for Operation *Iceberg*.

19 February–16 March, V Amphibious Corps assaults and captures Iwo Jima.

11 March (L-21), Tenth Army Operation Plan 1-45 put into effect.

21–27 March (L-11 to L-5), Operation *Iceberg* task forces and task groups sortie for Okinawa.

26–29 March (L-6 to L-3), 77th Inf. Div. assaults and captures Kerama Retto.

31 March (L-1), 420th Field Artillery Group lands on Keise Shima.

1 April (L-Day), Tenth Army assaults Okinawa's Hagushi Beaches with four divisions.

1–2 April, 2nd Mar. Div. conducts demonstrations off southwest coast.

2 April, Forward elements of 7th Inf. Div. reach east coast severing the island.

6/7 April, First of ten major *Kamikaze* attacks on TF 51 ships.

7 April, TF 58 aircraft sink battleship *Yamato* and four other warships.

6–11 April (L+5), 3rd Battalion, 105th Infantry secures Eastern Islands, Tsugen Shima on 10 April.

10 April, 27th Inf. Div. lands to reinforce XXIV Corps.

11 April, 2nd Mar. Div. (Tenth Army Floating Reserve) departs for Saipan.

16–21 April (W-Day), 77th Inf. Div. assaults and captures Ie Shima.

18 April, Ernie Pyle, the popular war correspondent, killed on Ie Shima.

19 April, XXIV Corps conducts major attack on outer Shuri defenses.

20 April, 6th Mar. div. secures Motobu Peninsula in the north.

27 April, 77th Inf. Div. lands on Okinawa.

30 April, 77th Inf. Div. relieves 96th Inf. Div. in the south.

1 May, 1st Mar. Div. relieves 27th Inf. Div. in the south. The 1st is attached to XXIV Corps.

4 May, 27th Inf. Div. relieves 6th Mar. Div. in the north.

4–6 May, XXIV Corps repulses major Japanese counterattack.

7 May, III Amphibious Corps enters the southern line in the Tenth Army western sector and 1st Mar. Div. reattached to IIIAC.

8 May, 6th Mar. Div. enters the line in the south.

9 May, 96th Inf. Div. relieves 7th Inf. Div. in the south.

11 May, Tenth Army conducts major attack on inner Shuri defenses.

17 May, Admiral Turner relieved by Admiral Hill as Commander, TF 51. General Buckner now directly subordinate to Admiral Spruance, Commander, TF 50.

27 May, Third Fleet relieved Fifth Fleet (TF 51 becomes TF 31). General Buckner now directly subordinate to Admiral Nimitz, CinCPOA.

30 May, 8th Marines (Special Landing Force) returns from Saipan and secures unoccupied islands 3 and 9 June.

30 May–4 June, Japanese 32nd Army withdraws from Shuri defenses south to the Kiyamu Peninsula.

31 May, 5th Marines secure Shuri Castle.

4 June (K-Day), 4th Marines conduct shore-to-shore assault on Oroku Peninsula; last opposed amphibious assault in World War Two.

14 June, Marines secure Oroku Peninsula.

15 June, 8th Marines land at Naha and attach to 1st Mar. Div.

18 June, General Buckner killed. General Geiger (USMC) assumes command of Tenth Army.

21 June (L+82), End of organized resistance on Okinawa.

23 June, General Stillwell assumes command of Tenth Army.

26–30 June, Amphibious Reconnaissance Battalion, FMFPac assaults and secures Kume Shima; last amphibious assault in World War II.

30 June, Mopping-up of southern Okinawa completed.

1 July, TF 31 dissolved.

4 August, 27th Inf. Div. completes mopping-up of northern Okinawa.

6 August, Atomic bomb dropped on Hiroshima.

9 August, Atomic bomb dropped on Nagasaki.

10 August, Japan sues for peace.

14 August, Ceasefire in the Pacific Theater.

2 September (VJ-Day), Japan formally surrenders.

7 September, All remaining Japanese forces in the Ryukyus surrender.

POST-WAR

24 April 1946, Local government representation established on Okinawa by US Military Governor, Ryukyus.

15 May 1972, US Government returns Ryukyu Islands to Japanese Government control.

OPPOSING PLANS

THE JAPANESE PLAN

The great Japanese bastion on Truk in the Caroline Islands was neutralized by air in February 1944; a move followed by the fall of the crucial Mariana Islands (Saipan, Tinian, Guam) that summer. Heavily fortified Iwo Jima was seized in February and March 1945. All of the Pacific islands, taken in the glorious days of 1941 and early 1942, were now back in Allied hands or enduring the process of being bombed and strafed into submission. Only scattered remnants of the Imperial Japanese Army (IJA) *(Kogun)* held out in the Philippines. Much of the Imperial Japanese Navy (IJN) *(Kaigun)* rested on the bottom of the Pacific. Its once feared carrier air arm had virtually ceased to exist. US submarines had cut Japan's sea lanes. B-29 bombers rained explosives and incendiaries on Japan's teaming cities at will.

Expecting attacks on Formosa and the Ryukyus, Japan prepared to battle the Americans to a stalemate. Hoping that Japanese spirit would endure massed American firepower and limitless material resources, she strove to inflict unacceptable losses and sue for peace.

Nicknamed the *Baka* (Japanese for Fool) bomb by the Americans, the Imperial Japanese Navy's Yokosuka MXY-7 *Ohka* (Cherry Blossom) rocket-propelled bomb was dropped from a Mitsubishi "Betty" G4M twin-engine attack bomber and flown by a pilot into enemy ships. It had a range of 43 miles (69 km) carrying a 1,200-kg warhead, shown here with the nose piece removed. It had a 16 ft (5 m) wingspan and length of 20 ft (6.07 m). Only a few reached their targets as the mother aircraft were often shot down, but those that hit a ship sank it or inflicted major damage. Their 533 mph (860 km/h) speed and small size made them difficult to down with gunfire.

Japan began the Pacific War with a light infantry-based doctrine and concepts "validated" by combat in China against an ill-armed, poorly supplied, weakly led and disunited army. The initial onslaught into the Pacific and Southeast Asia against little or unprepared opposition only strengthened the illusion of the superiority of Japanese doctrine and military abilities.

The Japanese concept of warfare focused on the offensive spirit of *Bushido*[7]. This doctrine, approaching religious fervor, was applied to the defense of Pacific islands. Its early failure in the Solomons and New Guinea forced a reluctant change. As observed in the Tenth US Army's

This 100-ft (30-m) long heavily log-reinforced tunnel had five rooms branching off it. The tunnel was found on Ie Shima, but was typical of those on the main island. They served as troop shelters during bombardments, housed command posts, aid stations, ammunition, and supplies. (USMC)

G-2 Intelligence Monograph of August 1945, "an army trained to attack on any and every occasion, irrespective of conditions, and with no calculation as to the real chances of success, could be beaten soundly." The concept of "impregnable defenses" was behind attempts to destroy the attackers on the beaches, but it proved a failure and was also unsuccessful in the Gilberts, Marshalls, and Marianas. The supposedly impenetrable beach obstacles and dense fortifications, designed to stop the attackers at the water's edge, were crushed by overwhelming American esprit de corps, firepower, and materiel. The senseless *banzai* charges, intended as local counterattacks to drive back a demoralized enemy, served only to hasten the inevitable end as Japanese soldiers died en masse for the Emperor under devastating American firepower.

A third defense strategy was introduced on Peleliu and then Iwo Jima. It sought to prolong the action and gradually grind down the attacking Americans as they battered themselves against heavily fortified defensive lines established in depth across the island. The goal was to inflict the maximum losses of troops, ships, aircraft, and material. It was to wear down the enemy's morale and break his spirit. There were no *banzai* charges on Peleliu or Iwo Jima and none were seen on Okinawa. The 32nd Army's battle slogan expressed this tactic in blunt terms:

> *One plane for one warship*
> *One boat for one ship*
> *One man for ten of the enemy or one tank*

In February 1944, after Truk was blasted into impotence, plans for the *Ten–Go* Operation were laid. Japan reinforced the defenses of Formosa and Okinawa and established the 32nd Army on the latter in April. *Ten-Go* envisioned a network of inter-supporting air bases to destroy American air and sea forces venturing into their zones. Thirteen groups of air bases were established in the Ryukyu chain and on Formosa. A group of bases might contain three to five airfields defended by anti-aircraft guns and the islands by strong IJA garrisons. Multiple airfields in a group allowed damaged ones to be repaired and aircraft to use the remaining fields.

Ten–Go was suspended after the Marianas fell and a new plan, *Sho–Go 2*, instituted. It called for massive air attacks by aircraft swarming from the Home Islands, Formosa, and the Philippines if the Ryukyus were attacked. The 32nd Army on Okinawa was reinforced through the summer to boast three infantry divisions, an independent mixed brigade, and substantial support and service troops. The 32nd received a blow in November when the 9th Division, its best, was withdrawn for duty on Leyte[8]. Additional forces were sent to other Nansai Shoto islands[9] further diluting the defenses of Okinawa.

Only 30 aircraft remained on Okinawa, although extensive air service establishments existed. Most aircraft had been withdrawn to Formosa and Kyushu. Those few remaining were destroyed by US air and naval gunfire by early March. In February 1945, IJA Air Service (*Kokygun*) air regiments of the 6th Air Army and IJN Air Force (*Koku Buntai*) air groups were consolidated into the Combined Air Fleet under an IJN admiral. Besides massed conventional air attacks, invading Americans would face the *Kamikaze*, the "Divine Wind," or Special Attack *(Tokko)* as the Japanese designated them[10]. They were codenamed *Kikusui* (floating chrysanthemums). American naval forces first experienced *Kamikaze* attacks mounted as a last resort by the IJN in the Philippines.

The plans for the defense of Okinawa went through several iterations before that which the Americans faced was adopted. While the Imperial General Headquarters advocated a policy of "decisive battle" to aggressively attack the enemy in close combat and defend the island's airfields, the 32nd Army faced reality and chose to pursue a "war of attrition" *(Jikyusen)*. Even with the arrival of the promised 84th Division in January to replace the 9th Division, the 32nd Army could not have defended the entire island, even though that course of action was desired by IGHQ. The 84th never arrived and the 32nd Army possessed the resources to defend only approximately one-third of the island. Two options were quickly rejected. The 10th Area Army on Formosa, to which 32nd Army was subordinate, desired the defense of the central plains with the Yontan and Kadena Airfields. Lieutenant-General Ushijima knew that with the arrival of the American fleet the airfields could not be used and his 32nd Army would be quickly destroyed on the exposed plains. Moving the 32nd Army to the rugged north might ensure, or at least prolong, its survival. But, this option would deprive it of its resources in the south and prevent it from forcing the Americans into close combat and inflicting unacceptable losses on them. The north lacked a viable road network and the 32nd Army did not have the transportation means to move what it needed into the northern hills.

To appease 10th Area Army, Ushijima thinly deployed the 44th Independent Mixed Brigade (IMB) to defend the central plains in December 1944. His two divisions were in the south. Ushijima's operations officer, Colonel Yahara, studied the deployment of the Army's units and felt they were still stretched too thin. By doctrine, a

A heavily constructed concrete, limestone, and log bunker line on Mezado Ridge 500–600 yds (455–546 m) southwest of Kunishi and 1,200 yds (1,092 m) south of Itoman, 21 June. While used as bomb shelters, an embrasure was provided for a light machine-gun. Only a direct hit by a large-caliber projectile or a heavy bomb would breach such bunkers. (US Army)

Japanese division defended a six-mile (9.6-km) front. Ushijima's two divisions and single brigade actively defended 24 miles (39 km) and covered a further 12 miles (19 km) of cross-island and coastal defenses. The Americans would pour through such a broad, thinly held front. To shorten the fronts Yahara withdrew the 44th IMB from the central plains in January 1945 and assigned it some of the 62nd Division's sector.

IGHQ insisted that the Americans, after their Marianas victory, would first seize small Daito Jima 180 miles (240 km) to the east as a base of operations and wished it heavily defended. Yahara felt the Americans would not bother, but would instead strike straight at Okinawa. He rightfully resisted the effort to squander forces on the insignificant rock.

The 32nd Army's deployment found the 62nd Division covering an area in the south from Naha and Shuri north to a line anchored on the east and west coasts on the second narrowest neck of the island, the three-and-a-half mile (5.5-km) wide Chatan Isthmus. This north-facing front was dug in on some of the first high ground encountered south of the central plains where the Americans would land. A more formidable defense line behind this was centered on the rugged 4,500-yd (4.1-km) long Urasoe–Mura Escarpment, Tanabaru Escarpment, and several ridges running from northwest to southeast across the island. The main defense line, however, was still further south and centered on Shuri Castle and a vast, rugged cross-island ridge and hill complex. Forces on this line were withheld from the first week's fighting. The weary advancing Americans would run headlong into well-prepared and formidable defenses. The 24th Division secured the southern end of the island to prevent landings and act as the 32nd Army reserve. The 44th IMB was southeast of the 62nd defending the Chinen Peninsula, where it was thought the Americans might land on the island's southeast Minatogawa Beaches (Minatoga in most US documents). The Okinawa

Naval Base Force secured the Oroku Peninsula southwest of the 62nd Division and was prepared to fight the Americans at the water's edge as was IJN doctrine. The island's north was not completely abandoned. The 1st Specially Established Regiment (formed from airfield service personnel) screened the Yontan and Kadena Airfields on the central plains. The regimental-size 2nd Infantry Unit, detached from the 44th IMB, was established on the Motobu Peninsula on the island's northwest coast to distract the Americans and tie up forces. One of its battalions was on Ie Shima just west of the Motobu along with other small elements. All of the main units in Okinawa Gunto would be augmented by specially established units formed from service troops in March in a further effort to thicken the 32nd Army's overextended lines.

The 32nd Army had little faith in promised Japanese air support. In order to survive and slow the Americans to the maximum extent, the Army would dig. Thousands of pillboxes, bunkers, weapons emplacements, and fighting positions were dug. Terrain features were incorporated into the defense and weapons were well-sited with excellent overlapping fields of fire. Multiple defense lines were established across the island anchored on dominating terrain. The construction and improvement of these repeating lines would continue through the battle as the Japanese were painfully pushed south. Supplies and munitions were protected in dugouts and caves. Extensive tunnel systems were dug, over 60 miles (96.54 km), enough to protect the Army's 100,000 troops.

The Imperial Japanese Army provided four battalion-size sea-raiding regiments each with 100 *Kamikaze* boats in the Kerama Retto. They were to launch night suicide attacks on the invading fleet. It was a tactic first used in the Philippines, and considerable faith was misplaced in it.

When this plan was proposed, the 10th Area Army ordered Ushijima's chief of staff, Major-General Cho, to justify why the airfields were to be left virtually undefended and the doctrine of destroying the invaders on the beaches ignored. Cho argued that previous events had proven it was impossible to destroy an American landing force at the water's edge, that the airfields would be untenable, and their defense would only expose the 32nd Army leading to its early annihilation. Let the Americans land where they chose, but once ashore and with little room to maneuver, they would encounter dug-in defenses on coast-to-coast ridge lines defended by an army prepared to maneuver and attack the enemy in a decisive battle. The 10th Area Army, to appease Ushijima for the self-serving withdrawal of the 9th Division, offered no more resistance to the plan.

Cho also flew to Tokyo in January for a final conference on the defense of Okinawa. He was told that *Kamikaze* air and sea attacks would be the sole means of destroying the American fleet. Imperial Japanese Army artillery and coast defense guns would hold their fire so as not to reveal their positions. They would be preserved to engage the Americans ashore when they became intermingled among the dense Japanese defenses. This would also help negate American air and naval gunfire support, the power of which the Japanese fully appreciated after recent battles.

A few weeks before the invasion, the 32nd Army was alerted by the Imperial General Headquarters that Admirals King and Nimitz had held a conference in Washington in early March. The Japanese had found that new operations occurred from 20–30 days after such high-level strategy conferences were held. Formosa or Okinawa was identified as the likely target.

However, any fortified defensive line, be it the Maginot, Gothic, *Westwall,* or the dug-in 32nd Army, can be defeated.

THE AMERICAN PLAN

The Joint Expeditionary Force (Task Force 51) faced a daunting challenge when plans for *Iceberg* began to be developed. First, intelligence on the area had to be collected. Accurate maps and sea charts were not available. The initial photo-mapping mission was flown during B-29 strikes in September 1944. All of Okinawa was photographed as were many of the outlying islands. Most of the north of the island, however, was hidden by clouds. Contour lines from captured Japanese maps were overprinted on the white areas, but it was not until midway through the campaign that complete photo-maps were available. Additional photo coverage, including photos of specific target areas, was obtained during the October carrier strikes.

American estimates of enemy strength and disposition were moderately accurate and erred on the low side. Estimates were revised over the months prior to the landing as the Japanese 9th Division was withdrawn and small numbers of reinforcements arrived on supply ships. By March 1945 it was estimated that 75,000 troops organized into 2½ divisions were on the island. It was understood that the enemy were concentrated on the southern third of the island and preparing a defense in-depth. As on Guam, a small force screened the north. Like the Japanese, the Americans felt this was more effective than a water's edge defense and potentially more dangerous to the landing force. They did, however, contemplate more resistance on the beaches than Ushijima had prepared and expected up to 80 percent casualties among the assault troops.

Initial planning began in September 1944 and called for a three-phase operation. The plan assumed that B-29s bombing Japan from the Marianas, the seizure of Iwo Jima, and carrier strikes on the Home Islands would concentrate all available Japanese aircraft there. The Okinawa landings would provoke violent air attacks on the fleet. One of the plan's main goals was the early seizure of the Yontan and Kadena Airfields for land-based aircraft to protect the fleet and provide close air support. The original plan preferred the west-coast beaches, but Admiral Turner expressed reservations because of expected winds and high surf conditions on 1 March. The east-coast Nakagusuka Wan (Bay) beaches were less favorable and the operation's postponement to April dispelled his concerns about the west-coast beaches.

Phase I called for the early securing of southern Okinawa and the development of its airfields along with seizing many of the offshore islands. The seizure of Ie Shima (codenamed *Indispensable*) and the rest of Okinawa was to take place in Phase II, and additional islands in the Ryukyus would also be seized. In Phase III Kikai Shima north of Okinawa was to be seized by 1st Mar. Div. and Miyako Shima in Sakishima Gunto near Formosa by V Amphibious Corps. In fact, V

From left to right: Admiral Raymond A. Spruance, Commander, Central Pacific Task Forces and Fifth Fleet; Fleet Admiral Chester W. Nimitz, Commander-in-Chief, Pacific Ocean Areas; and Lieutenant-General Simon B. Buckner Jr., Commanding General, Tenth Army. (USMC)

This formidable defensive position, made from reinforced concrete approximately 2 ft (60 cm) thick, utilizes a converted cave. Similar multiple positions and other, simpler fighting positions covered each other along limestone ridge lines. The larger embrasure could accommodate a light or heavy-machine gun while the smaller upper firing-slit allowed a rifleman to provide close-in protection and spot targets for the machine gunner whose vision might be obscured by dust. The "stepped" design of the embrasure helped prevent bullets from ricocheting into the opening. The 5-gal. (23-litre) water can was included in the photograph to give a sense of scale. Torn tree limbs in front originally camouflaged the position, which was connected to others by caves and tunnels. This position was near Beach "Yellow 2" in the 1st Marine Division's sector. (USMC)

Amphibious Corps was too badly mauled at Iwo Jima to undertake the operation. In the final plan, approved on 6 January 1945, Phase III was eliminated due to logistical considerations and Phases I and II were reversed, but the seizure of other islands was later canceled.

The new Phase I called for the early capture of Kerama Retto, 15 miles (24 km) west, by the 77th Inf. Div. beginning almost a week before the main landing. Kerama Retto would provide an ideal anchorage for refueling, rearming, and repairing ships of the bombardment line. A seaplane base for anti-submarine patrols was to be established there as well. One day before the main landing, an Army infantry battalion would secure Keise Shima, 11 miles (18 km) southwest of the Hagushi Beaches, and a field artillery group's long-range guns emplaced for fire support. An elaborate deception operation was to begin off the southeast coast of Okinawa two days before the Kerama Retto operation. Minesweepers, covered by fighters, would clear the waters while battleships bombarded positions ashore. The 2nd Mar. Div. would reinforce this deception by demonstrating off the beaches in hope the Japanese would rush reinforcements to the south and tie down counterattack forces that could be used against the real landing. Air strikes on Kyushu airfields would delay Japanese air attacks from the Home Islands.

The main landing would begin at 0830hrs, 1 April 1945, H-Hour, L-Day. The largest simultaneous amphibious assault in the Pacific War would see the landing of two Marine and two Army divisions abreast on eight miles (12.8 km) of beach. III Amphibious Corps (IIIAC) would land opposite Yontan Airfield with its 6th Mar. Div. on the left. The Division would move rapidly inland, seize the airfield and protect Tenth

Army's north flank by severing the island at the narrow Ishikawa Isthmus. Its 22nd Marines would land on the left flank. The 4th Marines would land on the right, its 2nd Battalion in Division Reserve, and would focus on the airfield. The Division's 29th Marines was in IIIAC Reserve to land to order. On the IIIAC's right, the 1st Marine Division would storm ashore south of the airfield and maintain contact with XXIV Corps on its right. The 7th Marines would land on the Division's left and the 5th on the right. The 1st Marines would be in Division Reserve and follow the 7th ashore. IIIAC Artillery would land on order in two groups of three battalions, with one group supporting each division. The Eastern Islands would be secured as required to further protect Tenth Army's seaward eastern flank.

The Bishi Gawa (stream) served as the initial physical boundary between IIIAC and XXIV Corps. The veteran 7th Infantry Division would land on the Corps' left, maintain contact with IIIAC, and seize Kadena Airfield. Its 17th Infantry would be on the left and the 32nd on the right. The 184th Infantry was the Division Reserve. The 96th Inf. Div. would land south of the airfield with its 381st Infantry on the left and the 383rd Infantry on the right. Its 382nd Infantry was the Corps Reserve. There was no division reserve, but the 382nd would land behind the 381st and be prepared to respond to a Japanese counterattack from the south. XXIV Artillery (less the group on Keise Shima) would land as necessary to support the Corps attack. The Corps' main mission, after capturing Kadena Airfield, was to swing south and secure an eastwest line through Kuba Saki and seal off the Japanese in the south.

The 2nd Mar. Div., after conducting its demonstration off the southeast beaches, would remain as the Tenth Army Floating Reserve along with the 27th Inf. Div. as the Expeditionary Troops Floating Reserve. The 81st Inf. Div. was held on New Caledonia as the Area Reserve.

Once the island was severed and the Japanese forces divided and isolated, the central portion of the island secured, and logistical build-up under way, XXIV Corps would advance south with the 7th Inf. Div. on the left (east) and the 96th on the right (west) to seize the main objective area; the island's southern end. IIIAC would back up XXIV Corps, securing the occupied sector across the island with its 1st Mar. Div. while the 6th advanced to clear the north end of the island. The 77th Inf. Div. would seize Ie Shima when ordered. The 27th Inf. Div., would land as necessary as XXIV Corps' frontline lengthened as the advance pressed south to where the island widened.

Initial air support for the landing forces would be provided by 14 escort carriers. Over 220 Marine fighters of Tactical Air Force, Tenth Army, a joint air force under Marine command, would be moved ashore from four escort carriers as airfields were captured and developed. Additional shore-based aircraft would be staged ashore at a later date.

The Navy task forces assigned to Task Force 51 would transport and deliver the landing forces, sustain them ashore, provide air cover and close air support, and deliver naval gunfire support. The Fifth Fleet's Fast Carrier Striking Force (TF 58) and British Carrier Force (TF 57) would attack Japanese air bases in the Home Islands, on Formosa, and the Ryukyus. They would also be prepared to engage any remnants of the Imperial Fleet that might attempt to sortie. Over 1,300 ships were committed to Operation *Iceberg*. Twentieth Air Force B-29 bombers would continue their pounding of Japan, especially air bases, and the Pacific Fleet Submarine Force would establish a barrier between Japan and Okinawa.

The logistic effort to mount and sustain such a massive campaign was enormous. Participating units staged at Espíritu Santo, Guadalcanal, the Russells, Saipan, Guam, Eniwetok, New Caledonia, Leyte, Oahu, and the West Coast of the United States. They formed up at Ulithi over 1,000 miles (1,609 km) to the southeast of Okinawa while other forces moved directly from Leyte. Just the effort and resources required to support all these far flung bases and maintain a supply line 4,000 miles (6,437 km) and 17 days steaming from Pearl Harbor – 6,200 miles (9,978 km), 26 days steaming from the West Coast – were phenomenal. The ability of the landing beaches to receive troops and supplies and availability of shipping were other governing factors. A total of 458 ships were required to transport and support the landing forces. Ammunition expenditure rates would be so high, over three times that used in the Marianas, that shortages were experienced from the West Coast all the way across the Pacific. Four major airfields would be constructed on Okinawa, requiring an effort much more than simply capturing existing crude strips. The new fields would be more extensive and the construction projects would literally change the island's landscape. The port of Naha would be rebuilt and expanded, and a massive advanced fleet operating base established at Nakagusuku Wan on the east side. Bases and facilities would be constructed from which to launch an even larger operation – the invasion of Japan.

---

7 Literally Bushi (warrior), Do (way or moral doctrine), i.e., "way of the warrior."

8 The 9th Division was actually sent to Formosa under the 32nd Army's superior, 10th Area Army, a self-serving act still bitterly debated among Japanese historians.

9 These forces were deployed to defend the Amami Gunto with the 21st IMR on Amami O Shima and 64th IMB on Tokuno Shima. The Sakishima Gunto was defended by the 28th Division and 60th IMB on Miyako Jima, 59th IMB on Irabu Jima, and 45th IMB on Ishigaki Jima.

10 While Westerners are intrigued and baffled by the *Kamikaze* concept, it was practical and honorable to the Japanese. *Koku Buntai* Captain Rikibei Inoguchi explained, "We must give our lives to the Emperor and Country, this is our inborn feeling. We Japanese base our lives on obedience to Emperor and Country. On the other hand, we wish for the best place in death, according to *Bushido*. *Kamikaze* was the incarnation of these feelings."

OPPOSING COMMANDERS

AMERICAN COMMANDERS

Task Force 50, the Fifth Fleet and Central Pacific Task Forces, was a joint command in the purest definition. This is reflected in its senior commanders, who represented the US Navy, Army, Marine Corps, and those services' air arms. By the time of the battle for Okinawa, the committed US forces had been forged into an efficient fighting machine capable of defeating any foe challenging them. Of all the many factors contributing to this skill at arms – planning, intelligence, training, logistics, and materiel resources – the diversified experiences of the task force's commanders was paramount.

The American system of command allowed a remarkable degree of latitude to subordinate commanders at all levels. Higher commanders developed strategic plans, after a great deal of coordination to accommodate the capabilities and limitations of each service. Their staffs refined the plans' details and allocated combat forces and logistics to execute the mission. Subordinate commanders and their staffs then developed their own operational and tactical plans to accomplish the mission. How they allocated and employed their own forces was, with some minor exceptions, left entirely to them. This degree of freedom

Troops of the 1st Mar. Div. board a landing craft, vehicle and personnel (LCVP) alongside an assault transport on the morning of L-Day. Rather than the rope cargo nets used earlier, these men have the benefit of more stable chain and wooden rung ladders. An LCVP, the most used landing craft, could carry 36 troops or a 6,000-lb (2,722-kg) vehicle or 8,100 lb (3,674 kg) of cargo. The 35-ft 9-in. (11-m) craft were armed with two .30cal. M1919A4 machine guns. (USMC)

Assault troops of the 1st Mar. Div. churn ashore aboard a landing vehicle, tracked Mk 3 (LVT[3]) amphibian tractor. This view is toward the Amtrac's stern and shows a .50cal. HB-M2 machine gun. Five-gallon (23-litre) water cans line the Amtrac's sides for use ashore and for protection from small-arms fire. (USMC)

was seldom realized in any other nations' armed forces. It was not uncommon for a senior commander to disagree with a subordinate's employment of his forces, but, generally, so long as the mission could be accomplished and the plan supported the overall plan, it was executed as the subordinate commander desired. It typified a basic American trait, "Tell me what needs to be done, then let me do it."

Raymond A. Spruance graduated from the Naval Academy in 1906 serving on battleships, then commanding destroyers, and finally a battleship in 1938–39. In the 1920s he served on numerous staffs in such varied disciplines as engineering and intelligence. His early operational experience saw him as Commander, Caribbean Sea Frontier, where he dealt with a potentially hostile Vichy French force and marauding U-boats attacking Allied shipping. The US entry into the war found him in command of a cruiser division, which escorted the USS *Hornet* during Doolittle's Tokyo raid. He commanded a two-carrier task force during the Battle of Midway and sank four Japanese carriers, inflicting a crippling blow on Japan. In rapid succession he became Nimitz's chief-of-staff, deputy commander of the Pacific Fleet, and then took command of the Central Pacific Force, which became the Fifth Fleet. In that capacity he directed Army and Marine forces seizing the Gilberts, Marshalls (after his promotion to admiral), and Marianas; some of the most complex joint amphibious operations to date. Forces under his command were victorious in the Battle of the Philippine Sea. The Fifth Fleet had grown into arguably the world's most powerful fleet. Spruance went on to seize Iwo Jima in February 1945 and then marshaled his forces for the final battle. As Commander, Task Force 50, Fifth Fleet and Central Pacific Task Forces, Spruance executed the largest amphibious operation of the war. He went on to command the Pacific Fleet after the war, but soon relinquished command to become president of the Naval War College. Retiring in 1948, he later served as ambassador to the Philippines. He died in 1969.

Richmond K. Turner graduated from the Naval Academy two years after his immediate superior at Okinawa, Spruance. Turner served on

LEFT **A soldier is treated by his buddies. He was one of the 104 wounded suffered on L-Day. Note that the soldier to the far left wears a Browning automatic rifle belt holding 12 20-round magazines. (US Army)**

BELOW **Troops of the 32nd Infantry, 7th Inf. Div. rest during the push inland toward Kadena Airfield from the "Orange" Beaches, 1 April. The man in the foreground carries an M2 tripod for a .30cal. M1919A4 machine gun and a 250-round M1 ammunition can. A gas mask case and M1910 pick-mattock are on his left hip. The flame gunner behind him carries an M2-2 flamethrower. (US Army)**

270795

battleships during the Great War, but in 1926 he made a major career change and was rated a Naval Aviator. Numerous aviation staff assignments followed, including as executive officer of the carrier USS *Saratoga* and culminating as Commander, Aircraft, Battle Force for the US Fleet. He next commanded a cruiser and then attended the Naval War College. The opening shots of the war found him as director of the Navy Department's War Plans Division. In the summer of 1942 Turner took over command of amphibious forces in the South Pacific. His experience on planning staffs and the command of air units and ships of the line were to serve him well as he launched the grueling Solomon Islands campaign. Here he experienced his only defeat during the Savo Island Battle. In August 1943, he assumed command of Admiral Spruance's amphibious forces to perfect landing force operations in the Gilberts, Marshalls (after promotion to vice-admiral), Marianas, and Iwo Jima. As Commander, Joint Expeditionary Force (TF 51), during the Okinawa landings, Turner directed all amphibious forces of the Third and Fifth Fleets. He was promoted to admiral in May 1945 while the battle still raged. After the war he served as the US Navy representative to the UN Military Staff Committee until retiring in 1947. Turner died in 1961.

Simon B. Buckner, Jr., the son of a Confederate general, attended the Virginia Military Institute before acceptance to the Military Academy at West Point. Graduating in 1908, he served as an infantry officer alternating mainly between Mexican border duty and the Philippines. In 1917 he, like his future commander, became an aviator. He spent little time in the air, however, as he attended the Infantry School, Command and General Staff College (C&GSC), and Army War College. Between schools he served as an instructor at each as well as at West Point. In the late 1930s he commanded infantry regiments and served on a division staff. In 1940 he took command of US forces in Alaska. In 1942 he countered Japanese landing attempts in the Aleutians and retook the islands they had seized by the next summer. He was promoted to

A landing craft, infantry (gun) (LCI[G]) type D. It mounts five 4.5-in. Mk 7 rocket launchers on either side along with three 40-mm and four 20-mm guns. Each Mk 7 launcher rack holds 12 high explosive rockets with a range of 1,100 yds (1,006 m). These craft preceded the assault waves toward shore firing suppressive barrages. Three of the same Mk 7 launcher racks were mounted on Marine 1-ton trucks. (USMC)

lieutenant-general in May 1943 and remained in command in Alaska until June 1944. Ordered to Hawaii, Buckner organized and took command of the Tenth Army. He quickly welded his new joint Army/Marine command into an effective force and led it to Okinawa as Commanding General, Expeditionary Troops and Tenth Army (TF 56). Three days before the island was declared secure, Buckner was killed observing his troops' advance on the final organized resistance.

While the most senior commanders of Operation *Iceberg* were products of the service academies, **John R. Hodge** received a Reserve Officers Training Corps commission from the University of Illinois in 1917. Soon receiving a regular commission in the infantry, he served in France in 1918–19. He taught military science at a college before attending the Infantry School and then served in Hawaii. In the mid-1930s he attended C&GSC and the Army War College. The Pearl Harbor attack found Hodge on the VII Corps staff. As assistant commander of the 25th Inf. Div. he fought on Guadalcanal alongside the Marines. Promoted to major-general in April 1943, he took command of the bloodied Americal Division leading it at Bougainville. His next assignment was commander of XXIV Corps in April 1944. Under the Sixth Army and landed by the Seventh Fleet in October, Hodge led his corps through the bitter Leyte campaign to secure the island by the year's end. Besides his experience with the Marines on Guadalcanal and Bougainville, the Marine V Amphibious Corps Artillery supported him on Leyte (while his own XXIV Corps Artillery supported the Marines on Saipan and Tinian). Returned to Hawaii, XXIV Corps joined the new Tenth Army to prepare for the assault on Okinawa. At the war's end Lieutenant-General Hodge led his corps to Korea for occupation duty. From 1948 he held further corps and army commands until retirement in 1953. He died ten years later.

Roy S. Geiger was considered an oddity by many – he was a Naval Aviator[11], the fifth Marine to become a pilot, and an amphibious corps commander. He flew in and commanded Marine aviation units from 1917 right up to assuming command of I Marine Amphibious Corps in November 1943. Geiger enlisted in the Marine Corps in 1907 after graduating from college. He was commissioned an infantry officer two years later to serve in Central America, China, and elsewhere. Between major aviation commands he attended the Army's C&GSC and War College, and then the Naval War College. In August 1941, Geiger took command of the 1st Marine Aircraft Wing taking it to Guadalcanal where he was promoted to major-general. In May 1943, he was assigned as Director, Division of Aviation, Headquarters, Marine Corps. In November he took command of the 1st Marine Amphibious Corps, considered an unusual move by many due to his flying vocation. But he excelled in two areas critical to successful corps operations, fire support (artillery, naval, air) and logistics. He led the corps on Bougainville, then to Guam (the Corps was redesignated III Amphibious Corps in April 1944), and Peleliu. On both Guadalcanal and Bougainville Geiger worked with John R. Hodge, his future sister corps commander on Okinawa. With the death of Lieutenant-General Buckner on 18 June 1945, Geiger assumed command of Tenth Army, the only Marine officer to command a field army, while retaining command of IIIAC. The next day he was promoted to lieutenant-general. General Buckner had expressly picked Geiger to assume command in the event of his death. Five days later, Geiger was relieved by Lieutenant-General Joseph W. Stilwell. In July 1945 Geiger took command of Fleet Marine Force, Pacific. In late 1946 he was assigned to Headquarters, Marine Corps, but became ill just before his scheduled retirement and died in January 1947. Later in the year he was given posthumous promotion to full general by a grateful Congress.

JAPANESE COMMANDERS

The Imperial Headquarters appointed **Lieutenant-General Mitsuru Ushijima**[12] as commander of the Japanese 32nd Army on 8 August 1944. He arrived two days later to replace the ailing Lieutenant-General Masao Watanabe. A 1908 graduate of the Japanese Military Academy, Ushijima was an infantry officer who had progressed through the usual command and staff duties, eventually serving as a vice minister in the Ministry of the Army. In 1942 he commanded an infantry group in Burma, a brigade-equivalent command. His assignment to the 32nd Army relieved him from his duties as commandant of the Military Academy. Ushijima believed in mentoring his subordinates and rather than taking sides when his staff frequently disagreed as to a course of action, he resolved disputes through mediation. As a commander he was described as coolly appreciative of reality.

The steady and reserved Ushijima selected a very different individual as his chief-of-staff. **Major-General Isamu Cho** was known for his strong emotions, enthusiasm, and boldness. As a regimental commander in the 19th Division, he once napped on a hillside in full view of Soviet troops during the 1938 Manchuria border dispute. He enjoyed good food and drink, often performing a wild sword dance when sufficiently inebriated. Graduating from the Military Academy in 1916, he progressed rapidly, although his career was marred by involvement in

This aerial view of the beachhead on L+4 gives some idea of the logistical effort required to sustain a landing force ashore. Six Landing Ships, Tank (LST) are off-loading at center right of the picture. The reef prevents them from grounding closer to shore. The small bay above and to the left of the LSTs is the mouth of the Bishi Gawa (Stream). (USMC)

several coup attempts by the radical right-wing Cherry Society (*Sakura-kai*). In the 1931 coup attempt he was promised the position of police chief of Tokyo. His reward was banishment to China. There he helped plan the occupation of Manchuria and later the Marco Polo Bridge Incident in Peking. Serving as the chief-of-staff to Prince Yasuhiko Asaka (Emperor Hirohito's uncle) in 1937, he was responsible for relaying the prince's orders to massacre up to 300,000 Chinese in Nanking. He served on the Southern Army staff during the invasion of Burma and briefly commanded the 10th Division in Manchuria before being sent to the Philippines in 1942. Cho was finally allowed to return to Japan in 1944 to take part in the planned recapture of Saipan. When this operation was canceled, he was assigned to the Ministry of War's Military Affairs Bureau and then as the 32nd Army's chief-of-staff on 8 July 1944. He was promoted to lieutenant-general on 1 March 1945. Cho was the main advocate of the underground defense of Okinawa, but he was also responsible for the disastrous all-out May offensive. While widely different in background and temperament, the team of Ushijima and Cho has been compared to that of Hindenburg and Ludendorf.

While of comparatively junior rank, an equally important, and unique, member of the 32nd Army staff was **Colonel Hiromichi Yahara**, the senior operations officer. Yahara was an expert in developing operation plans and had long experience on staffs. A 1923 graduate of the Military Academy, where he later instructed, he served on staffs in

Used by both the Army and Marines, the 2½-ton amphibious truck or "Duck" (derived for their designation, DUKW-353) was mainly used to haul light-artillery pieces and ammunition ashore. They were able to move inland and deliver their cargo where necessary to prevent congestion on the beaches. Here a hoist-equipped D-9 dozer tractor unloads ammunition. (US Army)

China, Malaya, and Burma, and at the War Office. His higher military education included the Japanese War College and he spent two years as an exchange officer in the United States. Aloof and cool, he was widely recognized as an expert in his field. His personality was the exact opposite of Cho's, his immediate superior.

A Japanese staff functioned very differently from its Western counterpart. The commander bore the burden of spiritual responsibility, maintained contact with higher headquarters, and guided his staff. The chief-of-staff and operations officer possessed far more power than a Western chief-of-staff and G-3. Staff officers presented options to the chief and decisions were derived by negotiation, guided by the commander, to reach a common consensus. In reality, aggressive and opinionated staff officers, concerned with face-saving, often battled their way through planning sessions with factions of officers taking sides. Planning was made more difficult in an environment where anyone advising caution was branded a coward, where major commanders took complete operational freedom *(Dokudan Senko)* from higher headquarters, and subordinates often ignored their commanders *(Gekokujo)*. It can be assumed that 32nd Army staff meetings were lively in an atmosphere where Cho's and Yahara's "discussions" were described as theatrical. Yahara was the most senior Japanese officer to survive the battle and wrote a book on his experiences.

---

11 Marine pilots were rated as Naval Aviators.
12 The Japanese place the surname first and the personal name second. Contemporary and post-war writings usually reversed the two. This book continues that practice. Many different spellings of Japanese names will be encountered due to interpretations of the two or more *Kanji* ideographs making up a man's name. The personal name of an adult male is almost never spoken with even close friends using a formal address. The actual meaning of the ideograph selected by a man's parents may not even be known to his closest friends.

OPPOSING FORCES

TASK FORCE 51

As a joint command, **Task Force 51** (TF 51), the Joint Expeditionary Force, contained elements from the US Army, Navy, Marine Corps, and the three services' air arms. It was a completely self-contained force capable of delivering itself to its area of operations, sustaining itself for 30 days, and executing combat actions in the air, on land, and on and under the sea. TF 51 was itself a component of another task force, TF 50, the Fifth Fleet and Central Pacific Forces under Admiral Raymond A. Spruance. Spruance, as the commander tasked with carrying out the invasion, directly controlled two other task forces participating in the Okinawa campaign.

The **Fast Carrier Force** (TF 58), under Vice-Admiral Marc A. Mitscher, had 88 ships including 11 fleet carriers and six light carriers with almost 1,400 aircraft backed by seven battleships, 18 cruisers, scores of destroyers and escorts, and a massive logistics support group. Vice-Admiral Sir Bernard Rawlings' **British Carrier Force** (TF 57) contributed four carriers, two battleships, five cruisers, and 14 destroyers plus a fleet train. Most of its 260 aircraft were American-built. Task Force 50 could also depend on support from other commands to include Submarine Force, Pacific Fleet; US Army Air Forces in China, and B-29s of the Twentieth Air Force flying out of the Marianas.

A D-18 bulldozer disembarks from a landing craft, tank Mk 6 (LCT[6]). Other engineer equipment will follow. The 119½-foot (36.4-m) long craft could carry four medium tanks or 150 tons of cargo. It was armed with two 20-mm guns. The stern could be opened and several LCTs could be anchored end-to-end to serve as a floating causeway between shore and an LST, as vehicles could simply drive through the connected craft. (US Army)

Task Force 51, the Joint Expeditionary Force, consisted of five smaller task forces and three task groups under Vice-Admiral Richmond K. Turner, Commander, Amphibious Forces, Pacific. Many of the Task Force's Navy units had little respite after the February Iwo Jima operation. This actually eased planning as command and communications systems had been battle-tested and refined. Task Force 51's command relationships, tasks, and subordinate forces were complex and are paraphrased here:

Amphibious Support Force (TF 52), Rear-Admiral William H.P. Blandy, included 18 escort carriers with 450 close air support aircraft in Support Carrier Group (TG 52.1), four more escort carriers (Special Escort Carrier Group) to deliver Marine Aircraft Groups 31 and 33 ashore, escorting destroyers, over 60 minesweepers (Mine Flotilla, TG 52.2) to clear approaches to the island, and ten 100-man underwater demolition teams (UDT) with each aboard a destroyer transport (Underwater Demolition Flotilla, TG 52.11) along with 170 fire support landing craft armed with guns, rockets, and mortars.

Western Islands Attack Group (TG 51.1), Rear-Admiral Ingolf N. Kiland, with the 77th Inf. Div. embarked, were to secure Kerama Retto and other offshore islands prior to L-Day. It was then to seize Ie Shima. It had 17 attack and attack cargo transports, 56 LSTs (Landing Ship, Tank), and numerous smaller support craft, destroyers, and escorts.

Northern Attack Force (TF 53), Rear-Admiral Lawrence F. Reifsnider, had two transport groups, each with over 20 attack and attack cargo transports with III Amphibious Corps' 1st and 6th Marine Divisions embarked. With them were 67 LSTs transporting amphibious tractors and pontoon causeways plus screening destroyers.

Gunfire and Covering Force (TF 54), Rear-Admiral Morton L. Deyo, would provide naval gunfire support with nine battleships, ten cruisers, and numerous destroyers.

Southern Attack Force (TF 55), Rear Admiral John L. Hall, was organized roughly the same as TF 53 , but with three transport groups. Embarked aboard these were XXIV Corps' 7th, 27th, and 96th Infantry Divisions. The 27th was TF 51's Floating Reserve (TG 51.3).

Demonstration Group (TG 51.2) consisted of a transport group carrying the 2nd Marine Division, the Tenth Army's Floating Reserve.

The **Expeditionary Troops** (TF 56) controlled all ground forces involved in the assault and the follow-on Island Command. In terms of manpower, it was the largest force within TF 50. Under the command of Lieutenant-General Simon B. Buckner, it was built around the Tenth Army.

US ARMY

Tenth Army was activated at Ft. Sam Houston, Texas, on 20 June 1944. It deployed to Schofield Barracks, Oahu, Hawaii, in August and prepared to assault Okinawa Gunto. Tenth Army was composed of two corps, one Army and the other Marine. It was unique in that it controlled its own tactical air force, a joint Marine and Army command. Tenth Army comprised over 102,000 Army troops of which over 38,000 were non-divisional artillery, combat support, and headquarters troops and some 9,000 service troops. Over 88,000 Marines were

A twin 40-mm antiaircraft gun mounted on an unidentified type of landing ship. The 40-mm Bofors was mounted on virtually all ships in either single, twin, or quad mountings (the latter two being liquid-cooled) for antiaircraft defense, which was essential at Okinawa because of the unrelenting *Kamikaze* attacks. Landing ships operating close inshore used antiaircraft guns to place suppressive fire on shore targets. Scores of four-round clips line the gun tub. (USMC)

assigned along with 18,000 Navy (mainly Seabees and medical personnel). Tenth Army assault troops, those landing in the initial assault, totaled 182,821 men.

Directly under Tenth Army was the **53rd Antiaircraft Artillery Brigade** with five AAA groups, six 90-mm and three 40-mm AAA battalions. All participating units had more than the usual allocation of AAA units due to Okinawa's proximity to Japan and Formosa. Additional military police (MP) and military government units were assigned in anticipation of an increased need to provide traffic control, guard prisoners of war and civilian internees, and conduct rear area security. This was due to lessons learned on Saipan and Tinian where the US first experienced large numbers of enemy civilians and refugees. Other troops included a medical group and signal units.

XXIV Corps (Southern Landing Force) was a relative late-comer in the Pacific. Activated at Ft. Shafter, Oahu, Hawaii, on 8 April 1944, it fought on Leyte from October to December with its 7th and 96th Infantry Divisions. It then secured undefended islands and prepared for Okinawa, departing Leyte at the end of March 1945. Under the command of Lieutenant-General John R. Hodge, the Corps already had valuable experience working with Marines. V Amphibious Corps (VAC) and XXIV Corps Artillery had been positioned to support the Yap Island assault, but this was canceled in August 1944. Due to unit positioning, VAC Artillery supported XXIV Corps on Leyte while XXIV Corps Artillery went with VAC to Saipan and Tinian.

XXIV Corps Artillery, under Brigadier-General Josef R. Sheetz, had three artillery groups with 14 battalions of various calibers. Okinawa saw the first use of the 8-in. howitzer in the Pacific. Rounding out the Corps was an engineer construction group, quartermaster group, medical group, and numerous combat support battalions.

Four infantry divisions were assigned to XXIV Corps. The reinforced 7th, 77th, and 96th averaged almost 22,000 troops, but each was some

1,000 infantrymen understrength. Stateside replacement centers were unable to keep pace with the increasing tempo of the war in the Pacific and Europe. The divisions were reinforced by an engineer combat group for shore party duty, tank, amphibian tank, two amphibian tractor, and two AAA battalions plus additional medical units.

The Regular Army **7th Infantry Division** was reactivated (it had served in World War One) at Ft. Ord, California, on 1 July 1940. Its experiences were varied. After first receiving desert training, and then amphibious training from the Marines, it seized Attu Island in the Aleutians in May 1943. It moved to Hawaii and assaulted Kwajalein Atoll in January 1944. After returning to Hawaii, it fought on Leyte in October then prepared for Okinawa. The "Bayonet Division" was commanded by Major-General Archibald V. Arnold.

The **96th Infantry Division**, an Army Reserve unit, was activated at the end of World War One, but did not serve overseas. It was reactivated at Camp Adair, Oregon on 15 August 1942. After extensive training, which included amphibious training under the Marines, it assaulted Leyte in October 1944. The "Deadeye Division" was under the command of Major-General James L. Bradley for its entire World War Two service.

The **27th Infantry Division**, the floating reserve, would be the next to arrive on Okinawa. It fielded only just over 16,000 troops and was 2,000 infantrymen short. This was a New York National Guard unit and had served on the Mexican border in 1916 and fought in World War One. It was inducted into Federal service on 15 October 1940 in New York City and had a rather checkered relationship with the Marines. After training in the South, it moved to Hawaii and assaulted Saipan under VAC. Accused of excessive caution and lack of aggression, its commanding officer was relieved of command by the Marine VAC commander, souring Army-Marine relations. On Okinawa the "New York Division" was commanded by Major-General George W. Griner, Jr.

The last division to land on Okinawa, but the first to see combat in the Ryukyus, was the **77th Infantry Division**. Like the 96th, it was an Army Reserve division, but it had seen combat in World War One. It was reactivated on 25 March 1942 at Ft. Jackson, South Carolina. After deploying to Hawaii, it landed on Guam under IIIAC in July 1944 to fight under Marine command. It next fought on Leyte under Sixth Army from December 1944 through February 1945. Under the command of Major-General Andrew B. Bruce, the "Statue of Liberty Division" served as the Western Landing Force to first seize islands west of Okinawa.

The **81st Infantry Division**, under Major-General Paul J. Mueller, on New Caledonia was assigned as the Area Reserve and was not committed to Okinawa.

US MARINE CORPS

The Marine Corps' contribution to Tenth Army was **III Amphibious Corps**. IIIAC, so designated as it had previously served as the Third Fleet's landing force, had originated as I Marine Amphibious Corps (IMAC) on 1 October 1942 at San Diego, California. It initially served as an operational headquarters for most Marine forces in the South Pacific to control Marine operations on Guadalcanal, Russell Islands, New Georgia, and Bougainville into 1944. Besides Marine units, it had operational control of US Army and New Zealand units. On 15 April 1944, IMAC's support units were transferred to the new VAC Marine Administrative Command and IMAC's tactical elements were redesignated IIIAC on Guadalcanal. It was given the mission of seizing Guam in July followed by the Peleliu operation in September. IIIAC returned to Guadalcanal to prepare for the Okinawa Gunto assault under Major-General Roy S. Geiger.

III Amphibious Corps Artillery, under Brigadier-General David R. Nimmer, consisted of two three-battalion provisional groups to support the Corps' two divisions. Other IIIAC units included a provisional AAA group with four battalions, an engineer group with a four-battalion naval construction regiment and one Army and one Marine engineer battalion, and a service group built around the 7th Field Depot. The Corps' non-divisional troops totaled over 12,000.

Only two Marine divisions were to fight on Okinawa, although a third was to play an important role. Unlike Army divisions, the Marine divisions deployed with 100 per cent infantry strength plus 2,500 replacements (initially used as a shore party). The Marine Corps' efficient Replacement and Training Command was responsible for this. The Marine Corps, with only six divisions, was able to funnel replacements to IIIAC's divisions while they recovered from their last operation and prepared for the next. Their replacements had already been absorbed before the other three divisions were committed to Iwo Jima under VAC. Now those divisions were being rebuilt for the invasion of Japan. Each assault division was reinforced with a naval construction[13], an armored amphibian tractor, and two amphibian tractor battalions, plus numerous smaller Marine and Army support units.

The **1st Marine Division**, the "Old Breed," was formed from the 1st Marine Brigade at Guantánamo Bay, Cuba, on 1 February 1941 (the 1st

F4U Corsair fighters of four Marine Aircraft Group 31 (MAG-31) fighting squadrons were operating from Yontan Airfield after 7 April, providing close air support and combat air patrols. This was the first air unit to arrive on the island. Conditions were crude, requiring the fighters' 234-gal. (1,064-litre) fuel tanks be filled from 5-gal. (23-litres) cans. (US Army)

Brigade was organized in 1935). It was the first US division committed to combat when it landed on Guadalcanal in August 1942. It fought on New Britain from December 1943 and into 1944, and then assaulted Peleliu in August. There it experienced the first Japanese cave defenses, making it the division best prepared for Okinawa. It staged on Pavuvu for the Okinawa assault under Major-General Pedro A. del Valle with over 26,000 troops.

The **6th Marine Division** was the newest in the Corps, but seven of its nine infantry battalions were combat experienced. The 1st Provisional Marine Brigade was formed from separate units on 19 April 1944 on Guadalcanal and fought on Guam in July. The 6th Mar. Div. was activated on 7 September 1944 at Tassafaronga, Guadalcanal using the Brigade as a core with the 4th and 22nd Marines. The 4th Marines, made up of the former raider battalions (Midway, Guadalcanal, Makin, Pavuvu, New Georgia, Bougainville), had secured Emirau and fought on Guam. The 22nd Marines had fought on Eniwetok and Guam and secured islands in the Marshalls. The then separate 1st Battalion, 29th Marines had fought on Saipan and Tinian. These units were joined by the remainder of the 29th Marines, activated in the States. The Division's more than 24,000 troops were commanded by Major-General Lemuel C. Shepherd, Jr.

The **2nd Marine Division** was formed from the 2nd Marine Brigade on 1 February 1941 at San Diego (the 2nd Brigade was formed there in 1936 and later served in China). Most of the division fought on Guadalcanal in 1942–43. Its next fight was the brutal Betio Island assault in Tarawa Atoll in November 1943. It then fought on Saipan and Tinian in the summer of 1944. The 22,000-man division, under Major-General Thomas E. Watson, served as the demonstration force off Okinawa and then as a floating reserve. It soon departed for Saipan to serve as an area reserve. Its 8th Marines Special Landing Force returned to secure offshore islands in June and then came ashore to be attached to the 1st Marine Division for the rest of the campaign.

US TACTICAL ORGANIZATION

On the surface US Army and Marine divisions appear to have been organized similarly, but there were many internal differences in structure, manning, weapons, and equipment. It would be wrong to suggest the structure of either was superior. Both Army and Marine divisions conducted extensive amphibious operations and fought the same enemy on the same terrain, and both demonstrated strengths and weaknesses. Marine divisions may have been designed specifically for amphibious assault, but Army divisions, even though more heavily equipped and lavishly supplied with motor transport, were easily tailored for the mission. In 1945 Army divisions were smaller than Marine divisions; some 14,000 troops as opposed to 19,000 in the Marines, but were more heavily armed in many categories of weapons. The Army reinforced its divisions with support units to 22,000 troops and the Marines up to 26,000 (including attached replacements). Organic and attached units for both services' divisions are listed in the Order of Battle tables (see pages 90–93).

ABOVE **On 9 April F4U Corsairs of Marine Aircraft Group 33 (MAG-33) arrived on Kadena Airfield. These fighters belong to Marine Fighting Squadron 312 (VMF-312), obviously known as the "Checkerboards" because of their checkered black and yellow cowlings and tail fins. A ¼-ton M3 utility truck ("jeep") sits in the foreground. (US Army)**

LEFT **Each Marine division had a detachment of 12 1-ton truck-mounted 4.5-in. rocket launchers organized into two six-truck sections. The crewmen were called "Buck Rogers Men" after a contemporary science fiction hero. Each truck, nicknamed a "Sandy Andy" after a popular toy, mounted three Mk 7 launcher racks with each holding 12 rockets. They could fire 36 high explosive and white phosphorus rockets in four seconds to a range of 1,100 yds (1,006 m). (USMC)**

It should be noted that while both divisions had four howitzer battalions, the Army had three 105-mm and one 155-mm while the Marines had four 105-mm (except 1/11, 1st Mar. Div., which still had 75-mm pack howitzers). Marine divisions had a rocket detachment with 12 truck-mounted 4.5-in. Mk 7 launchers. The Army employed a 4.5-in. rocket battalion. A total of 35 American artillery battalions fought on Okinawa. Army and Marine artillery battalions had three batteries of four howitzers regardless of caliber.

Army and Marine infantry regiments differed greatly, although they used much the same weaponry. Both had three battalions, each with three rifle companies of three rifle platoons of three rifle squads – there the similarity ends. Army regimental strength was 3,068, but those on Okinawa began about 300 men under strength[14]. They were task organized for combat into regimental combat teams (RCT) by attaching engineer combat and medical collecting companies, and special troops detachments. The regimental cannon company had six 105-mm M7 self-propelled howitzers, excellent assault guns to blast caves and pillboxes, and the antitank company had nine 37-mm M3A1 guns. The 860-man infantry battalions had a headquarters company and a heavy weapons company with eight .30cal. M1917A1 water-cooled machine guns and six 81mm M1 mortars. The three 193-man rifle companies had three 39-man rifle platoons with three 12-man squads, each with a Browning automatic rifle (M1918A2 BAR), 11 M1 rifles, and one M7 rifle grenade launcher. The weapons platoon had two .30cal. M1919A4 air-cooled machine guns and three 60mm M2 mortars. Several 2.36in. M9 rocket launchers (bazookas) and M2-2 flamethrowers were available.

Companies were lettered in sequence through the regiment: 1st Bn – A–D, 2nd Bn – E–H, and 3rd Bn – I–M (no J); D, H, and M were heavy weapons. There were also regimental headquarters (with a reconnaissance and intelligence platoon) and service companies. Regimental companies (HQ, Service, Cannon, AT) were unlettered.

While the Army infantry regiment had changed little during the war, the Marine regiment[15] had evolved considerably. The divisions were still ostensibly organized under the May 1944 tables, but the 3,400-man regiments destined for Okinawa were organized under the 1 May 1945 tables, which were implemented earlier in the year. The 996-man infantry battalion no longer had a separate weapons company (they were disbanded and the weapons reassigned to the units that habitually used them). The battalion headquarters company's mortar platoon had four 81-mm mortars. The company also had a 55-man assault platoon with three assault sections (two seven-man squads with a flamethrower, a 2.36-in. bazooka, and demolition men) to support each rifle company. The 242-man rifle company had a 51-man headquarters with a section of three 60-mm mortars while the 46-man machine gun platoon had eight .30cal. air-cooled and six .30cal. water-cooled machine guns. The 45-man rifle platoons had three 13-man squads: squad leader (M1 carbine) and three fire teams each with team leader (M1 rifle, M7 grenade launcher), rifleman (M1 rifle, M7 GL), automatic rifleman (BAR), and assistant automatic rifleman (M1 rifle, M7 GL)[16]. The regimental weapons company had two antitank platoons with four 37-mm guns each and a platoon of four 105-mm M7 self-propelled howitzers. The regimental headquarters and service company included a 43-man scout and sniper platoon.

Marine companies were lettered the same as in Army regiments, but there were no D, H, and M weapons companies (companies were not re-lettered after the reorganization, except in the new 29th Marines where they were lettered in sequence). Marine infantry regiments were task organized into combat teams (CT) by attaching engineer, pioneer (shore party), motor transport, and medical companies, plus smaller service elements.

Army medium tank battalions had 17 M4A3 Shermans (75-mm gun) in each of their three companies and three in the headquarters. Marine tank battalions had 15 M4A2s (1st Battalion) or M4A3s (6th Battalion) in their three companies plus one more in the headquarters. The Army employed the M4A1-equipped 713th Tank Battalion (Armored Flamethrower), the first of its kind; its Company B supported the Marines. Army companies had three five-tank platoons, while the Marines used four three-tank platoons; both companies had two tanks in the headquarters. The seven tank battalions on Okinawa would lose 153 tanks (51 were Marine) to mines, antitank guns, artillery, and suicide squads – in that order.

The six Army and five Marine amphibian tractor battalions had three companies with about 30 LVT(3) or LVT(4) Amtracs each. The three Army amphibian tank, and two Marine armored amphibian tractor battalions each had four companies with 18 LVT(A)(4) 75-mm howitzer-armed amphibian tanks each. These were used as self-propelled artillery once ashore.

To control land-based aircraft supporting the campaign, a joint air command was organized in the form of **Tactical Air Force, Tenth Army** (TG 99.2). TAF was activated on 21 November 1944 at Schofield Barracks, Hawaii. The 2nd Marine Aircraft Wing (2nd MAW) doubled as Headquarters, TAF under Major-General Francis P. Mulcahy, who was relieved due to poor health by Louis E. Woods on 11 June 1945.

Initial close air support (CAS) for troops ashore was provided by Marine and Navy units aboard TF 51 escort carriers, but as airfields were seized and repaired, TAF units staged ashore to assume increasing CAS responsibilities. Besides CAS, TAF was also responsible for photo reconnaissance, resupply drops to front-line troops, and offensive air missions against *Kamikazes* and conventional air raids to protect the fleet and troops ashore. Besides TAF's CAS aircraft, Navy aircraft from TFs 51 and 58 also provided CAS. TAF, along with TF 58, attacked enemy airfields in the northern Ryukyus and Japan to stifle increasing air raids. On 1 July 1945, TAF, Tenth Army was redesignated TAF, Ryukyus. TAF was dissolved on 14 July 1945.

TAF was composed of four Marine aircraft groups with 15 fighting squadrons (three with night fighters), two Marine torpedo-bombing squadrons, plus three US Army Air Force (USAAF) fighter groups with ten fighter squadrons, two heavy (B-24), one medium (B-25), and one light (A-26) bombardment groups to eventually total over 750 aircraft. Marine landing force air support control units accompanied Army and Marine units ashore to direct CAS.

IMPERIAL JAPANESE FORCES

Prior to the neutralization of Truk in early 1944 Okinawa Gunto was lightly defended by the battalion-size *Nakagusuku Wan* Fortress Artillery Unit and a few guard companies. To bolster the island's defenses, the Japanese **32nd Army** was organized on 1 April 1944, one year to the day before the Americans landed. The first combat unit to arrive was the veteran 17,000-man 9th Division[17] from Manchuria in June 1944 while Saipan was under attack. In late June, a mere 600 survivors of the 44th Independent Mixed Brigade (IMB) arrived. US submarines had attacked its convoy sending 5,000 troops to the bottom. The 15th Independent

Mixed Regiment was flown in during July, Japan's first attempt to airlift such a large force, followed by the 24th Division shipped from Manchuria. The 62nd Division arrived in August from China.

The Imperial Japanese Army (IJA) was organized into army groups (named major regional command with two or more area armies), area armies (named or numbered area command with two or more armies and an air army), armies (corps-size with two or more divisions, one or more IMBs, and numerous army support troops; there were no formations designated corps), divisions, and independent mixed brigades (IMB).

The infantry regiment was the main tactical maneuver unit. Support troops for armies and divisions consisted of numerous independent battalions, units, and companies. The nondescript term "unit" is frequently encountered. A unit could range in size from a small platoon to a battalion or larger size support unit. The internal structure of infantry and artillery regiments was not unlike US practices with three battalions. However, certain combat and support "regiments" (tank, reconnaissance, engineer, transport) were battalion-size consisting of three to five companies with no battalion structure. Companies and batteries were numbered in sequence within regiments and independent battalions. Construction and pioneer units were manned mainly by Koreans and to a lesser degree by impressed labor from other occupied areas (Formosa, Okinawa, Manchuria).

IJA infantry divisions (*Shidan*) were found organized into one of two very different structures: the traditional three-infantry regiment "triangular division" and the "brigaded division", which appeared early in the war in an effort to conserve manpower but retain firepower. Supporting units were streamlined and the infantry were concentrated into two brigades. Both types of division relied largely on army-level units for service support.

The **62nd Division**, under the command of Lieutenant-General Takeo Fujioka, was activated in June 1943 in Shansi Province, China

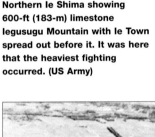

Northern Ie Shima showing 600-ft (183-m) limestone Iegusugu Mountain with Ie Town spread out before it. It was here that the heaviest fighting occurred. (US Army)

from the 4th and 6th IMBs, themselves formed in 1938. Both brigades and the Division had fought in China. The 62nd was a "brigaded division" comprising the 63rd and 64th Infantry Brigades. Both arrived with four 1,080-man independent infantry battalions (IIB), each with a machine gun company, an infantry gun company, and five rifle companies. In January both brigades received an additional 683-man IIB, but with only a machine gun company and three rifle companies and a platoon-size gun unit. Roughly 300-man engineer, signal, and transport units completed the 62nd Division along with a field hospital. It had no organic artillery.

With the withdrawal of the 9th Division in December, the strongest formation on Okinawa was the **24th Division** under Lieutenant-General Tatsumi Amamiya. Raised in Manchuria in December 1939, it had seen no combat, but was well trained. It was a "triangular division" with the roughly 2,800-man 22nd, 32nd, and 89th infantry regiments. Each had three battalions and a regimental gun company. The battalions had one machine gun, antitank, and infantry gun company each (the 3rd Battalions had an 81-mm mortar platoon in lieu of the gun company), and three rifle companies. The 42nd Artillery Regiment had three battalions, the 1st and 2nd with one 75-mm gun and two 100-mm howitzer batteries. The 3rd Battalion had three 150-mm howitzer batteries (Japanese batteries had four pieces). The 24th Reconnaissance Regiment had a machine gun and two rifle companies, 24th Engineer Regiment had three companies and the 24th Transport Regiment had five (three motor and two horse). There were also 200–300-man signal, water supply, and medical units.

The battered **44th Independent Mixed Brigade** had to be completely rebuilt on Okinawa and Kyushu, but it never achieved full strength and some elements were detached to Okinawa's north end. Under the command of Major-General Suzuki Shigeki, it had been organized on Kyushu for service on Okinawa. Its regimental-sized 2nd Infantry Unit was rebuilt, unlike the 1st, which was replaced by the 15th Independent Mixed Regiment (IMR). Both the 2nd Unit and 15th IMR were organized the same, with three battalions and regimental gun and antitank companies. The 700-man battalions had one machine-gun company and three rifle companies and a gun unit. Brigade units included a two-battery 75-mm howitzer unit, signal unit, and an engineer company. Most of the 2nd Unit – 1st and 2nd Battalions, gun and antitank companies – was detached to form the "*Udo* Force" (also known as "*Kunigami* Detachment") for service in the north.

While infantry regiments and battalions were of varied organization and strength, there were similarities. Regimental gun companies usually had four 75-mm Model 41 infantry guns and regimental and battalion antitank companies had 4–6 x 37-mm Model 94 "antitank" guns (actually rapid-fire infantry support guns). Battalion machine gun companies had eight or 12 x 7.7-mm Model 92 tripod-mounted heavy machine guns. Battalion gun companies had four 70-mm Model 92 infantry guns (sometimes substituted by 81-mm Model 97 mortars) while "gun units" had only two. Rifle companies varied widely; at full-strength they usually had three rifle platoons with three 13–15-man light machine sections (actually rifle squads with a Model 11, 96, or 99 bipod-mounted machine gun and one or two 50-mm Model 89 grenade dischargers – "knee mortars") and a 13–15-man grenade discharger section with three more "knee mortars" and more riflemen. Larger battalions' rifle companies often had a weapons' platoon with two heavy machine guns and two 20-mm Model 97 antitank rifles.

Non-divisional artillery units were under the **5th Artillery Group** to include Imperial Japanese Navy (IJN) coast defense gun companies. Major-General Kosuke Wada controlled the equivalent of nine IJA artillery battalions with 36 x 150-mm howitzers, 8 x 150-mm guns, 8 x 240-mm howitzers, 24 x 320-mm spigot mortars, and 96 x 81-mm mortars. Additionally, the artillery units of the 24th Division and 44th IMB were attached to the Group. The **21st Antiaircraft Artillery Group** fielded four AAA battalions with 72 x 75-mm AA guns and three machine cannon battalions with 54 x 20-mm cannons total. The two shipping engineer regiments of the **11th Shipping Group** operated IJA landing craft and later served as an ill-fated seaborne raiding force. The battalion-size **27th Tank Regiment** contained the 32nd Army's armor in the form of 13 Model 95 (1935) *Ha-Go* 37-mm light tanks and 14 Model 97 (1937) *Chi-Ha* 57-mm medium tanks plus a rifle company. There were also three independent antitank battalions with 18 excellent 47-mm Model 1 guns each and four independent [heavy] machine gun battalions.

Significant service, support, engineer, and signal units were under the control of either the 32nd Army or the 49th Line of Communications Sector. Airfield and aircraft service units were subordinate to the 19th Air Sector Command.

In June 1944, the IGHQ authorized the establishment of a Labor Unit (*Boeitai*) in the 20–50 age group. About 16,600 Okinawans augmented regular units (100 per battalion); others formed the "Blood and Iron for the Emperor" Duty Unit (*Tekketsu Kinnotai*) and special guard engineer units, while most simply reinforced the labor troops and were unarmed. Up to 39,000 *Boeitai* were conscripted. There were other organizations such as the Civil Defense Unit (*Keibotai*), organized in each town in February 1945 to fight air raid fires and maintain order, and the Home Defense Unit (*Keibitai*), raised in October 1944 with lightly armed 65-man self-defense platoons. A further manpower pool was tapped on 1 January 1945 when 32nd Army directed that all fit male islanders between the ages of 17 and 45 could be mobilized to augment the *Boeitai* laborers. This included thousands more on other Nansei

Shoto islands. Unknown thousands were conscripted[18]. Okinawans had no warrior tradition and they frustrated the Japanese with their indifference to military service. Some 600 middle school girls were trained as nurses.

IJA troops numbered 67,000. About 5,000 were Okinawan conscripts assigned to regular Japanese units. Over 12,000 Korean laborers and comfort women were present.

About 29,000 32nd Army troops belonged to labor, service, and specialized support units. In March, 18,500 service troops were reorganized into ad hoc "specially established" rifle units. These units' strength are not included in the listed strength of the divisions and 44th IMB to which they were attached. The 11th Shipping Group formed the 1st Specially Established Brigade with the 2nd–4th Specially Established Regiments and attached to the 24th Division. Ground service units of the 49th Line of Communications Sector were organized into the 2nd Specially Established Brigade with the 5th and 6th Specially Established Regiments and attached to the 62nd Division. The 6th was reattached to the 44th IMB in late May. The 1st Especially Established Regiment was raised by the 19th Air Sector Command and also attached to the 62nd to defend Yontan and Kadena Airfields. The 1st–3rd and 26th Independent battalions were formed from like-numbered IJA sea raiding base battalions in February. They were attached to the 24th and 62nd Divisions, and 44th IMB. A final ad hoc unit was the 50th Specially Established Battalion on Ie Shima. These units were armed only with rifles, hand grenades, and a few "knee mortars" and light machine guns. They were employed to screen flanks, man secondary lines, and eventually were fed into regular units as replacements. The Japanese often astounded the American command by their ability to reconstitute battered units from survivors and ad hoc replacements to include the use of captured weapons.

Some 3,825 **Imperial Japanese Navy** personnel and over 6,000 civilian combatant employees were assigned to the Okinawa Naval Base Force's 15 coast defense companies (120-mm and 140-mm guns), four antiaircraft company groups (20 x 120-mm, 77 x 25-mm, 60 x 13.2-mm AA); Oroku Detachment, 951st Air Group, Nansei Shoto Air Group; 226th and 3210th Construction Units, a mortar battery (18 x 81-mm), and naval base service personnel. Other units included the 27th Torpedo Boat, 33rd Midget Submarine, and 37th Torpedo Maintenance Units. The Base Force was formed in April 1944 and was under the command of Rear-Admiral Teiso Nippa. It defended the Oroku Peninsula and was headquartered at Tomigusuki south of Naha. Most IJN air group, construction, and service personnel, who included Okinawan conscripts and Korean laborers, were reorganized into several small untrained "naval attack force" rifle battalions. Additionally, some 1,100 *Boeitai* were assigned to the IJN.

---

13 Naval construction battalions were commonly known as "Seabees" due to their "CB" initials.
14 The subordinate unit strengths given are the authorized full strength.
15 Marine regiments did not bear functional designations, but were referred to simply as, for example, 4th Marines. Thus on Okinawa the 1st, 4th, 5th, 7th, 8th, 22nd, and 29th Marines were infantry and the 10th, 11th, and 15th Marines were artillery.
16 The fire team concept evolved from the Banana Wars in the 1920s and 1930s. The team was built around an automatic weapon and proved very successful.
17 The 9th Division was organized in 1895 and fought in the 1904–05 Russo-Japanese War and in China from 1937 to 1939. It consisted of the 7th, 19th, and 35th Infantry and 9th Mountain Artillery Regiments.
18 It is unclear what the organization and relationship of these units was. Most post-war writers refer to them collectively only as the *Boeitai*.

INITIAL OPERATIONS

PRELIMINARY STRIKES

The war first reached Okinawa Gunto on 29 September 1944 when B-29s bombed the airfields. This raid's main purpose was to photograph as much of Okinawa and its outlying islands as possible. The first raid by carrier aircraft followed on 10 October, an operation intended to neutralize the air threat to the approaching Leyte invasion force. The Japanese referred to this action as the Air Battle of Formosa. The Japanese lost 500 aircraft and 36 ships in three days. Okinawa was granted a respite until the new year brought a massive carrier raid on 3 January. The Fast Carrier Force (TF 38) returned on 10 January for an even more punishing raid. The January operations were in conjunction with raids on Formosa and the China coast. The Fast Carrier Force (now designated TF 58) struck targets in the Tokyo area through late February. While retiring to Ulithi, TF 58 struck Okinawa on 1 March with an extremely vicious raid.

American submarines and patrol bombers effectively isolated the Ryukyus from Japan and Formosa, sinking scores of cargo ships. Between attacks on Japan, B-29s conducted numerous attacks on Okinawa. By the end of March there were almost no operational Japanese aircraft in the Ryukyus. Naha City and its port were completely destroyed as was Shuri and its ancient treasures. Between 18 and 31 March, TF 58 conducted further strikes on Kyushu airfields and

Looking south from Hill 178 in the 7th Inf. Div. zone near Okinawa's east coast. It was from the far ridge that the Japanese 89th Infantry, 24th Division had launched its futile 4 May counteroffensive. The 7th Inf. Div. soon seized the ridgeline as it fought through the Shuri outer defenses. (US Army)

Marines in a water-filled 60-mm M2 mortar pit, 5 May. Its leather combination M4 muzzle cap and carrying sling are in place to keep rain out of the barrel. Adjacent to the pit a poncho has been staked out to provide some degree of shelter from the heavy rains. The gunner to the left carries a Mk 2 "K-Bar" fighting and utility knife. The term "K-Bar" is the firm's name and was derived from the endorsement of a satisfied pre-war customer who stated he had "killed a bar" (bear) with one of their knives, with the result that the company adopted the new name. (USMC)

An Army rifle squad checks out a tomb strongpoint it has just destroyed with large satchel charges, 7 May. The force of the explosion shattered the entrance and blew the defenders through the opening. (US Army)

Japanese warships in preparation for *Iceberg*. The Japanese counter-attacked the carriers, almost sinking the USS *Franklin* (CV-13), but failed to inflict serious damage on the task force. On 24 March, the force sank an entire eight-ship convoy northwest of Okinawa. On the same date, five 16-in. gun battleships and 11 destroyers shelled targets on Okinawa. Between 26 and 31 March, the British Carrier Force struck Sakishima Gunto to the southwest of Okinawa neutralizing its airfields.

The Japanese, expecting a landing on Okinawa or Formosa at any time, alerted its air forces for the *Ten-Go* Operation on 25 March. On 27 and 31 March, massive B-29 strikes on the Kyushu airfields effectively shut them down. The Japanese managed to launch only 50 two-aircraft attacks prior to L-Day damaging eight US ships. *Ten-Go* was not able to launch until 6 April, five days after the main landing.

Task Force 52's Mine Flotilla (TG 52.2) began sweeping the approaches to Okinawa on 22 March with 122 mine and patrol craft. By L-Day, 3,000 square miles of ocean were swept, resulting in the discovery of six minefields and the destruction of another 257 mines.

On 25 March, the Gunfire and Covering Force moved in with three 16-in., five 14-in., and one 12-in. gun battleships; seven 8-in. and three 6-in. gun cruisers, 32 destroyers and escorts, and 177 gunboats. Some 37,000 rounds of 5-in. and larger, 33,000 4.5-in. rockets, and 22,500 4.2-in. mortar rounds were fired in the seven days before L-Day. The Carrier Force delivered 3,100 strike sorties. They had little effect, although the few remaining Japanese aircraft on the island were destroyed. The Japanese had pulled back from the beaches to their underground shelters and refused to respond to attacks.

In the meantime, elements of the amphibious forces departed Leyte and Ulithi. They encountered rough weather en route with many groups barely making their target date.

INITIAL LANDINGS

Kerama Retto is a group of eight rugged islands (plus smaller islets) 15 miles (24 km) west of Okinawa. Unsuited for airfields, they were an ideal anchorage capable of accommodating over 70 large ships. The Keramas would become the fleet's refueling, rearming, and repair base. The proposal for its early capture was initially resisted because of the fear of air attack. The need for such a base was realized during the Iwo Jima assault. The Western Island Attack Group, 77th Inf. Div. embarked, swept through the Keramas from the west on 26 March (L-6). Five of the

Troops of the 305th Infantry, 77th Inf. Div. fire on attacking Japanese with M1 rifles during the approach to the Shuri Line, 11 May. Note that the two soldiers to the right carry .45cal. M1919A1 pistols, indicating they may be members of a weapons crew. Note the helmet marking in the shape of the division's patch on the man to the left. (US Army)

Division's infantry battalions (1/305, 3/305, 1/306, 2/306, 2/307) and two artillery battalions (304, 305 FA) secured the islands with little resistance by 29 May. Only four of the islands were defended by 975 IJN troops. Japanese losses were 530 dead and 121 prisoners. Some 1,200 civilians were interned, after almost 150 had committed suicide. Over 350 suicide boats were captured. American losses were 31 dead and 81 wounded. About 300 IJN troops remained unmolested on Tokashiki under a gentlemen's agreement until they surrendered after V-J Day. The 77th Inf. Div. re-embarked on 30 March leaving 2/305 behind for security. It was relieved by a provisional infantry battalion formed from the 870th Antiaircraft Artillery Battalion on 23 May. The floating fleet base and a seaplane base were in operation before the islands were fully secured. On 31 March, PB4Y Catalinas of Fleet Air Wing 1, operating from seaplane tenders, began anti-shipping patrols over the East China Sea, local anti-submarine patrols, and air-sea rescue support for carrier operations.

Keise Shima (actually four sand islets), 11 miles (18 km) southwest of the Hagushi Beaches, was secured unopposed by 2/306 Infantry early on 31 March. Marine scouts had previously confirmed the islets were unoccupied. The 420th Field Artillery Group came ashore with the 531st and 532nd FA Battalions to support the main landing and cover southern Okinawa with their 155-mm guns. The Japanese made several unsuccessful attempts to destroy the guns.

Underwater demolition teams (UDT) reconnoitered the Hagushi Beaches on 29 March. Spotter aircraft over Okinawa reported no human beings were visible. The entire island appeared deserted. At 1000hrs, 30 March, frogmen of UDTs 4, 7, 11, 16, 17, and 21 swam in to demolish anti-boat obstacles. The water temperature was a debilitating 70°F (21°C).

The amphibious force assembled just west of Okinawa. The Carrier Force took up station some 50 miles (80 km) to the east. On 31 March, the Demonstration Group, 2nd Mar. Div. embarked, arriving off the southeast Minatogawa Beaches, which the Japanese considered the most likely site for the main landing. This deception was reinforced by UDT scouts and minesweepers operating offshore since 29 March.

MAIN LANDING

Easter Sunday and April Fool's Day, 1 April 1945 – L-Day. Sunrise 0621hrs, temperature 74°F (23.3°C), 5–7 miles (8–11 km) visibility with smoke and haze, moderate east–northeast winds, sea conditions – light swell, no surf on the Hagushi Beaches, high tide (5 ft 11 in./1.79 km) at 0900hrs.

Over 1,300 TF 51, 52, 53, 54, and 55 ships were assembled off Okinawa. Transports and LSTs dropped anchor 3–7 miles (4.8–11 km) – offshore. Admiral Kelly Turner gave the order, "Land the landing force" at 0406hrs. Troops began to load their amphibian tractors and landing craft to launch at 0630hrs and circle awaiting the final signal.

At 0530hrs the pre-landing barrage smothered a zone 1,000 yds (914 m) inland with some 25 rounds per 100 sq yds (84 sq m). As the sun rose behind the hilly island, seasick soldiers and marines saw smoke-shrouded Okinawa Shima for the first time. At 0800hrs, dozens of

THE LANDING BEACHES, 1 APRIL 1945

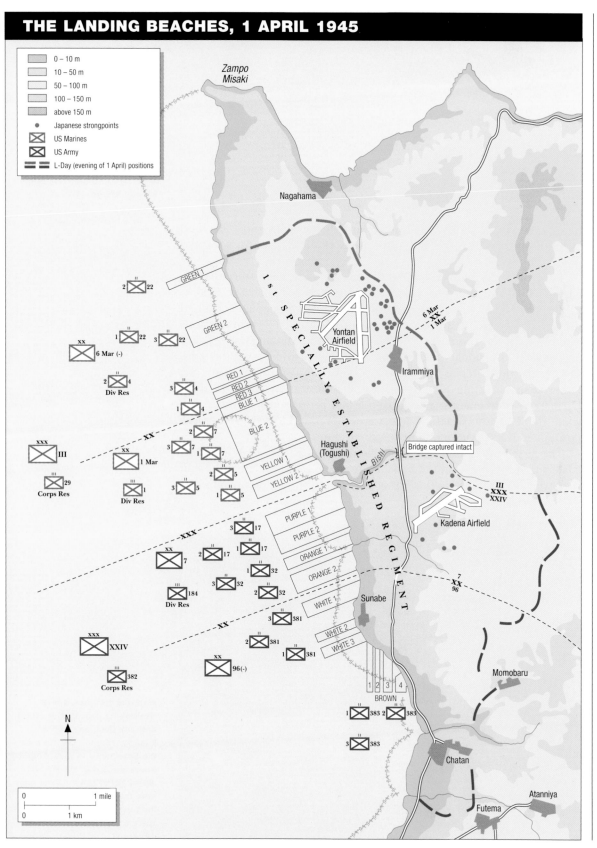

Legend:
- 0 – 10 m
- 10 – 50 m
- 50 – 100 m
- 100 – 150 m
- above 150 m
- Japanese strongpoints
- US Marines
- US Army
- L-Day (evening of 1 April) positions

Zampo Misaki

Nagahama

GREEN 1

2 | 22

1 | 22   3 | 22   GREEN 2

XX
6 Mar (-)

2 | 4
Div Res   3 | 4   RED 1
RED 2
RED 3
1 | 4   BLUE 1

XXX
III   2 | 7   BLUE 2

XX
1 Mar   3 | 7   1 | 7

III 29
Corps Res   III 1
Div Res   3 | 5   2 | 5   YELLOW 1
YELLOW 2
1 | 5

1st SPECIALLY ESTABLISHED REGIMENT

Yontan Airfield

Irammiya

Bishi

Hagushi (Togushi)   Bridge captured intact

6 Mar
XX
1 Mar

III
XXX
XXIV

Kadena Airfield

PURPLE 1
3 | 17   PURPLE 2
XX
7   2 | 17   1 | 17   ORANGE 1
1 | 32   ORANGE 2
III 184
Div Res   3 | 32   2 | 32

XXX
3 | 381   WHITE 1   Sunabe

XXX
XXIV   2 | 381   1 | 381   WHITE 2
WHITE 3

III 382
Corps Res   XX
96(-)

7
XX
96

Momobaru

1 | 2 | 3 | 4
BROWN

1 | 383   2 | 383

3 | 383

Chatan

N

Futema   Atanniya

0 ——— 1 mile
0 ——— 1 km

A Marine F4U Corsair fighter unleashes a full load of eight 5-in. high-velocity aircraft rockets (HVAR) at a ground target. These were effective for battering an area to suppress artillery and troop movement, but were too inaccurate for point targets such as bunkers and caves. The rockets were nicknamed the "Holy Moses" after the general reaction of observers to the effects of their impact. (US Army)

LCI(G) gunboats cruised on line toward the beaches with 3-in. and 40-mm guns blazing. At 0815hrs hundreds of circling Amtracs formed into assault waves.

Control craft pennants came down five minutes later and an eight-mile line of churning Amtracs began their 4,000-yard (3,658-m) run to the beaches. Two groups of 64 carrier planes strafed and bombed the beaches as naval gunfire shifted inland. As four American divisions ran in toward the shore, the 2nd Mar. Div. at the Minatogawa Beaches executed its diversionary feint. Ironically, the first troop casualties were suffered by this force as *Kamikazes* crashed into a transport and LST. Other than attracting air attacks, the demonstration failed to draw Japanese reinforcements. The Japanese had no reason to send troops from the Hagushi Beaches; few were there and other units were positioned exactly where Ushijima wanted them.

The first wave soon passed the battleship USS *Tennessee* (BB-43), 2,000 yds (1,829-m) from the beaches, its 14-in. guns leveled and firing shattering broadsides into the sea walls. Most assault regimental landing

A 76-mm gun-armed M18 "Hellcat" tank destroyer of the Antitank Company, 306th Infantry, 77th Inf. Div. fires on the Shuri Line, 11 May. Atop the turret are .50cal. HB-M2 and .30cal. M1919A4 machine guns. Note the crew's haversacks in the turret bustle rack and the spare treads on the turret rear. (US Army)

A .30cal. M1917A1 water-cooled heavy machine gun provides covering fire for advancing marines on 11 May. This weapon could maintain accurate long-range supporting fire for prolonged periods. The ground is littered with discarded ammunition boxes, damaged weapons, and discarded equipment. (USMC)

teams, two battalions abreast, consisted of eight waves: 1st – 28 LVT(A)(4) amtanks firing 75-mm howitzers to "shoot ashore" the following waves; 2nd – 16 LVT(4) Amtracs with assault troops; 3rd through 6th – 12 LVT(4)s each with more assault troops and crew-served weapons; 7th – varied numbers of LSMs or LCMs with flotation device-equipped Sherman tanks; and 8th – LVT(4)s with support troops.

The LCI(G) gunboats halted outside the reef and the assault waves passed landing at 0830hrs – H-Hour. Only sporadic Japanese mortar and artillery fire fell. The sea walls were breached by naval gunfire at numerous points. Resistance ashore was virtually nil as the untrained 3,473 airfield service troops of the 1st Specially Established Regiment dissolved. Only half of the unit was armed and there were virtually no heavy weapons. Okinawa was not the feared repeat of Peleliu and Iwo Jima with troops slaughtered on the beaches. In the first hour 50,000 troops landed. Blasted suicide boats and small craft were found choking the Bishi Gawa separating IIIAC and XXIV Corps zones. As soldiers and marines pressed inland the Amtracs swarmed back to pick up reserve battalions. These were followed by LCVPs with regimental support troops and supplies. Larger landing craft and ships began delivering divisional artillery and support troops at 1400hrs. The receding tide exposed the reef and the unloading of heavy equipment slowed. Late morning found the 4th Marines on the edge of Yontan Airfield and the 17th Infantry at Kadena. The two airfields were not expected to be captured until L+3.

By nightfall a 15,000-yd (13,716-m) beachhead, 5,000 yds (4,572 m) deep in places, was firmly established and another 10,000 troops had landed. The units were deployed, left to right, 6th Mar. Div, 1st Mar. Div, 7th Inf. Div, and 96th Inf. Div. A 600-yd (549-m) gap existed between IIIAC and XXIV Corps, but this was closed the next day. The four assault divisions reported only 28 dead, 27 missing, and 104 wounded this first day on Okinawa Shima.

While ineffective in Europe, the little 37-mm M3A1 antitank gun still had value in the Pacific Theater. Its compact size and comparatively light weight allowed it to be manhandled into position over rough ground to engage pillboxes and caves with armor-piercing, high explosive, and canister rounds. The latter was useful for countering infantry attacks and stripping camouflaging foliage from enemy positions. It remained effective against Japanese tanks as well. Note that this crew has attached a scalloped section of sheet metal to the shield to distort its distinctive straight upper edge. (USMC)

SPLITTING THE ISLAND

On the morning of L+1 the 2nd Mar. Div. conducted another demonstration off the southeast beaches to no avail, other than allowing Ushijima to claim he had forced their withdrawal. The two airfields were securely in American hands as were the surrounding hills. The defenders failed to place demolitions on the airfields, and by the afternoon of L+1 Kadena was usable for emergency landings. Yontan was usable on L+2. The main bridge over the Bishi Gawa was captured intact and the defenders had destroyed few bridges over smaller streams. The question in every one's mind was, "Where is the enemy?"

The weather remained favorable for the next two days and the Americans continued their rapid advance. The 6th Mar. Div. moved north and by 4 April had secured the narrow Ishikawa Isthmus. The 1st Mar. and 7th Inf. Divisions reached the east coast on the afternoon of the 3rd and the Marines secured the Katchin Peninsula on the 5th. The 96th Inf. Div. wheeled to its right and began moving south as did elements of the 7th on the east coast. By L+3 they were established on a line across the Chatan Isthmus facing south. All units were in positions they had expected to reach after two weeks of hard fighting.

The supply build-up continued and more support units landed. Empty transports departed and each night the fleet dispersed, but some fell victim to increasing air attacks. Hundreds of civilians were rounded up and interrogated. Military government units took over responsibility for their care. The information gleaned was sketchy and conflicting, but a picture emerged of a general Japanese withdrawal to the south prior to L-Day.

The weather turned for the worse on 4 April. The sea conditions were such that unloading was sometimes suspended. Rain turned roads into quagmires. Entire new roads were built between rain periods and the weak native bridges were replaced by steel Bailey bridges. The west coast highway was redesignated "US 1." Marine fighting squadrons arrived at Yontan on 7 April and at Kadena two days later to provide close air support (CAS).

To fully protect Tenth Army's eastern flank, the Eastern Islands lying northeast of the Katchin Peninsula in the Chimu Wan had to be secured. This was accomplished from 6–11 April by 3/105 of the 27th Inf. Div. supported by Fleet Marine Force Pacific (FMFPac) Amphibious Recon Battalion, UDT 7, and Army amtrac units; the remainder of the 105th Infantry served as the floating reserve aboard Eastern Islands Attack and Fire Support Group (TG 51.19). Most of the islands were unoccupied, except for Tsugen Shima, which was defended by Japanese 1st Battery, 7th Heavy Artillery Regiment. The battery lost 243 men and no prisoners were taken, but 30 escaped. US losses were 14 dead.

The American command could only guess at Japanese intentions. Air reconnaissance revealed nothing in the south (the Japanese remained underground). Some thought the enemy may have evacuated to other

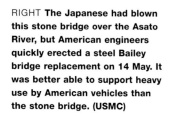

RIGHT **The Japanese had blown this stone bridge over the Asato River, but American engineers quickly erected a steel Bailey bridge replacement on 14 May. It was better able to support heavy use by American vehicles than the stone bridge. (USMC)**

BELOW **A platoon of Marine 75-mm howitzer-armed landing vehicles, tracked (armored) Mk 4 (LVT[A]4) provide fire support. After landing armored amphibian tractor battalions were often attached to divisional artillery regiments to augment their indirect fire. Thought of as tanks by some, they were inferior to genuine tanks due to their high silhouette, thin armor, and poorer cross-country performance. (USMC)**

A rifle platoon of 2nd Battalion, 306th Infantry, 77th Inf. Div. atop the crest of a ridge searches for a sniper firing on them, 14 May. The soldier in the foreground is armed with a .30cal. M1918A2 Browning automatic rifle, around which a rifle squad built its base of fire. Note that many of the troops have dabbed light-colored mud on their dark olive drab helmets for camouflage. (US Army)

islands, or had been drawn to the southeast by the demonstrations, or were waiting to counterattack; that opportunity came and passed. Still, there was little response from the enemy.

The impact of the invasion was initially more devastating in the Home Islands than to Japanese forces on Okinawa. On 3 April, news of the landing was released. This was Emperor Jimmu Day, who 2,500 years earlier, had launched the conquest of Yamato (after which the battleship was named) to "make the universe our home." Premier Kuniaki Koiso claimed the Americans would be driven from Okinawa and Saipan recaptured. He was forced to resign the next day. Admiral (Baron) Kantaro Suzuki was appointed by the Emperor on 7 April to find an honorable way for Japan to end the war.

THE OFFENSIVE CONTINUES

TENTH ARMY ADVANCES

On 4 April General Hodge ordered the 7th and 96th Inf. divisions to attack south. The Japanese plan was to use the 62nd Division to hold the main northern defense line while the 24th Division and 44th IMB were held in reserve to destroy any new American landings on the southern coasts. The 62nd Division and its supporting artillery were in excellent positions on commanding terrain and had clear line of sight right across XXIV Corps' area on the plain below with its sparse vegetation. The artillery could fire on the Hagushi Beaches and Nakagusuku Wan. The 62nd Division's defense was echeloned with its 63rd Brigade dug-in across the island and the 64th defending the west coast on its flank.

Punching through the outposts, the two American divisions cautiously pushed south, meeting strong resistance on Cactus, Kaniku, and Tombstone Ridges[19]. A crag called "the Pinnacle" was captured on 6 April by the 184th Infantry after a tough fight. It was thought to be the point on which Commodore Perry raised the American flag in 1853. The 63rd Brigade put up a stiff enough resistance to halt XXIV Corps elements from 6–8 April. The covering force had held the Americans off for eight days inflicting over 1,500 casualties on the Corps but at a cost of almost 4,500 dead. The outer Shuri defenses were now uncovered and the Corps would continue its advance against even tougher resistance.

The 1,000-yd (914 m) long Kakazu Ridge stretched northwest to southeast on the northeast side of Kakazu Village. The reinforced 63rd

A 105mm M7 self-propelled howitzer is directed forward by marines on 24 May. The M7 proved to be an excellent assault weapon for direct fire against pillboxes and cave positions. Spare track sections are fastened to its sides for additional protection from antitank guns. The man in the foreground carries an SCR-300 "walkie-talkie" radio, the standard company-level radio. (US Army)

The hillsides of southern Okinawa were dotted with tens of thousands of lyre-shaped tombs unique to the Okinawan culture. Generations of ancestors were buried in the limestone and concrete tombs. When a relative died the tomb was opened and the body interned in a front chamber to decompose. The bones were later cleaned and placed in ceramic urns in the tomb's main room. Families would have celebrations within the small wall-enclosed lawn fronting the tomb to honor their ancestors. The Japanese frequently converted the tombs to pillboxes by smashing in the small sealed entrance and emplacing a machine gun. The machine gun was supported by riflemen, and although the position lacked all-round fire, the flanks were protected by fire from other tombs and dug-in covering positions. There was, of course, no escape and they became tombs for Japanese soldiers as well. Thousands were destroyed along with the remains of many generations of ancestors. Many were blasted with artillery and tank fire merely on the suspicion that they might harbor Japanese defenders. The desecration of the tombs was a terrible affront to Okinawans. The reduction of a tomb required special tactics. An entire platoon might be required to reduce a fortified tomb and the adjacent covering positions. Artillery and mortars first saturated the tomb and surrounding area to kill any enemy on the surface and drive those within the defences away from firing positions. Under the cover of direct fire from tanks and self-propelled 105 mm howitzers the infantry would close in on the position's flanks staying out of the field of fire. Machine gun, BAR, rifle, and rifle grenade fire was directed at the firing port to cover bazooka, flamethrower, and demolition teams closing in from the flanks. The American's called this the "blowtorch and corkscrew," the Japanese called it "straddle tactics." (Howard Gerrard)

150

Brigade still manned the entire front. The 383rd Infantry, 96th Inf. Div. attacked the low hill mass on 9 April and was repulsed. After repeated attacks it was not until 12 April that the ridge was taken. The Japanese 63rd Brigade lost 5,750 men, the US 96th Division lost 451. During the Kakazu battles the 7th Inf. Div. to the east had made slow progress in rugged terrain against stiff resistance. The 7th Division's sector was only one-third of XXIV Corps' front, but the terrain forced narrow frontages and the almost nonexistent road system severely hampered logistics.

The 2nd Mar. Div, the Tenth Army Floating Reserve, departed for Saipan on 11 April. It was scheduled to land on Kikai, off Amami O Shima, northeast of Okinawa in July, but this landing never took place.

Chafing at their defensive strategy, the more aggressive Japanese officers clamored for a counterattack. Colonel Yahara held them at bay reasoning that even if a counterattack was successful, the troops would be exposed to massive American firepower on the plains. General Ushijima gave in when the Americans became stalled in the outer Shuri defenses. With difficulty the Japanese 22nd Infantry, 24th Division was moved north from the Oroku Peninsula to attack through the 63rd Brigade's line near the east coast. Elements of the 63rd Brigade would attack in the west along with the 272nd Independent Infantry Battalion (IIB), the 62nd Division reserve moved from Shuri.

The counterattack was launched at 1900hrs, 12 April with a 30-minute barrage to cover the infiltration. The attack was far too weak and uncoordinated as many commanders, realizing its folly, held back their troops. The 22nd Infantry, unfamiliar with the rugged terrain in front of the US 7th Inf. Div, foundered. The US 96th Inf. Div. faced a well-organized and sustained attack. The Japanese 272nd IIB's attack was well conducted and gave the US 381st Infantry a difficult night on Kakazu Ridge. The battle lasted into the night of 13/14 April. By dawn on the 14th it was all over. It delayed the American push a couple of days, but the Japanese lost hundreds of men and the Americans less than 100. The Americans continued to inch south and then prepared to assault the main Shuri defenses on even more rugged terrain. On 13 April President Franklin D. Roosevelt passed away, stunning most US personnel.

THE PUSH NORTH

While XXIV Corps fought slowly toward Shuri, IIIAC was engaged in a different kind of war. The 1st Mar. Div. defended Yontan Airfield, the landing beaches, and secured the zone behind XXIV Corps across the island. The 6th Mar. Div. had secured the Ishikawa Isthmus with the 22nd Marines to the north where the isthmus began to widen. On the morning of 6 April the 29th Marines launched a tank-supported push up the west coast while the 4th Marines moved up the east. Roads in the north were very limited and the terrain rugged with dense vegetation. Fire support was provided by the 2nd Field Artillery Group and 1st Armored Amphibian Tractor Battalion.

The Japanese had blown bridges and laid mines, but resistance was very light. Finally, on 8 April, after combing the hills, it was determined the enemy had concentrated on the Motobu Peninsula on the island's upper west coast. The 29th Marines now moved across the base of the

An 81-mm M1 mortar crew of 3rd Battalion, 22nd Marines, 6th Mar. Div. provides fire support. They are firing heavy high explosive rounds. These had a shorter range than the light HE, but their effect was equivalent to that of a 105-mm howitzer. (USMC)

An Army tank company prepares to advance from behind a ridge line. These M4A3 Shermans have had their large white stars painted over in black to prevent them from being used as aim points for antitank guns. The Japanese 47-mm Model 1 (1941) antitank gun, while of moderate performance when compared to similar contemporary weapons, was effective against Shermans. (US Army)

peninsula and westward. The 4th and 22nd Marines patrolled north and protected the 29th Marines' rear. Contacts increased over the next few days, but no decisive engagements were fought. Enemy resistance, exacerbated by worsening terrain, increased as the Marines moved west.

The enemy was positioned in a 6 x 8-mile (9.6 x 13-km) redoubt around the 1,200-ft (366-m) high Yae Take (Mount). The broken ground precluded the use of armor and was ideal for the defenders, the heavily armed 1,500-man "Udo Force" detached from the 44th IMB. Initial skirmishing and maneuvering lasted for days, but on 14 April the attack was begun in earnest by the 29th and 4th Marines. Numerous hills and ridges had to be taken during the approach to Yae Take. The 17th saw the final assault on the Take, but it was not cleared until the next day. Some 700 Japanese dead were counted; although enough managed to escape to conduct a lengthy guerrilla war in the wild north.

The guerrilla war was fought in countless small skirmishes, hit-and-run attacks, and sniping. To make matters worse, due to an effective propaganda effort many Okinawan irregulars fought with the Japanese and committed sabotage. Okinawan veterans with experience in China trained their fellows as home defense units. The 7th Marines, securing the Ishikawa Isthmus, was drawn into the guerrilla war as Japanese troops attempted to evade to the south.

On 4 May, the understrength 27th Inf. Div. relieved the 6th Mar. Div. in the north. The 6th had lost 236 dead and 1,601 wounded. Subordinate to the Island Command, the 27th Inf. Div. swept north fighting a ten-day battle on the 1,000-ft (305-m) Onna Take in late May and early June. On 4 August, the north was finally declared secure, although small pockets remained. Over 1,000 Japanese had been killed and some 500 prisoners taken.

IE SHIMA LANDINGS

Ie Shima (infrequently called Ie Jima) was codenamed *Indispensable*. It lies 3½ miles (5.6 km) off the west end of the Motobu Peninsula and 20 miles (32 km) north of the Hagushi Beaches. It is located at 26°43' N 127°47' E. The oval-shaped island is 5½ miles (9 km) long from east to west and 2¾ miles (4–5 km) wide. The north and northwest coasts are faced with cliffs up to 100 ft (30 m) high pockmarked with hundreds of caves. The south coast is lined with beaches which range in width from 9–35 yds (8–32 m) and are broken into sections of between 125 and 900 yds (114–823 m) long separated by low cliffs and outcroppings. The ground slopes gently inland from the beaches. The southwest coast and parts of the south are backed by bluffs. The entire island is surrounded by a coral reef several hundred yards wide, but it was not a major obstacle. Inland the ground rises to a level plateau averaging 165 ft (50.3 m) above sea level. Most of the island was served by a

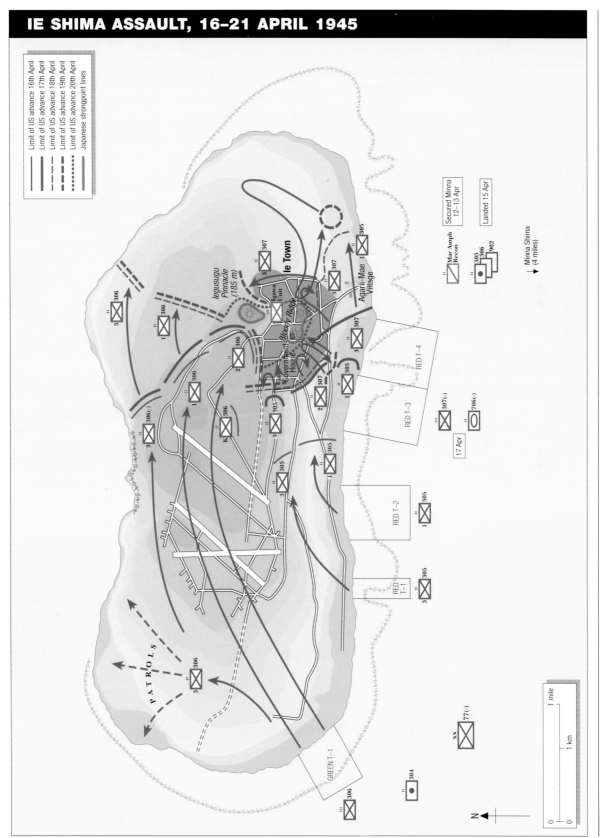

Limit of US advance 16th April
Limit of US advance 17th April
Limit of US advance 18th April
Limit of US advance 19th April
Limit of US advance 20th April
Japanese strongpoint lines

Iegusugu
Pinnacle
(185 m)

Ie Town

Igawa
Unit

Bloody Ridge

Government
House

Agarii-Mae
Village

Mar Amph
Recon

Secured Minna
12–13 Apr

Landed 15 Apr

305
306
902

Minna Shima
(4 miles)

RED T-4

RED T-3

307(-)

706(-)

17 Apr

RED T-2

305

RED
T-1

305

PATROLS

306

GREEN T-1

306

304

77(-)

N

1 mile

1 km

0

0

well-developed, but unsurfaced road network. Cultivated vegetable and sugarcane fields covered much of this land interspersed with clear areas of low grasses and clumps of scrub trees. Thrusting abruptly upward from the east portion of the island is Iegusugu Pinnacle. This is a conical limestone peak 600 ft (185 m) high, nicknamed "the Pinnacle" and covered with scrub brush and trees, and honeycombed with caves and ravines reinforced by tunnels and pillboxes. On the Pinnacle's south side is the sprawling Ie Town of stone buildings. On the island's center were three 6,000–7,000 ft (1,820–2,120 m) long airfields in the pattern of an "XI." The island had a population of 8,000, but about 3,000 had

been evacuated to Okinawa. Ie Shima was defended by 3,000 troops of the Igawa Unit, augmented by 1,500 armed civilians including women. Substantial defenses were built around the Pinnacle and within Ie Town.

Minna Shima, an islet four miles (6.4 km) south of Ie, was secured by Fleet Marine Force, Pacific Reconnaissance Battalion troops on 12/13 April and occupied by the three artillery battalions (305, 306, 902 FA) on the 15th. The 77th Inf. Div. was moved from its station 300 miles (483 km) southeast of Okinawa and assaulted Ie Shima on the morning of 16 April (W-Day) with full naval gunfire support as well as artillery firing from Motobu Peninsula. The 306th Infantry landed on Beach "Green T-1" at 0758hrs (S-Hour) on the southwest end while the 305th Infantry (less 2nd Battalion) hit "Red T-1" and "T-2" on the south-central coast. Initially, as on Okinawa, there was virtually no resistance with the airfields soon overrun as the regiments swept east across the island toward the Pinnacle and Ie Town. Resistance increased the next day as the town was approached. The 307th Infantry (less 1st Battalion) was landed on the morning of 17 April with part of the 706th Tank Battalion on "Red T-3". By 18 April the troops had closed in on the north, west, and south sides of the town and Pinnacle amid accusations of taking too long to accomplish the mission. The repeated attacks bogged down against fierce resistance, especially in the town's center around the administrative building, called Government House Hill, and the surrounding high ground known as Bloody Ridge. Most of the town was cleared on 20 April but the Pinnacle was not taken until the next day, and resistance continued on its slopes until 23 April. Ie Shima was declared secure at 1730hrs on 21 April, but mopping-up continued until the 26th. The Japanese lost 4,700, including most of the 1,500 armed civilians, and 409 prisoners were taken. About a third of the civilians remaining on the island died. American losses were 218 dead and missing and 900 wounded. Tragically, the popular war correspondent Ernie Pyle was killed by machine-gun fire on 18 April. On 25–28 April the 77th Inf. Div. was moved to Okinawa and was soon in combat again. The 1/305 Infantry remained on the island mopping-up until relieved by 2/106 Infantry on 6 May. The 2/305 occupied Zamami Shima. The entire civilian population was removed from Ie Shima within two weeks of it being secured to prevent interference with airfield construction. They were returned after the war.

THE ASSAULT ON THE SHURI DEFENSES

On Okinawa Shima XXIV Corps' Army divisions were now facing the Japanese main cross-island defense line – the Shuri defenses – built on a series of steep ridges and escarpments to the north of Shuri. The 7th Inf. Div. was to the east, the 96th in the center, and the 27th to the west. They had not moved since 14 April as preparations for the 19 April assault were undertaken. The entire Japanese front was still defended by the 62nd Division with its 64th Brigade defending the west and center and the 63rd Brigade the east, well dug in on the hills and ridges, mainly the Urasoe-Mura Escarpment in the west and center and the Tanabaru Escarpment in the east. The 44th IMB was to the rear in the Shuri area.

A preliminary attack was launched by the 27th Inf. Div. on the night of 18 April when bridges were secretly built across the Machinato Inlet

OVERLEAF
1400HRS, 19 APRIL 1945, KAKAZU RIDGE
On 19 April the US 193rd Tank Battalion advanced south on Route 5 between Kakazu and Nishibaru Ridges with 30 tanks and 105 mm M7 self-propelled howitzers, supporting an attack by 1/105th Infantry, 27th Infantry Division. It was overwhelmed by the Japanese 272nd Independent Infantry Battalion, supported by elements of the 2nd Mortar and 22nd Independent Antitank Gun Battalions. Heavy Japanese fire separated the infantry from the tanks. Mines, 47 mm Model 1 antitank guns, artillery, and suicide squads destroyed 18 M4A3 Sherman tanks and four attached 713th Tank Battalion M4A1 flame tanks. Suicide squads first blinded tank crews with hand-thrown Model 94 smoke candles, kept them buttoned up with Model 97 grenades and small arms fire, and flung 22 lb satchel charges beneath the tanks. Hand-placed Model 99 magnetic demolition charges were also used – their 1½ pounds of TNT could penetrate a Sherman tank's side and top armor. Some tank crews bolted 2 in. planks on the hull sides and festooned the tops of hatches with nails to counter the hand mines. Japanese swarmed over some disabled tanks forcing the hatches open and grenading the crews. Some crewmen dug-in under their disabled tanks and held out for two days before returning to American lines. Only eight tanks and self-propelled howitzers survived the attack and were reassigned to other battalions to replace their losses. The 193rd was not reconstituted for the remainder of the campaign. (Howard Gerrard)

separating Uchitomari and Machinato on the west coast. The 106th Infantry secured a valuable foothold on the northwest end of the Urasoe-Mura Escarpment and cleared Machinato Village during a bold night infiltration attack.

The main attack was launched at 0640hrs, 19 April, after a massive 27-battalion artillery barrage while naval gunfire and aircraft pounded the Japanese rear area. The 7th Inf. Div. attacked toward Skyline Ridge, the anchor at the east end of the Japanese line, but was thrown back in most sectors by withering fire. The 96th Inf. Div. in the center made little headway against the strongly defended Tombstone and Nishibaru Ridges, barely gaining any ground beyond its start line. The 27th Inf. Div. on the west flank merely held its ground on the south side of the Machinato Inlet, but made further gains on the Urasoe-Mura Escarpment. Its attack on the Kakazu Ridge failed, however, when the 193rd Tank Battalion was separated from 1/105th Infantry as they crossed a saddle between Kakazu and Nishibaru Ridges, resulting in the loss of 22 tanks and the attack's failure.

For the next week the three divisions continued the effort to push south against well dug-in resistance with no unit gaining more than 1,300 yds (1,188 m). The 27th Inf. Div. on the west flank was stalled on the north side of Gusukuma near the coast and on its inland flank at the Urasoe-Mura Escarpment, as was the 96th Infantry Division. Kakazu and Nishibaru Ridges and the Tanabaru were overcome, but the Japanese 22nd Infantry was holding up the 7th Inf. Div. on the east flank. The Bradford Task Force, assembled from reserve battalions of all three divisions in the line, and heavily supported by armor, overran the Kakazu Pocket on 24 April, but the Japanese had abandoned it. The Japanese also lost their one opportunity for a successful counterattack as there were no US reserves; everything had been committed to the line. By the end of the month most units had progressed comparatively well, gaining 1,000–2,000 yds (914–1,829 m) in many areas. The 96th Inf. Div. was still held up on its west flank by the Urasoe-Mura Escarpment defended by the Japanese 32nd Infantry. The US 7th Inf. Div. had made significant headway on its inland flank, but was held up there on Kochi Ridge by the Japanese 22nd Infantry. The divisions were exhausted and their strength low.

It was during this period that it was proposed to execute a flanking landing using the 77th Inf. Div. on the southwest coast north of Minatogawa in an effort to force the Japanese to pull troops out of the Shuri defenses. It was rejected by Buckner from 17–22 April as it was too much of a risk to land a single division so far behind Japanese lines, with the additional logistics burden and the ships required to protect the supporting anchorage.

The 1st Mar. Div. was attached to XXIV Corps on 30 April, relieving the 27th Inf. Div. on the east flank. The 77th Inf. Div, although short

The bodies of two paratroopers of the Japanese 1st Raiding Brigade who attempted an airlanded raid on Yontan Airfield on the night of 24 May. The wreckage of aircraft they destroyed with demolitions and grenades litter the area. They managed to destroy eight fighters and damage 24. (US Army)

1st Mar. Div. troops on the approaches to Shuri Castle view the carnage and devastation of this hotly contested portion of the battlefield, 25 May. (USMC)

three battalions on occupation duty on outlying islands, relieved the much battered 96th. The assault continued southward through the main Shuri defenses, an effort continued until 3 May, when the Japanese attempted their most determined counteroffensive.

THE JAPANESE COUNTEROFFENSIVE

Frustrated at the prolonged defensive battle, many Japanese commanders desired a counteroffensive to halt the American advance. Colonel Yahara, 32nd Army operations officer, warned of the folly of such an attack, but Major-General Cho, chief-of-staff, prevailed. The Japanese attacked on the night of 3 May with their main effort made in the center and the east by the 24th Division. The attack was supported by raids conducted by forces landed in the American rear on both coasts. Shallow penetrations were accomplished in some areas, but the attack was repulsed (see the Bird's Eye View map on pp.74–75 for details of the counterattack). Japanese losses, some 7,000 of the 76,000-man force, only served to further weaken their front. American units had suffered fewer than 700 casualties and they continued to push south. The counteroffensive was nothing short of a blunder.

The Japanese now rebuilt their units, largely with rear service troops, and prepared for a battle of attrition. The 62nd Division, with only a quarter of its strength surviving, defended the western third of the line while the 24th Division, reduced to two-thirds, defended from north of Shuri to the east coast. The 44th IMB, at four-fifths strength, supported the 62nd Division. Japanese artillery had been cut by half and its daily ammunition allotment drastically reduced.

---

19 The Americans used Japanese place names when so identified on the map, but many terrain features were unnamed and given nicknames or named after a nearby village.

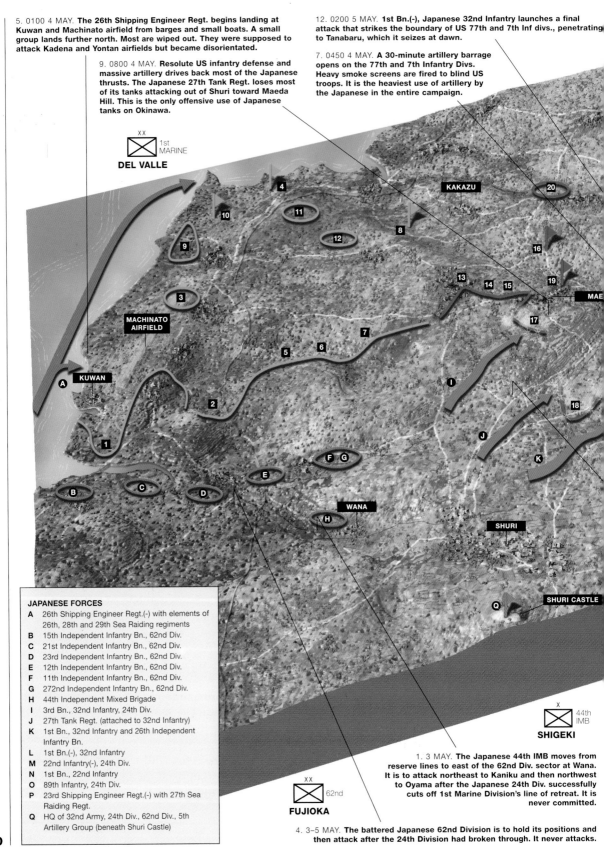

5. 0100 4 MAY. **The 26th Shipping Engineer Regt. begins landing at Kuwan and Machinato airfield from barges and small boats. A small group lands further north. Most are wiped out. They were supposed to attack Kadena and Yontan airfields but became disorientated.**

12. 0200 5 MAY. **1st Bn.(-), Japanese 32nd Infantry launches a final attack that strikes the boundary of US 77th and 7th Inf divs., penetrating to Tanabaru, which it seizes at dawn.**

9. 0800 4 MAY. **Resolute US infantry defense and massive artillery drives back most of the Japanese thrusts. The Japanese 27th Tank Regt. loses most of its tanks attacking out of Shuri toward Maeda Hill. This is the only offensive use of Japanese tanks on Okinawa.**

7. 0450 4 MAY. **A 30-minute artillery barrage opens on the 77th and 7th Infantry Divs. Heavy smoke screens are fired to blind US troops. It is the heaviest use of artillery by the Japanese in the entire campaign.**

XX
1st MARINE
DEL VALLE

KAKAZU

MACHINATO AIRFIELD

KUWAN

MAE

WANA

SHURI

SHURI CASTLE

JAPANESE FORCES

A 26th Shipping Engineer Regt.(-) with elements of 26th, 28th and 29th Sea Raiding regiments
B 15th Independent Infantry Bn., 62nd Div.
C 21st Independent Infantry Bn., 62nd Div.
D 23rd Independent Infantry Bn., 62nd Div.
E 12th Independent Infantry Bn., 62nd Div.
F 11th Independent Infantry Bn., 62nd Div.
G 272nd Independent Infantry Bn., 62nd Div.
H 44th Independent Mixed Brigade
I 3rd Bn., 32nd Infantry, 24th Div.
J 27th Tank Regt. (attached to 32nd Infantry)
K 1st Bn., 32nd Infantry and 26th Independent Infantry Bn.
L 1st Bn.(-), 32nd Infantry
M 22nd Infantry(-), 24th Div.
N 1st Bn., 22nd Infantry
O 89th Infantry, 24th Div.
P 23rd Shipping Engineer Regt.(-) with 27th Sea Raiding Regt.
Q HQ of 32nd Army, 24th Div., 62nd Div., 5th Artillery Group (beneath Shuri Castle)

X
44th IMB
SHIGEKI

1. 3 MAY. **The Japanese 44th IMB moves from reserve lines to east of the 62nd Div. sector at Wana. It is to attack northeast to Kaniku and then northwest to Oyama after the Japanese 24th Div. successfully cuts off 1st Marine Division's line of retreat. It is never committed.**

XX
62nd
FUJIOKA

4. 3–5 MAY. **The battered Japanese 62nd Division is to hold its positions and then attack after the 24th Division had broken through. It never attacks.**

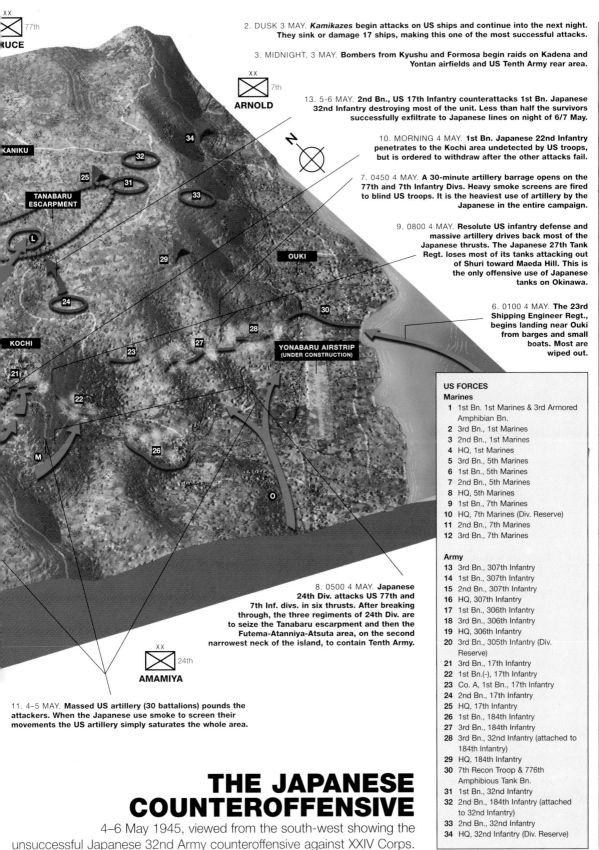

2. DUSK 3 MAY. *Kamikazes* begin attacks on US ships and continue into the next night. They sink or damage 17 ships, making this one of the most successful attacks.

3. MIDNIGHT, 3 MAY. **Bombers from Kyushu and Formosa begin raids on Kadena and Yontan airfields and US Tenth Army rear area.**

7th
ARNOLD

13. 5-6 MAY. **2nd Bn., US 17th Infantry counterattacks 1st Bn. Japanese 32nd Infantry destroying most of the unit. Less than half the survivors successfully exfiltrate to Japanese lines on night of 6/7 May.**

KANIKU

34

32

10. MORNING 4 MAY. **1st Bn. Japanese 22nd Infantry penetrates to the Kochi area undetected by US troops, but is ordered to withdraw after the other attacks fail.**

25

31

7. 0450 4 MAY. **A 30-minute artillery barrage opens on the 77th and 7th Infantry Divs. Heavy smoke screens are fired to blind US troops. It is the heaviest use of artillery by the Japanese in the entire campaign.**

33

TANABARU
ESCARPMENT

L

29

OUKI

9. 0800 4 MAY. **Resolute US infantry defense and massive artillery drives back most of the Japanese thrusts. The Japanese 27th Tank Regt. loses most of its tanks attacking out of Shuri toward Maeda Hill. This is the only offensive use of Japanese tanks on Okinawa.**

24

30

6. 0100 4 MAY. **The 23rd Shipping Engineer Regt., begins landing near Ouki from barges and small boats. Most are wiped out.**

KOCHI

28

23

27

21

YONABARU AIRSTRIP
(UNDER CONSTRUCTION)

22

M

26

O

8. 0500 4 MAY. **Japanese 24th Div. attacks US 77th and 7th Inf. divs. in six thrusts. After breaking through, the three regiments of 24th Div. are to seize the Tanabaru escarpment and then the Futema-Atanniya-Atsuta area, on the second narrowest neck of the island, to contain Tenth Army.**

24th
AMAMIYA

11. 4–5 MAY. **Massed US artillery (30 battalions) pounds the attackers. When the Japanese use smoke to screen their movements the US artillery simply saturates the whole area.**

US FORCES
Marines
1 1st Bn. 1st Marines & 3rd Armored Amphibian Bn.
2 3rd Bn., 1st Marines
3 2nd Bn., 1st Marines
4 HQ, 1st Marines
5 3rd Bn., 5th Marines
6 1st Bn., 5th Marines
7 2nd Bn., 5th Marines
8 HQ, 5th Marines
9 1st Bn., 7th Marines
10 HQ, 7th Marines (Div. Reserve)
11 2nd Bn., 7th Marines
12 3rd Bn., 7th Marines

Army
13 3rd Bn., 307th Infantry
14 1st Bn., 307th Infantry
15 2nd Bn., 307th Infantry
16 HQ, 307th Infantry
17 1st Bn., 306th Infantry
18 3rd Bn., 306th Infantry
19 HQ, 306th Infantry
20 3rd Bn., 305th Infantry (Div. Reserve)
21 3rd Bn., 17th Infantry
22 1st Bn.(-), 17th Infantry
23 Co. A, 1st Bn., 17th Infantry
24 2nd Bn., 17th Infantry
25 HQ, 17th Infantry
26 1st Bn., 184th Infantry
27 3rd Bn., 184th Infantry
28 3rd Bn., 32nd Infantry (attached to 184th Infantry)
29 HQ, 184th Infantry
30 7th Recon Troop & 776th Amphibious Tank Bn.
31 1st Bn., 32nd Infantry
32 2nd Bn., 184th Infantry (attached to 32nd Infantry)
33 2nd Bn., 32nd Infantry
34 HQ, 32nd Infantry (Div. Reserve)

THE JAPANESE COUNTEROFFENSIVE
4–6 May 1945, viewed from the south-west showing the unsuccessful Japanese 32nd Army counteroffensive against XXIV Corps.

ACTION AT SEA

Throughout the campaign TF 51 (Joint Expeditionary Force) provided close air support to the troops ashore, combat air patrols to protect from air attacks, interception of *Kamikazes*, reconnaissance and anti-submarine patrols, logistical support, floating hospitals, continuous gun fire support, and other indispensable services.

The first two weeks of the campaign saw TF 57 (British Carrier Force) operating off Saishima Gunto to neutralize airfields there. Prior to and during the campaign, the Fifth and Third Fleets' fast carriers executed attacks throughout the Ryukyus, on Formosa, mainland China, and Kyushu to neutralize Japanese airfields.

KAMIKAZE ATTACKS

The *Kamikaze*, or Special Attack, concept of intentional suicide attacks on Allied ships by volunteer pilots originated in the Philippines. Those early attacks were sporadically planned, but by the time of Okinawa a well-organized effort had been developed; *Ten-Go* Operation. The 1st Special Attack Force, under Admiral Soemu Toyoda, consisted of over 1,800 aircraft of the combined 5th Air Fleet and 6th Air Army based on Kyushu and Formosa. The Force launched its first attacks in mid-March during the fast carrier raids on Japan. Limited attacks were launched during the initial Okinawa landings, but the full fury of the *Kamikaze* was not felt until a massive 355-plane raid on 6–7 April was unleashed. In 19 hours the Navy suffered six ships sunk and 21 damaged with over 500 casualties. The Japanese lost almost 400 aircraft; *Kamikaze* and conventional covering fighters. The attacks continued unabated through April with a total of 14 US ships sunk and 90 damaged by *Kamikazes*, while conventional air attacks sank one and damaged 47. The Japanese paid a price of over 1,100 aircraft. The month of May saw more air attacks, which concentrated on the picket ships, transports, and carriers as well as the American airfields. Especially heavy attacks occurred in late May. Attacks continued to the end of the campaign, with the last launched on 21–22 June. In all there were ten main attacks, *Sho-Go 1* to *10*, with 1,465 aircraft interspersed with smaller attacks to total about 1,900 aircraft. The result was 26 US ships sunk and 225 damaged by *Kamikazes* as well as two sunk and 61 damaged by conventional air attack. The attacks on the fleet caused the highest US Navy casualty rate in the war.

Among the *Kamikazes* was the MXY7 *Ohka* (Cherry Blossom) rocket-propelled, manned bomb, better known by its American nickname, the *Baka* (Fool) bomb. Dropped from IJN G4M "Betty" twin-engine bombers, the first attack taking place on 21 March, only one ship was sunk and four damaged by the 2,646-lb (1,200-kg) guided bomb.

Dark blue-painted F4U-1 Corsair fighters of Marine Fighting Squadron 232 (VMF-232) roll in over southern Okinawa to hit ground targets. Close air support of ground troops was one of the main missions of Marine aviation. (US Army)

THE SINKING OF THE *YAMATO*

In a desperate effort the Japanese sortied the *Yamato* on 6 April on a suicide mission. The super battleship was to beach itself on Okinawa to the south of the American landing beaches and turn its 18.1-in. guns on American forces ashore and the transports. There was only enough fuel available for the *Yamato* and its accompanying ships to make a one-way trip. The *Ten-Ichi* Operation ("Heaven Number One") saw the *Yamato*, the light cruiser *Yahagi*, and eight destroyers sortie from Tokuyama Naval Base on southwest Honshu. One destroyer experienced engine trouble and turned back. Vice-Admiral Seiichi Ito's Surface Special Attack Force was detected by US submarines soon after it entered the open sea. Contact was lost during the night as the force turned west. American carrier planes found the *Yamato* on the morning of 7 April after it had turned southwest toward its target. TF 58 aircraft struck the force at noon, sinking the *Yamato* (ten torpedo, five bomb hits), the *Yahagi*, (seven torpedo, 12 bomb hits), and four destroyers in two hours at a cost of ten US aircraft. Without air cover the battleship did not even make it halfway to Okinawa and went down with 2,487 crew. Four damaged escort destroyers escaped back to Japan.

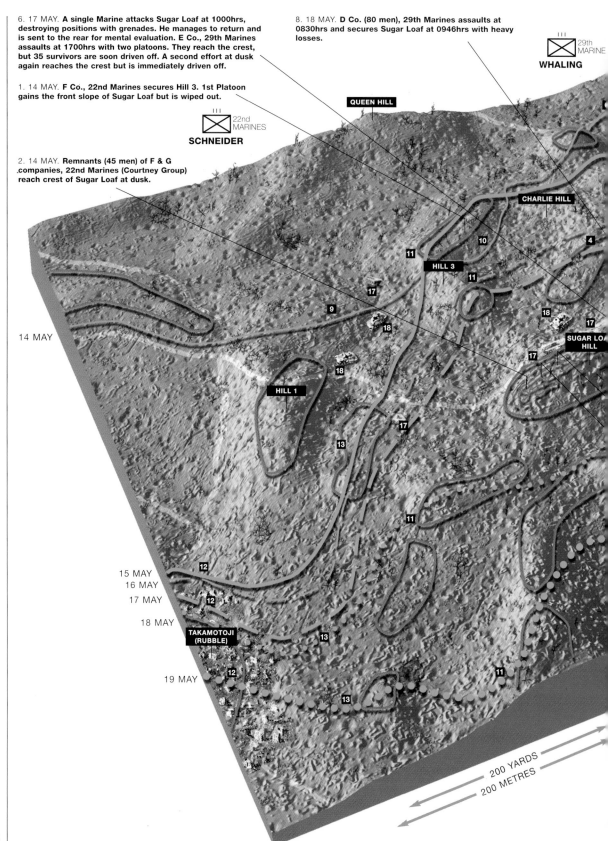

6. 17 MAY. **A single Marine attacks Sugar Loaf at 1000hrs, destroying positions with grenades. He manages to return and is sent to the rear for mental evaluation. E Co., 29th Marines assaults at 1700hrs with two platoons. They reach the crest, but 35 survivors are soon driven off. A second effort at dusk again reaches the crest but is immediately driven off.**

8. 18 MAY. **D Co. (80 men), 29th Marines assaults at 0830hrs and secures Sugar Loaf at 0946hrs with heavy losses.**

1. 14 MAY. **F Co., 22nd Marines secures Hill 3. 1st Platoon gains the front slope of Sugar Loaf but is wiped out.**

2. 14 MAY. **Remnants (45 men) of F & G .companies, 22nd Marines (Courtney Group) reach crest of Sugar Loaf at dusk.**

29th MARINE

WHALING

22nd MARINES

SCHNEIDER

QUEEN HILL

CHARLIE HILL

10

11

4

HILL 3

11

17

18

17

9

18

SUGAR LOAF HILL

17

14 MAY

18

17

HILL 1

17

13

11

15 MAY

16 MAY

17 MAY

12

18 MAY

12

TAKAMOTOJI (RUBBLE)

13

11

19 MAY

12

13

13

200 YARDS

200 METRES

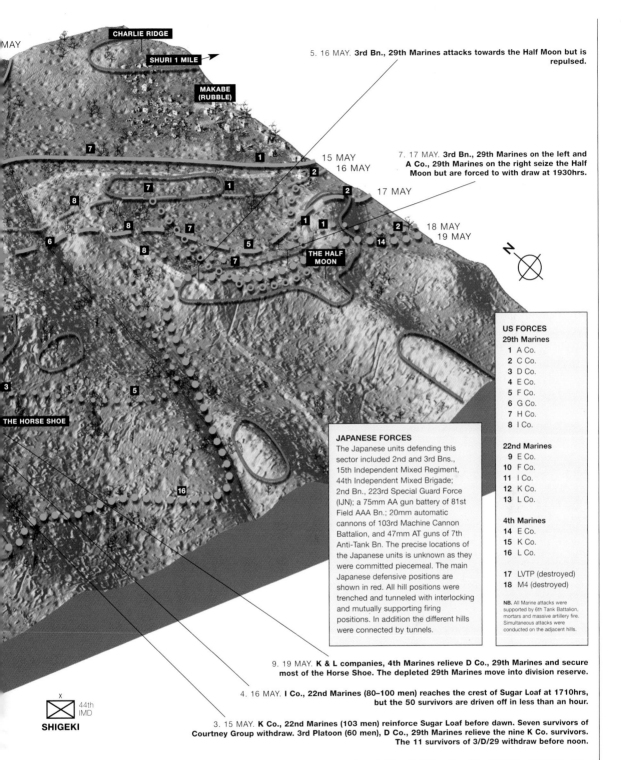

CHARLIE RIDGE

SHURI 1 MILE ➤

MAKABE (RUBBLE)

MAY

5. 16 MAY. **3rd Bn., 29th Marines attacks towards the Half Moon but is repulsed.**

7. 17 MAY. **3rd Bn., 29th Marines on the left and A Co., 29th Marines on the right seize the Half Moon but are forced to with draw at 1930hrs.**

15 MAY
16 MAY

17 MAY

18 MAY
19 MAY

THE HALF MOON

N

THE HORSE SHOE

US FORCES
29th Marines
1 A Co.
2 C Co.
3 D Co.
4 E Co.
5 F Co.
6 G Co.
7 H Co.
8 I Co.

22nd Marines
9 E Co.
10 F Co.
11 I Co.
12 K Co.
13 L Co.

4th Marines
14 E Co.
15 K Co.
16 L Co.

17 LVTP (destroyed)
18 M4 (destroyed)

NB. All Marine attacks were supported by 6th Tank Battalion, mortars and massive artillery fire. Simultaneous attacks were conducted on the adjacent hills.

JAPANESE FORCES
The Japanese units defending this sector included 2nd and 3rd Bns., 15th Independent Mixed Regiment, 44th Independent Mixed Brigade; 2nd Bn., 223rd Special Guard Force (IJN); a 75mm AA gun battery of 81st Field AAA Bn.; 20mm automatic cannons of 103rd Machine Cannon Battalion, and 47mm AT guns of 7th Anti-Tank Bn. The precise locations of the Japanese units is unknown as they were committed piecemeal. The main Japanese defensive positions are shown in red. All hill positions were trenched and tunneled with interlocking and mutually supporting firing positions. In addition the different hills were connected by tunnels.

9. 19 MAY. **K & L companies, 4th Marines relieve D Co., 29th Marines and secure most of the Horse Shoe. The depleted 29th Marines move into division reserve.**

4. 16 MAY. **I Co., 22nd Marines (80–100 men) reaches the crest of Sugar Loaf at 1710hrs, but the 50 survivors are driven off in less than an hour.**

3. 15 MAY. **K Co., 22nd Marines (103 men) reinforce Sugar Loaf before dawn. Seven survivors of Courtney Group withdraw. 3rd Platoon (60 men), D Co., 29th Marines relieve the nine K Co. survivors. The 11 survivors of 3/D/29 withdraw before noon.**

X
44th
IMD
SHIGEKI

BATTLE FOR SUGAR LOAF HILL
13–19 May 1945, viewed from the south-west showing the initial 6th Marine Division assaults on Sugar Loaf Hill, the key to breaching the west flank of the Shuri Line. It required seven days to advance 520 yards. More than 3,000 Marines and untold thousands of Japanese were killed or wounded.

SEIZING THE SOUTH

SHURI FALLS

On 7 May, IIIAC resumed control of the 1st Marine Division on the west flank. As the Americans pushed south the island widened and it would be necessary to place a fourth division into the line. The 6th Mar. Div. was soon assigned a sector on the 1st Mar. Div.'s right and inserted a single regiment, the 22nd, into the line. The 77th Inf. Div. was strengthened by the arrival of its understrength 305th Infantry, relieved from garrisoning Ie Shima. The rested 96th Inf. Div. relieved the 7th Inf. Div. in the line on 8 May (the surrender of Germany was announced that day). The Tenth Army's renewed offensive began on 11 May with, from east to west, 96th Inf., 77th Inf., 1st Mar., and 6th Mar. divisions in the line.

There had been rain earlier but on 22 May heavy rains began. After ten days low ground, gullies, and ravines turned into thigh-deep seas of mud. Small streams and rivers overflowed their banks and the already overburdened roads became impassable in many areas.

The primary objective was Shuri. Progress was slow but steady, although the two center divisions had not driven as deeply into the Shuri defenses as those on the flanks. The 6th Mar. Div. was held up by furious fighting around Sugar Loaf Hill west of Shuri as the other divisions battled for stoutly defended ridges and hills. No complete Japanese unit remained in the lines, only remnants. On 29 May the 22nd Marines took Naha while an element of the 5th Marines, seizing the opportunity, crossed into the 77th Infantry Division's sector and captured Shuri Castle, much to the Army's exasperation. On the same date Army units broke through on the east coast as Japanese units were

A 4th Marines, 6th Mar. Div. .30cal. M1919A4 machine-gun squad maintains covering fire for assault troops on the southern portion of Oroku Peninsula as they enter the central hills, 7 June. (USMC)

ABOVE **A 4.2-in. M2 mortar of the Army's 91st Chemical Mortar Company (Separate) fires in support of the 22nd Marines, 6th Mar. Div., 18 June. The Marines, lacking such mortars, valued their support as they could quickly place high explosives and white phosphorus smoke on targets. (USMC)**

ABOVE, RIGHT **Seeing their still experimental first use in the Pacific, these Army 75-mm T25 recoilless rifles are being bore-sighted before going into action. They were mounted on the same tripod as the .30cal. M1917A1 heavy machine gun. The weapons could be man-packed relatively easily into terrain not accessible to heavier weapons. They were extremely accurate, making them valuable for knocking out caves and pillboxes. A small number of shoulder-fired 57-mm T15E1 recoilless rifles were also used. (US Army)**

routed creating a melee of intermingled US and Japanese units, with many units at times being attacked from both sides. The apparent confusion was due to a complex Japanese scheme of withdrawal.

THE PUSH SOUTH

On 25 May, the Japanese 62nd Division withdrew through a defensive line of the 44th IMB southeast of Naha and then attacked XXIV Corps elements to the east. The Japanese 24th Division then withdrew from that sector on 29 May as the 62nd Division established a new line to the rear. The 24th Division established a new line south of Itoman on the west coast as the 44th IMB withdrew on 31 May to establish a line linked to the 24th Division's and running to the east coast. The 62nd Division then conducted a fighting withdrawal through the new lines between 30 May and 4 June. The 10,000-man Naval Base Force on Oroku Peninsula, misinterpreting the order, withdrew to the south too early on 28 May. Dissatisfied with the positions there, they immediately returned to their base, preferring to die defending it rather than flight alongside the Imperial Japanese Army. US aerial observers, sighting large numbers of the enemy moving south and service troops moving north to reinforce the withdrawing units, thought that the Japanese were merely using the poor weather to mask a relief of line units. The Japanese 32nd Army successfully withdrew to the south, but of the 50,000 troops at the beginning of the operation, only 30,000 remained. Those wounded capable of action had been left behind to fight to the death with the rearguards, and the severely wounded were killed. The 32nd Army Headquarters left its tunnel command post beneath Shuri Castle on 27 May. It established a temporary CP at Tsukazan the next day and the following day moved to a small ridge (Hill 89) near Mabuni on the south coast. Heavy spring rains began at this time, arriving two weeks later than normal. Rains hindered both sides' operations, but the vehicle-dependent Americans were hampered most.

On 24 May paratroopers of the Japanese 1st Raiding Brigade attempted an airlanded raid on Yontan Airfield staged from Japan. Only

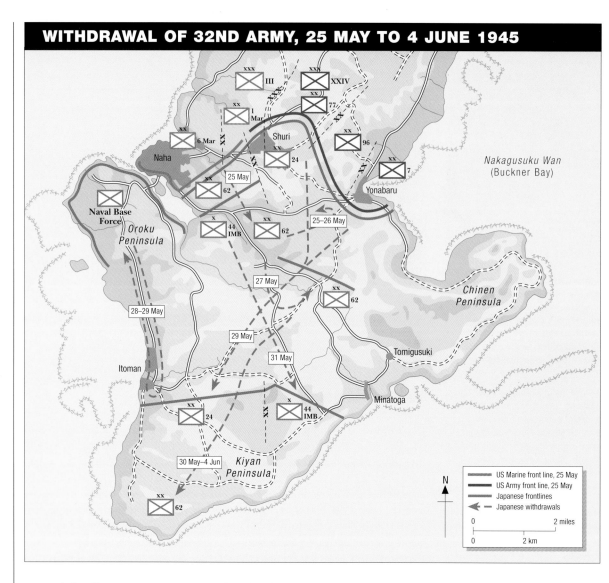

one of the five transports managed to land. A number of US aircraft were destroyed and damaged on the ground, but the raiders were quickly killed.

IJN forces still held the Oroku Peninsula on the southwest coast, south of Naha (*Brother*), where the 6th Mar. Div. was blocked by Naha Harbor. Not to be halted by a mere body of water, the Division did what was natural and executed a shore-to-shore amphibious assault launched from the west coast north of Naha and into Naha Harbor to flank enemy forces on the peninsula on 4 June (K-Day).

The 4th Marines landed on Beaches "Red 1" and "Red 2", south of Naha, at 0600hrs to be followed by the 29th Marines. While not given much attention, the two-regiment subsidiary operation was larger than some earlier amphibious assaults. It was also the last opposed amphibious assault in World War Two.

The 2nd Mar. Div.'s 8th Marines returned to Okinawa from Saipan on 30 May. Its 2nd and 3rd Battalions landed on Iheya Jima on 3 June and the 1st Battalion landed on Aguni Shima on 9 June. These islands,

A gunner of the 22nd Marines, 6th Mar. Div. turns a 7.7-mm Model 92 (1932) machine gun against its former owners. This was a copy of the British World War One-vintage Lewis machine gun used by the Imperial Japanese Navy. Its 47-round drum magazines and extra cartons of ammunition lie on the ground. (USMC)

north and west of Okinawa, were unoccupied. Radar and fighter direction centers were established on both islands.

The situation was stabilized by 31 May with most Japanese rear guards positioned in the central portion of the crumbling lines. By 3 June the 7th Inf. Div. had pushed south on to the Chinen Peninsula on the southeast coast. The 96th Inf. Div. and 1st Mar. Div. steadily drove south in the center as the 6th Marine Division cleared the Oroku Peninsula on the west coast.

THE LAST STAND

After hard fighting, the Japanese remnants were driven to the south end of the island, Kiyan Peninsula, by 11 June. There were still substantial pockets in the American rear areas. The Japanese intent now was to hold a line running from south of Itoman on the west coast through the Yuza-Dake and Yaeju-Dake hill masses in the center to a point on the east coast south of Minatogawa, an area approximately five miles across and three deep. The 8th Marines landed at Naha on 15 June and was attached to the 1st Mar. Div. to assist with the final operations ashore. The Tenth Army commander, Lieutenant-General Buckner, was killed observing his troops' advance against the final organized resistance on 18 June. Major-General Roy Geiger assumed command of Tenth Army, the only Marine officer to command a field army, while retaining command of IIIAC. The next day he was promoted to lieutenant-general. General Buckner had expressly picked Geiger to assume command in the event of his death. Five days later Geiger was relieved by Army Lieutenant-General Joseph W. Stilwell.

The assaulting divisions' sectors had narrowed to the point that only three to five of the freshest battalions were required in the line. The 7th Inf. Div. overran the Japanese 44th IMB's pocket on Hill 115 southwest of Nakaza on 17 June. The US 96th Inf. Div. was pinched out of the line on 20 June to deal with a large pocket of Japanese 24th Division in the peninsula's center at Medeera and Makabe. It was not reduced until 22 June. As the 6th Mar. Div. cleared the west coast of the peninsula, the 1st Mar. Div. wiped out the remaining Japanese 62nd Division pocket just inland of the island's south end on the Kiyamu-Gusuku Ridge. The 7th Inf. Div. closed in on the Japanese 32nd Army's Headquarters, defended by 24th Division survivors, on a coastal ridge (Hill 89) south of Mabuni. These pockets were largely wiped out on 21 June and Okinawa Shoito was declared secure at 1700hrs. Small pockets of resistance remained and the American mopping-up continued for days. At 0340hrs 22 June, Lieutenant-General Ushijima and Major-General Cho committed ritual suicide outside their cave on the south side of Hill 89. The other division and brigade commanders and staffs died during "honorable death attacks" between 21 and 30 June.

Kume Shima, 55 miles (89 km) west of Okinawa, was secured by the Fleet Marine Force, Pacific Amphibious Reconnaissance Battalion between 26 and 30 June to establish a radar site and fighter direction center. Landing on the island's southeast coast, the force met no opposition from the estimated 50-man garrison, which was later engaged. This was the final amphibious assault of World War Two.

AFTERMATH

The armed forces of America and Japan had met in an 82-day, no quarter battle, proving what was already known by both sides: the victor would have to utterly destroy his opponent. Both sides used their resources, whether limited or abundant, to the utmost of their ability to achieve their goals and gain the tactical advantage. Okinawa provided a glimpse of what would have happened if the United States had been forced to invade the Japanese Home Islands.

Only the much larger and longer Philippine Campaign saw higher casualties in the Pacific Theater than Okinawa. Marine ground and air losses were 2,938 dead and missing and 16,017 wounded. The Army lost 4,675 dead and missing and 18,099 wounded. There were over 26,200 US casualties due to combat fatigue, illness, and non-battle injuries. The joint US air services lost 763 aircraft, 458 in combat. US Navy losses were inordinately high with 36 ships sunk and 368 damaged, of which 43 were so badly damaged they were scrapped. These high rates were largely due to the suicide attacks on the fleet. These attacks were also the cause of the Navy's highest casualty rate of the war – 4,900 dead and missing and 4,800 wounded. The British Carrier Force (TF 57) suffered four ships damaged, 98 aircraft lost, 62 KIA, and 82 WIA.

The seven US divisions and IIIAC and XXIV Corps troops suffered the losses listed in the table below. To replace these losses Army units received 12,227 replacements and the Marines 11,147. Tenth Army troops and TAF are not included.

ARMY AND MARINE CORPS CASUALTIES

Division	KIA/DOW	WIA/IIA	MIA	Total
1st Mar. Div.	1,067	6,418	40	6,525
2nd Mar. Div.*	8/48	37/327	8/1	423
6th Mar. Div.	1,622	6,689	15	7,326
7th Inf. Div.	1,122	4,943	3	6,068
27th Inf. Div.	711	2,520	24	3,255
77th Inf. Div.	1,018	3,968	40	5,026
96th Inf. Div.	1,506	5,912	12	7,430
IIIAC	35	149	4	188
XXIV Corps	55	346	2	403

* Two sets of casualty figures are provided for the 2nd Mar. Div. The first number represents 3/2 Marines' losses during the L-Day demonstration and the second is the 8th Marines' losses while attached to the 1st Mar. Div. in June.

Over 100,000 Japanese troops and Okinawan *Boeitai* fought on Okinawa and other islands in the Ryukyus. Estimates of casualties are difficult to determine due to the duration of the action, numbers of enemy forces, inflated reporting of enemy dead, and the nature of combat on Okinawa. The US assessment of Japanese casualties came to over 142,000, more than were on the island. A more realistic assessment is that approximately

An exhausted marine rests on shell-blasted ground during the final stages of the last battle of World War II. (USMC)

66,000 combatants died and half of the survivors were wounded. A total of 7,400 combatants were taken prisoner during the campaign. Some 3,400 unarmed laborers (*Boeitai*, Koreans, and Chinese) were captured. Large numbers of troops turned themselves in after Japan surrendered. Approximately 10,000 IJA and IJN personnel and 8,000 Okinawan *Boeitai* and conscripts survived the battle. The Japanese lost 7,830 aircraft; 4,155 in combat, 2,655 operationally, and 1,020 destroyed on the ground on Kyushu and Formosa. Over 4,600 *Kamikaze* crews died along with hundreds of other pilots. Over 3,650 IJN sailors were lost during the *Yamato*'s sortie. Japan lost a total of 16 warships during the campaign with four damaged.

Island Command's military government and military police took charge of 285,272 Okinawan and Japanese civilians. At the conclusion of the operation, 42,000–50,000 Okinawan civilians were estimated to have died due to Japanese or American combat action or suicide, or were murdered by the Japanese (to prevent their surrender or to steal their food). Post-war studies found that over 122,000 civilians were killed (almost one-third of the indigenous population and a figure rivaling the combined death toll of over 120,000 at Hiroshima and Nagasaki) and a culture was shattered.

Ie Shima served a final role in the war when two white-painted Japanese G4M1 "Betty" bombers bearing green crosses in place of the rising sun arrived from Tokyo on 19 August with the Japanese surrender delegation. They were then flown to Manila on US aircraft. They returned the next day and set off for Japan. Because of misunderstandings, the American ground crew failed to provide sufficient fuel for the aircraft to return, and one crashed offshore of Japan, but the envoys were rescued and delivered the terms of unconditional surrender to the Emperor on schedule.

Large numbers of Japanese troops were killed in post-operation mopping-up and additional prisoners were taken, ultimately growing to 16,350 by the end of November 1945. It was the first time that large numbers of Japanese troops willingly surrendered. On 16 August, Japan announced its intention to surrender. On 29 August, those IJN troops still holding out in the Kerama Retto were among the first Japanese troops to surrender after the announcement. On 7 September, five days after V-J Day, the Ryukyu Islands were formerly surrendered at Kadena Airfield to Lieutenant-General Stilwell by Vice-Admiral Tadao Kato and Lieutenant-General Toshiro Nomi (both had been stationed in Sakishima Gunto). There were still approximately 105,000 IJA and IJN personnel on the other Ryukyus islands. Small numbers of Japanese renegades and Okinawan rebels conducted a low-level guerrilla war against US occupation forces into 1947 when the last surrendered.

The United States now possessed a base just 320 miles (515 km) southwest of Kyushu. A massive construction project began with 87,000

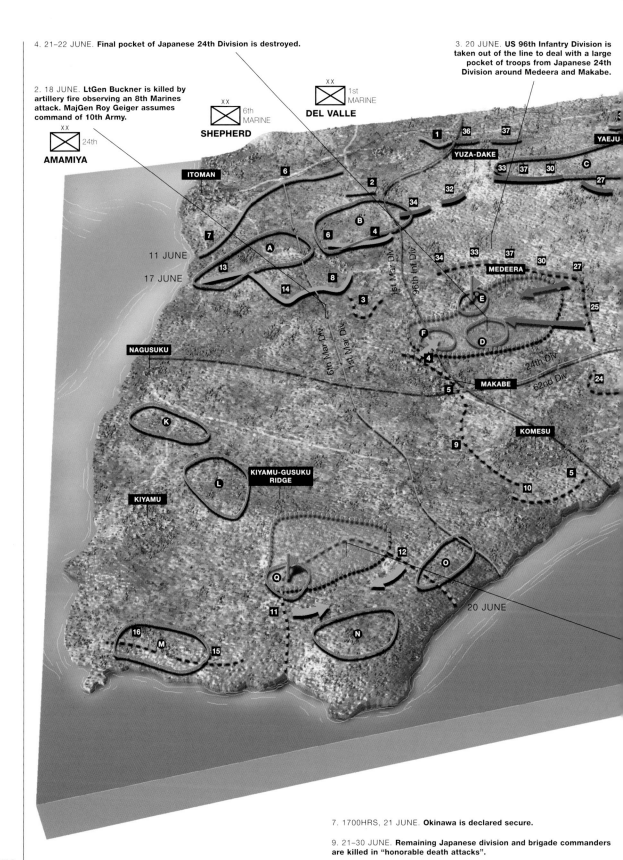

4. 21–22 JUNE. **Final pocket of Japanese 24th Division is destroyed.**

3. 20 JUNE. **US 96th Infantry Division is taken out of the line to deal with a large pocket of troops from Japanese 24th Division around Medeera and Makabe.**

2. 18 JUNE. **LtGen Buckner is killed by artillery fire observing an 8th Marines attack. MajGen Roy Geiger assumes command of 10th Army.**

XX
24th
AMAMIYA

XX
6th
MARINE
SHEPHERD

XX
1st
MARINE
DEL VALLE

ITOMAN

6

2

34

36

37

YAEJU

YUZA-DAKE

33   37   30   C

32   27

B

6   4

7

A

11 JUNE

13

17 JUNE

14

8

3

34   33   37   30

MEDEERA   27

E

1st Mar Div

96th Inf Div

25

F   D

NAGUSUKU

6th Mar Div

1st Mar Div

4

24th Div

MAKABE   62nd Div   24

5

KOMESU

K

9

5

KIYAMU-GUSUKU RIDGE

L

10

KIYAMU

12

O

Q

11

20 JUNE

16

M

N

15

7. 1700HRS, 21 JUNE. **Okinawa is declared secure.**

9. 21–30 JUNE. **Remaining Japanese division and brigade commanders are killed in "honorable death attacks".**

172

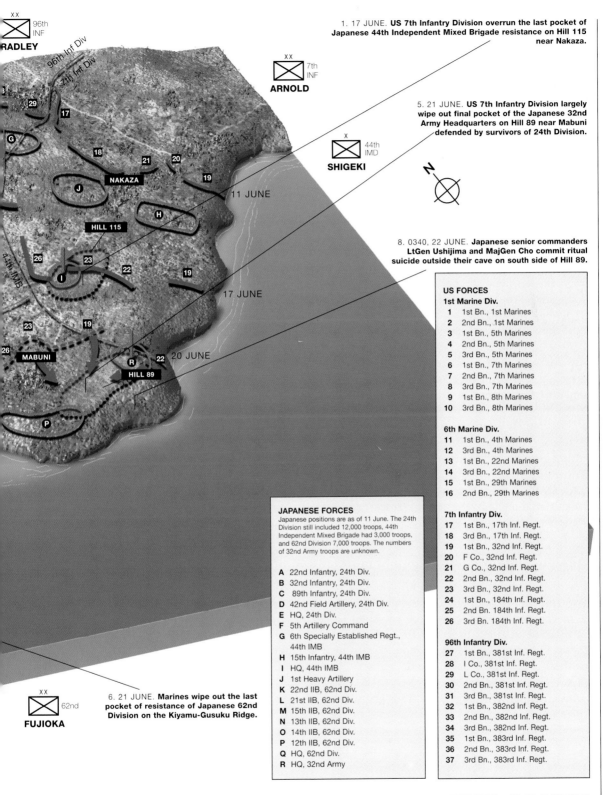

XX
96th
INF
RADLEY

96th Inf Div

7th Inf Div

29

17

G

18

21

20

J

NAKAZA

19

H

11 JUNE

HILL 115

26

23

22

19

44th IMB

I

17 JUNE

23

19

26

MABUNI

R

22

20 JUNE

HILL 89

P

XX
7th
INF
ARNOLD

X
44th
IMD
SHIGEKI

N

XX
62nd
FUJIOKA

1. 17 JUNE. US 7th Infantry Division overrun the last pocket of Japanese 44th Independent Mixed Brigade resistance on Hill 115 near Nakaza.

5. 21 JUNE. US 7th Infantry Division largely wipe out final pocket of the Japanese 32nd Army Headquarters on Hill 89 near Mabuni defended by survivors of 24th Division.

8. 0340, 22 JUNE. Japanese senior commanders LtGen Ushijima and MajGen Cho commit ritual suicide outside their cave on south side of Hill 89.

6. 21 JUNE. Marines wipe out the last pocket of resistance of Japanese 62nd Division on the Kiyamu-Gusuku Ridge.

US FORCES
1st Marine Div.
1   1st Bn., 1st Marines
2   2nd Bn., 1st Marines
3   1st Bn., 5th Marines
4   2nd Bn., 5th Marines
5   3rd Bn., 5th Marines
6   1st Bn., 7th Marines
7   2nd Bn., 7th Marines
8   3rd Bn., 7th Marines
9   1st Bn., 8th Marines
10 3rd Bn., 8th Marines

6th Marine Div.
11 1st Bn., 4th Marines
12 3rd Bn., 4th Marines
13 1st Bn., 22nd Marines
14 3rd Bn., 22nd Marines
15 1st Bn., 29th Marines
16 2nd Bn., 29th Marines

7th Infantry Div.
17 1st Bn., 17th Inf. Regt.
18 3rd Bn., 17th Inf. Regt.
19 1st Bn., 32nd Inf. Regt.
20 F Co., 32nd Inf. Regt.
21 G Co., 32nd Inf. Regt.
22 2nd Bn., 32nd Inf. Regt.
23 3rd Bn., 32nd Inf. Regt.
24 1st Bn., 184th Inf. Regt.
25 2nd Bn. 184th Inf. Regt.
26 3rd Bn., 184th Inf. Regt.

96th Infantry Div.
27 1st Bn., 381st Inf. Regt.
28 I Co., 381st Inf. Regt.
29 L Co., 381st Inf. Regt.
30 2nd Bn., 381st Inf. Regt.
31 3rd Bn., 381st Inf. Regt.
32 1st Bn., 382nd Inf. Regt.
33 2nd Bn., 382nd Inf. Regt.
34 3rd Bn., 382nd Inf. Regt.
35 1st Bn., 383rd Inf. Regt.
36 2nd Bn., 383rd Inf. Regt.
37 3rd Bn., 383rd Inf. Regt.

JAPANESE FORCES
Japanese positions are as of 11 June. The 24th Division still included 12,000 troops, 44th Independent Mixed Brigade had 3,000 troops, and 62nd Division 7,000 troops. The numbers of 32nd Army troops are unknown.

A   22nd Infantry, 24th Div.
B   32nd Infantry, 24th Div.
C   89th Infantry, 24th Div.
D   42nd Field Artillery, 24th Div.
E   HQ, 24th Div.
F   5th Artillery Command
G   6th Specially Established Regt., 44th IMB
H   15th Infantry, 44th IMB
I   HQ, 44th IMB
J   1st Heavy Artillery
K   22nd IIB, 62nd Div.
L   21st IIB, 62nd Div.
M   15th IIB, 62nd Div.
N   13th IIB, 62nd Div.
O   14th IIB, 62nd Div.
P   12th IIB, 62nd Div.
Q   HQ, 62nd Div.
R   HQ, 32nd Army

FINAL STAND IN THE SOUTH

11–21 June 1945, viewed from the south-west showing the final Japanese defense of the Kiyan peninsula on Okinawa's southern end and the Tenth Army's assault on the Yaeju-Dake line.

construction troops (US Army, Navy, and Royal Engineers), who planned to build 22 airfields to accommodate the Eighth Air Force deploying from Europe as well as Navy and Marine aviation units. Only a proportion of the fields were completed, among them six 10,000-ft (3,048-m) bomber fields. Navy and Marine fields were established at Awase and Chimu on Okinawa and Plumb Field on Ie Shima. These fields were known collectively as Naval Air Stations, Okinawa.

Naval Operating Base, Okinawa, was established at Baten Ko on the south end of Buckner Bay, the renamed Nakagusuku Wan. It controlled port facilities at Naha, Chimu Wan, Nago Wan, and Katchin Hanto on the north end of Buckner Bay. The island developed into a major staging base for Army and Marine units destined for the invasion of Japan. Two devastating typhoons in September and October caused major damage and forced the relocation of some naval base facilities. The main naval base was moved from Baten Ko to the southeast end of the Katchin Peninsula to what is still known as "White" Beach. The 1950–53 Korean War made Okinawa an important Army logistics and Navy operating base as did Vietnam into the 1970s.

The Army Air Forces maintained a major bomber base at Kadena Air Base and the US Air Force continued to do so when organized in 1947. B-29 bombers flew long-range missions to bomb North Korea during the Korean War. B-52 bombers habitually flew missions to Vietnam from Okinawa and strategic reconnaissance aircraft operated from there on missions throughout Asia. In 1973 the Navy moved its facilities from Naha Air Base to Kadena Air Base to locate alongside the Air Force.

As combat units departed for the States after the war, the 44th Infantry, Philippine Scouts (a US Army unit composed of Filipino troops) garrisoned the island in January 1947, leading to racial disputes. The 44th Infantry left in May 1949 and was replaced by the US Army's 29th Infantry to guard the air bases. Army, Air Force, and Navy units have remained on the island since, and Marine units have been stationed there since 1956.

The military administration of Okinawa and the Ryukyu Islands was initially the Navy's responsibility, with assistance from the Army, but on 1 July 1946 the military government was turned over to the Army. Progressively more responsibility was given to Okinawans as the government developed. Many Okinawans, especially students and leftists, desired that Okinawa be returned to Japanese control and the withdrawal of the US armed forces, despite the fact that the armed forces furnished 70 percent of the island's income. Increasingly violent protests were experienced into the early 1970s. Okinawa was returned to Japanese sovereignty on 15 May 1972. Buckner Bay reverted to its original name of Nakagusuku Wan. US military bases would be allowed to remain and have to this day. Some of the 39 separate US military installations are shared with Japanese Self-Defense Force units.

An IJN lieutenant, commander of the 183rd Naval Attack Force Rifle Battalion, surrenders to the 7th Marines, 1st Mar. Div. on Motobu Peninsula, 3 September. Japanese Navy field uniforms were a darker green than the olive drab worn by the Army. They were further identified by the yellow anchor insignia on their field caps. (USMC)

THE BATTLEFIELD TODAY

I n 1969, the author had the opportunity to visit Okinawa on a seven-day leave from Vietnam. He found a thriving community growing across the island in modern, sprawling urbanization. There were few reminders of the war and most war memorials had yet to be dedicated. Comparing wartime photos in history books to the healed landscape was like comparing a desert to a tropical rain forest. Other than a quick bus tour where battle sites around Naha were pointed out, with nothing much of the war to see, and a lecture by a bored tour guide on the battle with the aid of a huge 3-D terrain board complete with little lights to track events, the trip was anticlimactic.

Today, however, visitors to Okinawa are treated to an array of memorials and exhibit sites. These include restored underground tunnels and headquarters. Time, progress, and prosperity have much changed Okinawa. A veteran will be hard pressed to identify any of the areas in which he fought; urban sprawl and cultivation have transformed the island. Guided tours are available and island accommodations are top quality.

Shuri Castle was reconstructed and reopened in 1992. The Cornerstone of Peace Park was opened at Mabuni on Okinawa's south end in 1995. Its walls are inscribed with almost 240,000 names of Okinawans, Americans, Japanese, Koreans, and Formosans who died on the island.

Shuri Castle, an objective for which so many attackers and defenders died, was reopened in 1992 in all its pre-war splendor. The Japanese 32nd Army Headquarters tunnel complex was located beneath the castle. The walls, roads, and paths are white limestone, the building walls are red brick, and the roof tan tiles.

ORDER OF BATTLE

US Army Forces on Okinawa

The Army began the operation with 102,250 troops, which rose to 190,301 by the end of June. Only companies and larger size Army units are listed. Attached US Marine Corps and USAAF ground units are included. Unit task organization for combat is not detailed.

TENTH ARMY (JOINT EXPEDITIONARY TROOPS – TASK FORCE 56)

Headquarters and Headquarters Company, Tenth Army

Headquarters and Headquarters Company, 1st Engineer Special Brigade (shore party control)

    51st Military Police Battalion (Companies A, B, and C) (deployed as 1st Provisional MP Bn. and redesignated 9 April 45)

53rd Antiaircraft Artillery Brigade

    HQ and Headquarters Battery, 53rd AA Bde.

    43rd, 44th, 97th, 136th, and 137th AA Groups

    96th, 98th, 369th, 503rd, 505th, and 948th Antiaircraft Artillery Gun Battalions. (90-mm)

    834th (SP), 779th, and 870th Antiaircraft Artillery Auto Weapons Bns (40-mm/.50cal.)

    230th, 294th, 295th, and 325th Antiaircraft Artillery Battalions (Searchlight)

20th Armored Group

    713th Tank Battalion (Armored Flamethrower)

Tenth Army Troops

    3rd and 82nd Signal Construction Battalions, Light

    85th Signal Operation Battalion

        241st and 529th Signal Operation Companies

    318th Signal Service Battalion, Mobile

        3161st and 3373rd Signal Service Companies

    57th Signal Repair Company

    585th Signal Depot Company

    Provisional Radio Intelligence Company

80th Medical Group

    96th and 153rd Medical Battalions, Separate

        386th, 444th, 541st, and 646th Medical Collecting Companies, Separate

        665th and 668th Medical Clearing Companies, Separate

        Provisional Medical Service Unit

    3040th Quartermaster Car Company

    163rd Liaison Squadron (USAAF)

    1st Depot Army Unit (USAAF)

    Landing Force Air Support Control Unit 2 (USMC)

XXIV CORPS (SOUTHERN LANDING FORCE) – 7,032 MEN

    Headquarters and Headquarters Company, XXIV Corps

    XXIV Corps Artillery

    Headquarters and Headquarters Battery, XXIV Corps Artillery

        419th and 420th Field Artillery Groups (Motorized)

        145th, 198th, and 225th Field Artillery Battalions (155-mm Howitzer)

        226th, 531st, and 532nd Field Artillery Battalions (155-mm Gun)

        287th (Observation) and 421st (4.5in. Rocket) Field Artillery Battalions

        749th and 750th Field Artillery Battalions (8in. Howitzer)

        144th Coast Artillery Group

        38th, 179th, and 282nd Coast Artillery Battalions (155-mm gun)

    1181st Engineer Construction Group

    47th, 1397th, and 1398th Engineer Construction Battalions

    1901st Engineer Aviation Battalion

    968th Engineer Maintenance Company

    1088th Engineer Depot Company

    1445th Engineer Searchlight Repair Company

    XXIV Corps Troops

    521st Quartermaster Group

        187th and 492nd Quartermaster Battalions, Mobile

        504th Transportation Corps Port Battalion

        244th and 247th Quartermaster Depot Supply Companies

        3008th and 3063rd Quartermaster Graves Registration Companies

        3754th Quartermaster Truck Company

        4342nd Quartermaster Service Company

    71st Medical Battalion

        384th Medical Clearing Company, Separate

        556th Medical Motorized Ambulance Company

        644th and 645th Medical Collecting Companies, Separate

        594th Quartermaster Laundry Company

    88th Chemical Mortar Battalion

    101st Signal Battalion, Separate

    519th Military Police Battalion, Army

    866th Antiaircraft Artillery Automatic Weapons Battalion (40-mm)

    Landing Force Air Support Control Unit 3 (USMC)

    Detachment, Air Warning Squadron 7 (USMC)

XXIV CORPS ORGANIZATION

XXIV Corps Infantry Divisions	7th	27th	77th	96th
Landing Date	1 April 45	9 April 45	27 April 45	1 April 45
Assault Strength	21,929	16,143	20,981	22,330
Infantry Regiment	17th	105th	305th	381st
Infantry Regiment	32nd	106th	306th	382nd
Infantry Regiment	184th	165th	307th	383rd
Division Artillery				
Field Artillery Battalion (105mm)	48th	104th	304th	361st
Field Artillery Battalion (105mm)	49th	105th	305th	362nd
Field Artillery Battalion (105mm)	57th	249th	902nd	921st
Field Artillery Battalion (155mm)	31st	106th	306th	363rd
Division Troops				
Engineer Combat Battalion	13th	102nd	302nd	321st
Medical Battalion	7th	102nd	302nd	321st
Cavalry Reconnaissance Troop	7th	27th	77th	96th
Division Special Troops				
Signal Company	7th	27th	77th	96th
Quartermaster Company	7th	27th	77th	96th
Ordnance Light Maintenance Company	707th	727th	777th	796th
Attachments				
Engineer Combat Group (shore party)	1140th	1165th	1118th	1122nd
Engineer Combat Battalion	50th	34th	132nd	170th
Engineer Combat Battalion	104th	152nd	233rd	173rd
Engineer Combat Battalion	110th	1341st	242nd	174th
Tank Battalion, Medium	711th	193rd	706th	763rd
Amphibian Tank Battalion	776th	–	708th	780th
Amphibian Tractor Battalion	536th	-	715th	728th
Amphibian Tractor Battalion	718th	-	773rd	788th
Antiaircraft Artillery Gun Battalion (90mm)	502nd	-	93rd	504th
Antiaircraft Artillery AW Battalion (40mm)	861st	-	7th	485th
Ordnance Ammunition Company	644th	61st	793rd	632nd
Ordnance Bomb Disposal Sqn. (USAAF)	204th	-	92nd	206th
Medical Field Hospital	69th	68th	36th	31st
Medical Portable Surgical Hospitals	52nd, 66th	96th, 98th	68th, 95th	51st, 67th

US Marine Corps Forces on Okinawa

The Marine Corps began the operation with 88,500 troops, of which 66,636 participated in the assault. Attached US Army, USAAF, and USN units are included. Unit task organization for combat is not depicted.

III AMPHIBIOUS CORPS (NORTHERN LANDING FORCE) – 12,422 men
Headquarters and Service Battalion, III Amphibious Corps
   1st Bomb Disposal Company
   1st Separate Topographic Company
Medical Battalion, III Amphibious Corps
Signal Battalion, III Amphibious Corps
1st Military Police Battalion (Provisional)
Company A, 51st Military Police Battalion (USA) (deployed as
   1st Provisional MP Battalion and redesignated 9 April 1945)
1st Separate Engineer Battalion
802nd Engineer Aviation Battalion (USA)
11th Motor Transport Battalion (Provisional)
Corps Evacuation Hospitals No. 2 and No. 3 (USN)
Amphibious Reconnaissance Battalion, Fleet Marine Force, Pacific
7th Service Regiment (deployed as the 7th Field Depot and
   redesignated 1 June 1945)
   Headquarters and Service Battalion, 7th Service Regiment (only
   unit formed)

1st, 3rd, and 12th Marine Ammunition Companies
5th, 18th, 19th, 20th, 37th, and 38th Marine Depot Companies
Corps Artillery, III Amphibious Corps
   Headquarters Battery, Corps Artillery, III Amphibious Corps
   2nd Provisional Field Artillery Group
      1st, 3rd, and 6th 155-mm Howitzer Battalions
      7th, 8th, and 9th 155-mm Gun Battalions
   456th Transportation Corps Amphibious Truck Company (USA)
   Marine Observation Squadron 7
1st Provisional Antiaircraft Artillery Group
   2nd, 5th, 8th, and 16th Antiaircraft Artillery Battalions
   (90-mm/40-mm)
46th, 54th, 55th, 57th, 62nd, and 63rd Replacement Drafts

III AMPHIBIOUS CORPS ORGANIZATION

III Amphibious Corps Marine Divisions	1st	2nd	6th
Landing Date	1 April 45	*	1 April 45
Assault Strength	26,274	22,195	24,356
Marine Infantry Regiments	1st, 5th, 7th	2nd, 6th, 8th	4th, 22nd, 29th
Marine Artillery Regiment	11th	10th	15th
HQ Battalion, Marine Division	1st	2nd	6th
Tank Battalion	1st	2nd	6th
Engineer Battalion	1st	2nd	6th
Pioneer Battalion	1st	2nd	6th
Service Troops			
Motor Transport Battalion	1st	2nd	6th
Service Battalion	1st	2nd	6th
Medical Battalion	1st	2nd	6th
Attachments			
Armored Amphibian Tractor Battalion	3rd (Prov)	-	1st
Amphibian Tractor Battalions	1st, 8th	2nd	4th, 9th
Naval Construction Battalion	145th	130th	58th
Marine Observation Squadron	VMO-3	-	VMO-6
Assault Signal Company	1st, 4th	2nd	6th
Marine Amphibian Truck Company	3rd	2nd	6th
Amphibious Truck Company (USA)	454th	-	814th
Chemical Mortar Company (USA)	B/88th ChemBn	-	91st
Military Police Company (USA)	B/51st MP Bn	-	C/51st MP Bn
Provisional Rocket Detachment	4th	-	5th
Marine War Dog Platoon	4th	2nd	1st
Replacement Drafts	29th, 32nd	35th, 41st	26th, 33rd

* The 2nd Mar. Div. did not land and departed on 11 April. Its 8th Marines (Reinforced); 2nd Battalion: 10th Marines, and 2nd Amphibian Tractor Battalion returned on 30 May, landed as the Expeditionary Troops Special Landing Force on 15 June, and was attached to the 1st Mar. Division.

TACTICAL AIR FORCE, TENTH ARMY

TACTICAL AIR FORCE, TENTH ARMY (TASK GROUP 99.2)
HQ Squadron, 2nd Marine Aircraft Wing
Air Defense Command (Task Unit 99.2.1)
Marine Aircraft Group 43
    HQ Squadron 43 (HQ, Air Defense Command)
    Air Warning Squadron 1, 6, 7, 8, and 11
Company B, 568th Signal Air Warning Battalion (USAAF)
927th Signal Air Warning Company (USAAF)
Detachment 1, 305th Fighter Control Squadron (USAAF)
Marine Aircraft Group 14
    HQ and Service Squadrons 14
    Marine Fighting Squadrons 212, 222, and 223
Marine Aircraft Group 22
    HQ and Service Squadrons 22
    Marine Fighting Squadrons 113, 314, and 422
    Marine Fighting Squadron (Night) 533
Marine Aircraft Group 31
    HQ and Service Squadrons 31
    Marine Fighting Squadrons 224, 311, and 441
    Marine Fighting Squadron (Night) 542
Marine Aircraft Group 33
    HQ and Service Squadrons 33
    Marine Fighting Squadrons 312, 322, and 323
    Marine Fighting Squadron (Night) 543
301st Fighter Wing (USAAF)
    HQ and HQ Squadron, 301st Fighter Wing
    318th Fighter Group
19th, 73rd, and 333rd Fighter Squadrons
548th Night Fighter Squadron
364th Air Service Group
    413th Fighter Group

1st, 21st, and 34th Fighter Squadrons
337th Air Service Group
    507th Fighter Group
463rd, 464th, and 465th Fighter Squadrons
557th Air Service Group
    342nd Station Complement Squadron
    460th Aviation Squadron (Colored)
Bomber Command (VII Bomber Command – Task Unit 99.2.2)
HQ and HQ Squadron, VII Bomber Command (USAAF)
11th Bombardment Group, Heavy
    26th, 42nd, 98th, and 431st Bombardment Squadrons, Heavy
    57th Air Service Group
41st Bombardment Group, Medium
    47th, 48th, 396th, and 820th Bombardment Squadrons, Medium
    389th Air Service Group
319th Bombardment Group, Light
    437th, 438th, 439th, and 440th Bombardment Squadrons, Light
514th Air Service Group
494th Bombardment Group, Heavy
    864th, 865th, 866th, and 867th Bombardment Squadrons, Heavy
    13th Air Service Group
Antisubmarine Unit (Task Unit 99.2.3) Marine Torpedo-Bomber Squadrons 131 and 232
Photographic Unit (Task Unit 99.2.4) 28th Photographic Reconnaissance Squadron (USAAF)
Air Support Control Unit (Task Unit 99.2.5)
Commander, Marine Air Support Control Units, Amphibious Forces, Pacific Fleet
    Landing Force Air Support Control Units 1, 2, and 3

Imperial Japanese Army Forces on Okinawa

The ad hoc "specially established" units were attached to the 24th and 62nd Divisions, and 44th IMB, but are not included in those formations' total strengths.

32ND ARMY TROOPS
36th Signal Regiment
32nd Army Field Freight Depot
32nd Army Field Ordnance Depot
32nd Army service, medical, and construction units
66th Independent Engineer Battalion
Intelligence Unit *(Kempei tai)*

24th Division – 14,360 men
22nd, 32nd, and 89th Infantry Regiments
2nd Specially Established Brigade
5th and 6th Specially Established Regiments
24th Reconnaissance Regiment
24th Engineer Regiment
24th Transport Regiment
24th Division service units

62nd Division – 11,623 men
63rd Brigade
11th–14th, and 273rd Independent Infantry Battalions
64th Brigade
15th, 21st–23rd, and 272nd Independent Infantry Battalions
1st Specially Established Brigade
2nd–4th Specially Established Regiments
1st Especially Established Regiment
Engineer,Signal, Transport, and Service Units

44th Independent Mixed Brigade – 4,485 men
2nd Infantry Unit (less1st Bn. on Ie Shima and 2nd Bn.on Motobu Peninsula)
15th Independent Mixed Regiment
6th Especially Established Regiment (transferred from 24th Division in late May)
Engineer Unit

Attached to 24th and 62nd Divisions, and 44th IMB:
3rd, 4th, 14th, and 17th Independent Machine Gun Battalions
3rd, 7th, and 22nd Independent Antitank Battalions (47-mm)
1st–3rd, 26th–29th Independent Battalions (infantry)
27th Tank Regiment (-) (battalion-size combined arms unit)

5th Artillery Group – 5,300 men
1st, 4th, and 5th Companies, 1st Independent Artillery Mortar Regiment (320-mm)
2nd Battalion, 1st Medium Artillery Regiment (150-mm howitzer)
3 batteries, 7th Heavy Artillery Regiment (240-mm howitzer)
23rd Medium Artillery Regiment (150-mm howitzer)
42nd Field Artillery Regiment, 24th Division (75-mm gun, 100-mm howitzer, 150-mm howitzer)
1st and 2nd Light Mortar Battalions (81-mm)
100th Independent Heavy Artillery Battalion (150-mm gun)
Artillery Unit, 44th Independent Mixed Brigade (75-mm gun)
15 IJN coast artillery companies (attached) (120-mm & 140-mm)

21st Antiaircraft Artillery Group – 3,130 men
27th Independent Antiaircraft Artillery Battalion (75-mm)
70th, 80th, and 81st Field Antiaircraft Artillery Battalions (75-mm)
103rd–105th Independent Machine Cannon Battalions (20-mm)

11th Shipping Group
23rd and 26th Shipping Engineer Regiments (less one company each)
26th, 27th, 28th (plus 1st and 3rd Companies, 29th) Sea Raiding Regiments

Okinawan Labour Unit *(Boeitai)* – 39,000 men
"Blood and Iron for the Emperor" Duty Unit *(Tekketsu Kinnotai)* (battalion-size combat unit)
502nd–504th Special Guard Engineer Units
Boeitai assigned to the IJA as augmentees:16,600 men

Kerama Retto – 975 men
1st–3rd Sea Raiding Regiments

Ie Shima (Igawa Unit) – 3,000 men
1st Battalion, 2nd Infantry Unit
50th Specially Established Battalion
Aircraft service, construction, and engineer units

Eastern Islands (Tsugen Shima) – 250 men
1st Battery, 7th Heavy Artillery Regiment (240-mm howitzer)

FURTHER READING

Appleman, R.E., Burns, J.M., Gugeler, R.A., and Stevens, J., *The US Army In World War II, The War in the Pacific, Okinawa: The Last Battle* (Washington 1948)

Feifer, G., *Tennozan: The Battle for Okinawa and the Atomic Bomb* (New York 1992)

Fine, D.I., *Operation Iceberg: The Invasion and Conquest of Okinawa in World War II – An Oral History* (New York 1995)

Foster, S., *Okinawa 1945: Final Assault on the Empire* (New York 1994)

Garand, G.W., and Strobridge, T.R., *History of US Marine Operations In World War II, Victory and Occupation, Vol. V* (Washington 1968)

Hallas, J.H., *Killing Ground on Okinawa: The Battle for Sugar Loaf Hill* (Westport, Connecticut 1996)

Huber, T.M., "Japan's Battle for Okinawa: April to June 1945", *Leavenworth Papers* (Washington 1990)

Isely, J.A., and Crowl, P.A., *The US Marines and Amphibious Warfare: Its Theory, and its Practice in the Pacific* (Princeton, New Jersey 1951)

Leckie, R., *Okinawa: The Last Battle of World War II*, Viking (1995)

Leonard, C.J., *After the Battle No. 43, Okinawa* (London 1984)

Lorelli, J., *To Foreign Shores: US Amphibious Operations in World War II* (Annapolis 1994)

Moran, J., *US Marine Corps Uniforms and Equipment in World War II* (London 1992)

Morison, S.E., *History of United States Naval Operations in World War II, Victory in the Pacific, Vol. XIV* (Boston 1960)

Morris, M.D., *Okinawa: A Tiger by the Tail* (New York 1969)

Nichols, C.S., Jr., and Shaw, H.I., Jr., *Okinawa: Victory in the Pacific* (Washington 1955)

Rottman, Gordon L., *US Marine Corps World War II Order of Battle* (Westport, Connecticut 2001)

Rottman, Gordon L., *World War II Pacific Island Guide: A Geo-Military Study* (Westport, Connecticut 2001)

Sledge, E.B., *With the Old Breed at Peleliu and Okinawa* (Novato, California 1981)

Spur, R., *A Glorious Way to Die: The Kamikaze Mission of the Battleship* Yamato*, April 1945*, Newmarket Press (Scranton, Pennsylvania 1981)

Stanton, S., *US Army Uniforms of World War II* (Harrisburg, Pennsylvania 1991)

Winton, John, *The Forgotten Fleet: The Story of the British Pacific Fleet* (Wadhurst, United Kingdom 1991)

Wukovits, J.E., *Marines in World War II Commemorative Series, The Final Campaign: Marines in the Victory on Okinawa* (Washington 1996)

Yahara, Col. Hiromichi, *The Battle for Okinawa* (New York and Chichester 1995)

INDEX

Figures in **bold** refer to illustrations

Aguni Shima 168
aircraft
    F4U Corsair fighters **128, 130, 142, 163**
    Mitsubishi 'Betty' G4M twin-engine attack bomber **104**
    TBF Avenger torpedo-bomber **119**
airfields 7, 15, 18, 19, 30, 33, 36, 38, 44, 46, 53
Amamiya, LtGen Tatsumi 134
amphibious trucks (DUKW-353) ('Ducks') **123**
antiaircraft guns **126**
antitank guns, 37mm M3A1 **144**
Arkansas, USS 13
Arnold, MajGen Archibald V. 127
Asaka, Prince Yasuhiko 122
Atsuchi, Col Kanehiko 25, 32, 37
Awacha Pocket (Okinawa) **97**

Bailey bridges 144, **145**
banzai charges 106
beach landings *see* landings
beaches **13**, 15, **16**, 17, **17**, 18, 24, **29, 33,** 45, **48,** 75
Berry, Cpl Charles J. 85
Bishi Gawa (stream) 114, **122,** 143, 144
Bismarck Sea, USS 36
Blandy, RAdm William Henry Purnell (1890–1954) 20, 21
Blandy, RAdm William H.P. 125
Blue Beaches 15, 28, 29
Boehm, LtCol Harold 62–3
bombs, Yokosuka MXY-7 Ohka (Cherry Blossom) **104,** 162
bone diggers 75
Bradley, MajGen James L. 127
Bradley, Pharmacist's Mate John H. 83, **84**
British and Commonwealth forces 5
British Carrier Force (TF 57) 114, 124, 138, 162, 170
Bruce, MajGen Andrew B. 128
Buckner, Gen Simon B. **112,** 125, 158
    career 119–20
    death 169
    and Pacific strategy 96
bunkers 110

Bushido 105

Caddy, Pfc William 85
Callahan, Pfc R. F. **31**
Caroline Islands, neutralization of Truk 94, 104
casualties 25, 49
    Japanese 30, 44, 57, 65, 69, **69**
    US 11–12, 21, 28, 29, 30, 37, 39, **40,** 45, 46, 47, **56,** 57, 65, 68 71, 74, **88**
Cates, MajGen Clifton B. 11, **11,** 15, 41
Chambers, LtCol Justice M. 38, 85
Charlie Dog Ridge 45
Chatan Isthmus (Okinawa Shima) 110, 144
Cherry Society (*Sakurakai*) 122
Chinen Peninsula (Okinawa Shima) 110, 169
Cho, MajGen Isamu 111, 159
    career 121–2
    death 169
chronology 76
civilians 16
climate **36**
Cole, Sgt Darrell S. 28, 85
Cushman's Pocket 63, 65, 67, 68

Daito Jima 110
Death Valley 67, 68, 69
defensive positions **113, 138,** 155, **156–7** *see also* bunkers
del Valle, MajGen Pedro A. 129
Deyo, RAdm Morton L. 125
dispositions **18**
Dunlap, Capt Robert H. 85

Eldorado, USS 31, 82
Ente, Pharmacist's Mate Jack **36**
Erskine, MajGen Groves B **10,** 10–11, 55, 62, 68, 69

flag raised on Mount Suribachi 41, **47, 81,** 81–2
Formosa
    Japanese defense of 106–7
    US invasion plans 93–5, 95–6
Franklin, USS 138
Fujioka, LtGen Takeo 133

Gagnon, Rene 83, **84**
Geiger, LtGen Roy S. 128, 169
    career 120–1

Genaust, Sgt Bill (photographer) 81, 82
Gray, Sgt Ross F. 88
Green Beach 15, 25
Griner, MajGen George W. 127
gun emplacements **101**

Hagushi Beaches (Okinawa Shima) 100, 113
Hall, RAdm John L. 125
Halsey, Adm William F., and Pacific strategy 93
Hansell, BrigGen Haywood 7
Harmon, LtGen Millard F., and Pacific strategy 95–6
Harrell, Sgt William G. 60, 88
Hayes, Corporal Ira H. 83, **84**
Henry A. Wiley, USS 32´
Herring, Lt Rufus G. 88
Hill, RAdm Harry W. 20
Hill Peter 46, 47, 48–9
Hodge, LtGen John R. 126, 147
    career 120
Horie, Maj Yoshitaka 19, 69
howitzer, 105mm M7 **147**

Ichimaru, RAdm Toshinosuke 14
Idaho, USS 13, 41, 44
Ie Shima 111, 112, **133**
    geography 152, 154
    US landing on **153,** 154, 155
Iheya Jima 168
Ikeda, Col Masuo 44
Indianapolis, USS 21, 62
Inoue, LtGen 17
Inouye, Capt Samaji 63–4
Ishikawa Isthmus (Okinawa Shima) 98, 99, 100, 114, 144, 150
Ito, VAdm Seiichi 163
Iwo Jima **16,** 17–19, 75
    declared secure 68
    Japanese defense of 106
    strategic importance of 6–7, 7–8, 73
    terrain **67**
    US seizure of 94, 96, 97, 104

Jacobson, Pfc Douglas T. 48, 88, **88**
Japan 5, **6**
    air raids on **5,** 6–7, 7, **8,** 66–7, 74
    atomic bombs used against **73,** 74
    concept of warfare 105–6
    surrender 171

Japanese Forces 5, 13, 14, 31, 54, 57, 67, 74
  1st Raiding Brigade 167–8
  1st Specially Established Regiment 111, 136, 143
  5th Artillery Group 135
  11th Shipping Group 135
  15th Independent Mixed Regiment 132–3, 135
  21st Antiaircraft Artillery Group 135
  24th Division 134, 147, 150, 159, 167, 169, **172–3**
  27th Tank Regiment 135
  32nd Army 132, **160–1, 168**
  44th Independent Mixed Brigade (IMB) 107, 132, 134–5, 147, 159, **164–5**, 167, 169
  62nd Division 133–4, 147, 155, 159, 167, 169
  272nd Independent Infantry Battalion (IIB) 150
  artillery 19, **56**
  attack encampment 69
  banzai attack 63–5
  casualties 30, 44, 57, 65, 69, **69, 156–7**, 170–1
  Civil Defense Unit 135
  commanders 121–3
  counter-attacks 38–9
  'the Courageous Battle Vows' 13–14
  and Cushman's Pocket 67, 68
  Death Valley 69
  defend airfields 36, 38, 44
  defense sectors **18**
  equipment 135
  at Higashi 67, 68–9
  Home Defense Unit 135
  IJA Air Service 107
  IJN 5, 14, 64, 80
  IJN Air Force 107
  kamikaze attacks 36–7
  Labour Unit 135–6
  the 'Meatgrinder' 47, 56
  at Motoyama 52
  on Mount Suribachi 25, 32, 37, 38, 41
  navy 136
  order of battle 80
  rifle units 136
  supply drop 49
  tactical organization 133, 136
  tactics 17
  tanks 52
  uniforms **174**
  US landings 19, 24–5, 25, 28, 29, 30

Jikyusen (war of attrition) 107
Johnson, LtCol Chandler 39, 57
Julian, Sgt Joseph R. 88

Kamikaze attacks 107, **108–9,** 111, 132, 142, 162, 171
Katchin Hanto (peninsula) **93,** 144
Kato, VAdm Tadao 171
Keise Shima 113, 114
  US seizure of 140
Keokuk, USS 37
Kerama Retto 113, 171
  US seizure of 139–40
Kikai Shima 112
Kikusui (floating chrysanthemums) 107
Kiland, RAdm Ingolf N. 125
King, Adm Ernest J., and Pacific strategy 93, 96
Kiyan Peninsula (Okinawa Shima) 169, **172–3**
Koiso, Kuniaki 146
Korean laborers 16
Kuba Saki 114
Kume Shima 169
Kuribayashi, LtGen Tadamichi 8, 11–12, **12, 15,** 33, 49, 60
  and the banzai attack 64
  'the Courageous Battle Vows' 13–14
  death of 69, 72
  Death Valley 69
  and Mount Suribachi 32, 39
  plans 17, 19
  prepares final defense 67
  reorganises defenses **14,** 16
  US landings 24–5
Kuribayashi, Taro **88**

LaBelle, Pfc James D. 65, 88
landing craft, infantry (gun) (LCI[G]) type D **120**
landing craft, tank Mk 6 (LCT[6]) **124**
landing craft, vehicle and personnel (LCVP) **116**
landing ships, tank (LST) **122**
landing vehicle, tracked (armored) Mk 4 (LVT[A]4) **145**
landing vehicle, tracked Mk3 (LVT[3]) (Amtrac) **117,** 132
landings **18,** 19, 21, **21,** 22–5, **25, 28,** 28–31, **29, 32, 33, 45, 85**
Leims, Lt John H. 89
LeMay, Curtis Emerson (1906–90) 7, 66–7
Leutze, USS 21
Lowery, Lou (photographer) 41, 81

Lucas, Pfc Jacklyn H. 89
Lummus, Lt Jack 65, 89
Lurga Point, USS 37
Luzon, MacArthur's plans for invasion of 95, 96

MacArthur, Gen Douglas (1880–1964) 9, 10
  and Pacific strategy 95, 96
  in Southwest Pacific Area 94
McCarthy, Capt Joseph J 35, 36, 89
machine guns
  .30 cal. M1917Al heavy **143**
  7.7mm Model 92 **169**
Mariana Islands
  US seizure of 94, 104
Marine Corps Memorial, Arlington National Cemetery 81, **83,** 83–4, **84, 91**
Martin, Lt Harry L. 69, 89
'Meatgrinder,' the 46–7, 48, 49, 53, 56–7, 57, 60, 67
memorials 72, 81, **83,** 83–4, **84, 91**
military police 126, **127**
Minna Shima 155
Mitscher, VAdm Marc A. 124
Miyako Shima 112
mortars
  4.2-in.M2 **167**
  60mm M2 **138**
  81mm Ml **151, 152**
  320mm spigot **101**
Motobu Peninsula (Okinawa Shima) **95, 98,** 111
Motoyama 52
Mueller, MajGen Paul J. 128
Mulcahy, MajGen Francis P. 132

Nakagusuka Wan (bay) 112, 115
Nansei Shoto 97
Natoma Bay, USS 36
Nevada, USS 13
Nimitz, Adm Chester W. (1885–1966) 8, 9, **9,** 112
  and Pacific strategy 93, 95, 96
Nimmer, BrigGen David R. 128
Nippa, RAdm Teiso 136
Nishi, LtCol Baron Takeichi 52, 57, 68
Nishi Ridge 54, 57
Nomi, LtGen Toshiro 171

Okinawa Gunto (group) **105**
  geography 98
  history 98
  US plans for invasion of 96, 97
  villages **96**
Okinawa Shima (island) **94**

airfields 100, 101, 107, 111, 112, 114
battlefields today 175
buildings 101
civilians **127,** 171
coastline 100
geography 98
Hill 115 169
Hill 178 **137**
Japanese defense strategy 106–7, 110–12
Japanese defenses **99,** 155, **156–7**
Korean and Vietnam Wars, role in 174
language and culture 102
Naval Operating Base 174
population 100–1
recent history 174
Sugar Loaf Hill **154, 164–5,** 166
terrain 98–100
US offensive strategy 112–15
weather 101–2
Operation Bunkhouse 96
Operation Causeway 93–5, 95–6
Operation Downfall 74
Operation Iceberg
  bombing raids 137–8
  Eastern Islands, US seizure of 145
  Ie Shima, US landing on **153,** 154, 155
  Japanese forces
    absence of initial response 145–6
    counterattack (12 April) 150
    counteroffensive (3 May) 159
    final defeat of 169
    withdrawal to the south 167, **168**
  Kakazu Ridge, US attack on 147, **148–9,** 150, 158
  Kamikaze attacks 162
  Keise Shima, US seizure of 140
  Kerama Retto, US seizure of 139–40
  landing beaches **141**
  logistics 115
  main landing 140–3
  Naha, US assault on 168, 169
  Onna Take, battle for 152
  order of battle 176–9
  planning 96–7, 112–15
  shelling from sea 139
  Shuri defenses
    US attack on 155, 158–9
    US seizure of 166–7
  US forces
    casualties 170
    initial advances 144

Yae Take (Mount), US attack on 151
Yamato, sinking of 163, 171
Operation Indispensable 112, 152
Operation Scattering 96
Operation Sho-Go 107, 162
Operation Ten-Go 106–87, 138, 162
Operation Ten-Ichi 163
Oroku Peninsula (Okinawa Shima) 111, 150, 167, 169

Pacific War, Allied strategy 94, 97
Peleliu 17, 106
Pensacola, USS 20–1, 44
Perry, Codr Matthew 98, 147
Philippines
  MacArthur's plans for invasion of 95, 96
  US invasion of 94, 170
Phillips, Pvt George 89
Pierce, Pharmacist's Mate Francis, Jr. 89
prisoners 49, 68, **68**
Pyle, Ernie **134,** 155

Q-boats 107, **108–9**
Quarry, the 15, 25, 29, 32–3, 35

Rawlings, VAdm Sir Bernard 124
Red Beaches 15, 28
Reifsnider, RAdm Lawrence F. 125
Richardson, Gen Robert C., and Pacific strategy 96
rifle, 75mm T25 recoilless **167**
rocket launchers 130, **130**
Rockey, MajGen Keller E. 11, **11,** 41, 57
Roosevelt, Franklin D., 32nd President of the United States (1882–1945)
    death 150
    and Pacific strategy 95
Roselle, Lt Benjamin 28–9
Rosenthal, Joe (photographer) 41, **80, 81,** 81–2, 83
Ruhl, Pfc Donald J. 89
Ryukyu Islands
  geography 97–8
  history 98
  surrender of 171
  US plans for invasion of 96–7

Santoro, Pfc Pete 36
Saratoga, USS 36, 37
Schmidt, MajGen Harry 10, 11, **11,** 29, 36, 38, 41, 52, 69
  and naval bombardment 20, 21
  plans 15, 45–6

Senda, MajGen Sadasue 63, 68–51
Sheetz, BrigGen Josef R. 126
Shepherd, MajGen Lemuel C. 129
Shigeki, MajGen Suzuki 134
Shuri Castle (Okinawa Shima) 100–1, 110, **175**
Sigler, Pvt Franklin E. 89–90
Smith, LtGen Holland McTyeire (1882–1967) 8, 9–10, **10,** 31, 39
  criticism of Navy 20, 21
  on Kuribayashi 12, 69
soldiers
  dead **158, 159**
  wounded **118**
Spearfish, USS 17
Spruance, Adm Raymond A. (1886–1969) 9, **10,** 20, 21, 62, **112,** 124
  career 117
  and Pacific strategy 96
Stein, Cpl Tony 90
Stilwell, LtGen Joseph W. 121, 169, 171
strategic progress 30–1, 41, 45, **66,** 67
Suribachi, Mount 15, **16, 17,** 17–18, 25, 29, 64, 68, 75, **79**
  US assaults 28, 31–2, 34–5, **37,** 37–8, 39, 41
  US flag raised 41, **47, 81,** 81–2
Suzuki, Adm (Baron) Kantaro 146

Tanabaru Escarpment (Okinawa Shima) 110, 155
tank, M4A3 Sherman **151**
tank destroyer, 76mm gun-armed M18 'Hellcat' **142**
Tatum, 'Chuck' 34
Tennessee, USS 13, 142
Tojo, Gen Shigenori 94
Tokashiki Shima **100**
Tokko (Special Attack) 107
Toyoda, Adm Soemu 162
Truk, neutralization of 94, 104
Tsugen Shima 145
tunnel system **15,** 16–17
Turkey Knob, the 47, 48, 53, 56, 57, 67
Turner, Adm Richmond K. (1885–1961) 9, **10,** 30, 112, 125, 140
  career 117, 119

United States Air Force 7–8, 66–7, 73, 74, 75, 84
  Boeing B29 Superfortress **5,** 7, **7, 8, 60,** 61, 73, **73**
United States Forces 6, 13, **30, 35, 61**

1st Marine Division 128–89, 150, 166, 169, **172–3**

2nd Marine Division 129, 150

III Amphibious Corps Artillery (USMC) 128

III Amphibious Corps (USMC) 128

3rd Marine Division 10–11, 33, 52, 57, 61, 62, 65, 68

4th Marine Division 11, 35, 46, 49, 53, 54, 62, 65

5th Marine Division 11, 35, 46, 47–8, 53, 57, 61, 62, 68

6th Marine Division 129, 150, 152, **164–5,** 166, **166,** 168, 169, **172–3**

7th Infantry Division 127, 147, 150, 158, 166, 169, **172–3**

9th Regiment 47, 48–9, 52, 62–3

21st Regiment 33, 36, 38, 44, 52, 53–4, 62

22nd Marine Division 166

23rd Regiment 28, 34, 47, 48, 54, 57, 60, 63

24th Regiment 34, 35–6, 45, 47, 48, **49,** 54, 57, 60, 62, 63

XXIV Corps 126, 147, 150, 155, 158, **160–1,** 167

XXIV Corps Artillery 126–87

25th Regiment 28, 30, 48, 54–5, 56

26th Regiment 34, 35, 56–7, 63

27th Infantry Division 127, 145, 152, 155, 158

27th Regiment 28, 30, 34, 35, 62

28th Regiment 25, 28, 29, 31–2, 33, 34–5, 37, 39, 41, 54, 57, 69

44th Infantry, Philippine Scouts 174

53rd Antiaircraft Artillery Brigade 126

77th Infantry Division 128, **139, 146,** 155, 158–89, 166

81st Infantry Division 128

96th Infantry Division 127, 147, 150, 158, 166, 169, **172–3**

305th Infantry Division 166

306th Infantry Division 155

307th Infantry Division 155

air support 19, 31, 62, 68

and the airfields 32–3, 38, 39, 41, 44

amphibian tractor battalions 132, 150

Amphibious Support Force (TF 52) 125

Amtacs **44, 45, 48**

artillery **40, 53**

banzai attack 64–5

battle replacements 55

Bradford Task Force 158

breakthrough to the sea 65

casualties 11–12, 28, 29, 30, 39, **40,** 45, 46, 47, **56,** 57, 65, 68, 69, 74

evacuation **63, 64**

cemeteries **65**

close air support (CAS) 132, 144

combat efficiency 54–5

commanders 116–21

communications **39**

company designation 131

Cushman's Pocket 63, 65, 68

at Death Valley 69

Demonstration Group (TG51.2) 125

dogs **24–5**

Eastern Islands Attack and Fire Support Group (TG51.19) 145

engineers 57, 60

equipment 130–1

Expeditionary Troops (TF 56) 125

Fast Carrier Force (TF 58) 114, 124, 137

flamethrowers **41,** 52–3, **55**

Fleet Marine Force Pacific (FMFPac) 145, 169

Gunfire and Covering Force (TF 54) 125, 139

at Hill Peter 46, 48–9

infantry **118**

island hoping 5, 9

landings **18,** 21, **21,** 22–5, **25, 28,** 28–31, **29, 32, 33, 45, 85**

machine guns **34, 54**

in the 'Meatgrinder' 46–7, 48, 49, 53, 56–7, 57, 60

at Motoyama 52

on Mount Suribachi 31–2, 34–5, **37,** 37–8

flag raised 41, **47, 81,** 81–2

night attack 62–3

at Nishi Ridge 57

Northern Attack Force (TF 53) 125

order of battle 78–9

plans 15, 33–4

regimental combat teams (RCT) 131

rest 61–2

resupply points **154**

rocket trucks 38, **46,** 49, **52**

Southern Attack Force (TF 55) 125

Tactical Air Force, Tenth Army (TG 99.2) 132

tactical organization 129–32

tank battalions 131–2

tanks 24, 25, 29, 32, 35, 37, **38,** 41, 46, 48, 49, 56, 57, 60, 62, 69

Task Force 50 (TF 50) 124

Task Force 51 (TF 51) (Joint Expeditionary Force) 112, 114, 124, 162

Task Force 52 Mine Flotilla (TG 52.2) 139

Tenth Army 125–6

underwater demolition teams 21

Western Islands Attack Group (TG 51.1) 125, 139

United States Marine Corps *see under* United States Forces

United States Navy 13, 35, 41, 62, **63**

bombardments **20,** 20–1, **24,** 41, 44, 62, 67–8

casualties 21, 37, **88**

kamikaze attacks 36–7

the Seabees (Naval Construction Battalions) 30, 44–5, 46

Urasoe-Mura Escarpment (Okinawa Shima) 110, 155, 158

Ushijima, LtGen Mitsuru 107, 110, 111, 112, 150

career 121

death 169

Wada, MajGen Kosuke 135

Wake Island, USS 36

Walsh, Gunnery Sgt William G. 90

Washington, USS 33

Watanabe, LtGen Masao 121

Watson, MajGen Thomas E. 129

Whalen, Pharmacist's Mate George E. 90

Williams, Cpl Hershel W. 90, **90**

Williams, Pharmacist's Mate Jack 90

Willis, Pharmacist's Mate John H. 90

Woods, Louis E. 132

Yahara, Col Hiromichi 107, 110, 150, 159

career 122–3

Yamato, sinking of 163, 171

Yellow Beaches 15, 28

Youamata, Maj 37

Zamami Shima 155